T0342261

PENSION POWER

PENSION POWER

Unions, Pension Funds, and Social Investment in Canada

Isla Carmichael

UNIVERSITY OF TORONTO PRESS
Toronto Buffalo London

© University of Toronto Press Incorporated 2005
Toronto Buffalo London
Printed in Canada

ISBN 0-8020-3647-3

Printed on acid-free paper

Library and Archives Canada Cataloguing in Publication

Carmichael, Isla
Pension power : unions, pension funds and social investment
in Canada / Isla Carmichael.

Includes bibliographical references and index.
ISBN 0-8020-3647-3

1. Pension trusts – Investments – Canada.   2. Deferred compensation –
Canada.   3. Labor unions – Canada.   4. Capital investment – Canada.
5. Investments – Moral and ethical aspects.   I. Title.

HD7105.45.C3C42 2005   332.67'254'0971   C2005-901239-0

University of Toronto Press acknowledges the financial assistance to its
publishing program of the Canada Council and the Ontario Arts Council.

University of Toronto Press acknowledges the financial support for its
publishing activities of the Government of Canada through the Book
Publishing Industry Development Program (BPIDP).

This book is dedicated
to my mother,
Agnes Carmichael Huxham,
and the memory of my father,
Sydney Huxham.

Contents

Tables and Figures

Tables

Figures

Preface and Acknowledgments

This is a book about the potential for radical change in the role that the labour movement in Canada plays in the economy. I hope to reveal the changing relationship between labour and capital and show how, through the wise use of pension fund capital, unionists can play a part in shaping economic growth in this country.

This book will be controversial. I intend it to be. It will be controversial with the financial industry, who have had easy use of pension fund capital for the past twenty or thirty years; with employers who have enjoyed control and access to 'their' pension funds; and with some parts of the Canadian trade union movement and the left which have resisted getting involved in a deeper confrontation with employers and the financial industry over control of deferred wages. I argue that we can harness the power of our deferred wages as social capital to rebuild neglected communities and increase productivity, for the benefit of workers, communities, and our governments.

I would like to thank the people who assisted and supported me in completing my doctoral thesis and, hence, this book. My supervisor, Professor Jack Quarter, of the Ontario Institute for Studies in Education (OISE) of the University of Toronto, was persistent but patient in his constructive feedback, editorial comment, and insistence that this work was significant and valuable. My committee members – Professors Roy Adams of McMaster University, Edward Jackson of Carleton University, and Daniel Schugurensky also of OISE – were remarkable for their enthusiasm for this project, in spite of the inconveniences imposed on some of them by long distance travel. I also thank Professor Art Shostak of Drexel University, who provided insightful and valuable commentary as external examiner.

In 1999 I interviewed many trade unionists and others involved in pension fund investment. In particular, I must thank Bill Clark for his visionary work with the trade union movement in British Columbia and for telling me his story. Bill and his wife, Gwen, offered their friendship during my weeks in Vancouver. Ken Georgetti, now president of the Canadian Labour Congress (CLC), was generous with his time when there were many claims on his attention. Both he and his assistant at the B.C. Federation of Labour, Phil Legg, provided important documents regarding the relationship of labour and capital in British Columbia.

Staff at Concert Real Estate Development Company in Vancouver could not have been more courteous and helpful. David Podmore, the chief executive officer of Concert went to great lengths to provide data that could allow a fuller picture of the company's contribution to the economy of British Columbia; he also perceived that my questions that went beyond the 'bottom-line' could be important to other investors and communities. Wayne Stone and Jane Richey, then administrators of the Carpentry Workers Pension Plan of British Columbia provided commentary, based on an extensive involvement in social investment. Rod Hiebert, as president of the Telecommunications Workers Union and trustee of his members' pension plan, gave me a tour of the Collingwood neighbourhood of (Vancouver) in the midst of his very busy schedule. Audrey Howe, then president of Mortgage Fund One, and her staff, Allan Collings, Michael Taylor and Gordon Allan, set aside considerable time to work with me and answer many questions. Bruce Rollick, who was instrumental in the creation of Concert and Mortgage Fund One and actuary at the Wyatt Company for several pension funds, gave me the technical information essential to understanding the dynamic between the two investments. Chris Taulu, long-time community activist and director of the crime prevention unit in Collingwood, and Paula Carr, of the Collingwood Neighbourhood House, also went beyond the call of duty in explaining the history of the relationship between Collingwood and Concert.

I thank the Ontario Public Service Employees' Union (OPSEU). It is one of several unions that have had joint trusteeship of pension funds on their agendas for many years. This has taken a succession of leaders who have steadily built union strength and expertise in this area – James Clancy, Fred Upshaw, Leah Casselman, Bill Kuehnbaum, and David Rapaport. As well, I wish to thank the staff at OPSEU. Among the many who assisted me were Shirley McVittie, Jordan Berger, Terry Moore, Annie Keung, and Heather Gavin. I also thank Kim Macpherson, now of the OPSEU Joint Trusteed Benefit Fund, for her advice.

Many union activists and researchers have been so helpful over the years. I thank Darcie Beggs and Michel Lizée of the Canadian Union of Public Employees – a union leading the way in pension trustee education. Heartfelt thanks also to Bob Baldwin, director of social and economic policy at the Canadian Labour Congress, for his solid and thoughtful advice and insight.

Those who reviewed chapters, brainstormed, and answered questions were Tessa Hebb, then Canadian director of the Heartland Project, and Arlene Wortsman, then from the Canadian Labour and Business Centre. Kirk Falconer, now at Mary Macdonald and Associates, was an invaluable ally.

I have had the good fortune to work with, and learn from, the pension committee of the National Union of Public and General Employees (NUPGE). Larry Brown has provided excellent national leadership for this group. This book is to assist in training those pension activists following in their footsteps.

Many more gave me support, information, and critical expertise where needed. These include Chris Schenk, research director at the Ontario Federation of Labour, and Bob Hebdon of McGill University. Jack Layton, Canada's leading urban reformer and now leader of the New Democratic Party and Member of Parliament for Toronto-Danforth, provided me with important connections in economic development departments across the country. B.J. Richmond, Laurie Mook, and Sonja Greckol provided critical commentary on social accounting and gender issues surrounding social audits.

Finally, I thank Paula White from the Ontario Institute for Studies in Education of the University of Toronto for her assistance in editing on the final round.

Of course, I alone am responsible for this book's research and conclusions.

On a personal note, I thank my partner Tim Little, my son Julian Peters, and my daughter Sidney Peters for their love and faith in me. All three are stimulating and exciting people who challenge and inspire me to continue to work on issues of worker control.

Isla Carmichael,
Toronto, May 2005

PENSION POWER

Introduction

In 1968, as the new president of the Telecommunications Workers Union (TWU) in British Columbia, Bill Clark was astonished when he learned of the large amount of money in his members' pension fund. He considered pension money, 'just different wages,' even though the money was in a pension fund rather than a pay cheque. Clark was strongly influenced by Peter Drucker's *The Unseen Revolution* (1976). He reasoned that if other pension funds were similar, there must be a lot of money leaving British Columbia 'because Ontario, Quebec, New York, and places like that were better investments for fund managers.' This was the genesis of the Concert Real Estate Corporation and of Mortgage Fund One.

Trusteed pension funds are one of the largest pools of capital in Canada, with total assets estimated at approximately $624.2 billion as of the fourth quarter of 2003 (Canada, Statistics Canada, 2004). Neither workers nor their unions have control over this money, even though it represents the deferred wages of almost half the workers in this country. Instead, employers and governments have traditionally viewed pensions as workers' retirement income contingent on the good will of employers.

In this book, I examine the effect of worker control over pension fund investment through the social investments by twenty union pension funds in Concert Properties Real Estate Corporation of British Columbia. One union in particular – the Carpenters Union – is examined for the impact of its investments on the pension fund itself (the Carpentry Workers Pension Plan of British Columbia) in increased contributions, on members of the pension fund in job creation, on government in increased revenues, and on the community in increased jobs and services. I will present social accounting models for Concert that are transferable to other funds. Finally, I will consider the training implications for unions that flow from the argument that unions should have greater control over their members' pension funds.

Framework: Control of Capital Accumulation

Pension funds form one of the largest pools of capital in Canada, second in size only to the total financial assets of all the major banks (Canada, Statistics Canada, 2004). Until 1997, their assets were growing in the previous ten years by approximately 11 per cent annually – this measure is calculated by taking assets in current dollars for trusteed pension funds, and the annual change from 1987 to 1997, using Statistics Canada data (1997, Quarterly Estimates p. 5). By any account this is a staggering amount of money.

Worldwide, the picture is similar. Pension fund assets, by the end of 1994, amounted to U.S.$10 trillion (World Bank, 1994). As Minns (2003) points out, this figure is greater than the combined total market value of all the world's industrial, commercial, and financial corporations quoted on the three largest world stock markets (New York, Tokyo, and London). Pension funds in the United States control 47 per cent of all U.S. equity. In Canada, the comparable figure is 35 per cent, with 40 per cent of pension fund assets invested in equities (Patry and Poitevin, 1995).

Given the size of these funds, a greater level of control by workers of their investment could lead to a greater democratization of the economy through full employment, together with the growth and redistribution of wages. Yet workers, for the most part, have no control over the investment or accumulation of these funds. Pension funds are invested in the market primarily through fund managers employed by the major financial institutions and retained by the pension fund. In its survey of 147 fund managers, *Benefits Canada* (Bak, 1997) reports that pension assets under management in 1997 were $339.3 billion. This represents approximately 70 per cent of all pension assets in Canada at the time and is an increase of 29.5 per cent over the previous year of the proportion managed. Furthermore, the top ten money managers controlled almost 44 per cent of these assets.

The larger funds tend to hire their own investment staff, but 60 per cent of pension funds use external investment managers. Professional fund managers have almost total discretion over the investment of funds (Rifkin and Barber, 1980; Deaton, 1989; Roe, 1991; Minns, 1996). This discretion infuses their investment practices. Fund managers are retained for their specialization in certain types of asset allocation, their 'style,' and the prestige of their companies.

For the most part, pension fund managers retain the privileges of capital trusteeship, and through their exercise of voting rights for shares held by the fund, influence decisions on the purchase of companies, on takeovers, on corporate policies including downsizing, on privatization of government assets, on corporate behaviour such as health and safety and environmental standards, and finally, on corporate structures and compensation (Carmichael, 1996).

This does not include the increasing role of pension funds in international markets, as well as their role in foreign currencies, national debts, and other economic policies (Davis, 1995; Minns, 1996). The Canadian Labour Congress (CLC) has stated that 'the largely private nature of the investment process makes workers, communities and governments the hostages of those who control the investment process (1990, p. 3).

These investment managers often have a direct financial interest in takeovers and privatization. In 1994, in the United Kingdom, eight out of the top ten pension fund management companies were involved as advisers in takeovers. Of the eight U.K. banks involved in privatization sales, four were among the top ten pension fund managers. Financial institutions involved in the management of pension funds have a 'clear commercial interest' in the takeover business, privatization of public services, and the privatization of state pension systems (Minns, 1996, p. 386).

'State pension systems' more often than not are those social security systems designed to provide universal benefits. These systems have come under attack from the World Bank (1994, p. 174) for being inefficiently managed, that is, with too many 'political ties' and inherently unfair as later generations of contributors are paying in more than they will take out (ibid., p. 13). This is an implicit criticism of the role of the state in social welfare systems and a weakly disguised call for privatization. These systems, such as the Canada Pension Plan (CPP) and the Quebec Pension Plan (QPP) in Canada, are pay-as-you-go systems where funds are not invested, but are redistributive and intergenerational, in that income flows from those earning more to those earning less. Overall, the World Bank views this kind of system as a lost opportunity for the accumulation capital by of those who are wealthier, as well as inherently inefficient since the fund is not invested in the capital markets (ibid.).[1] Far preferable, according to the World Bank, is the Chilean system, which is providing a model for several 'emerging market' countries, such as Brazil,

---

1 Richard Minns (1996) offers an extensive, detailed critique of the World Bank Report *Averting the Old Age Crisis* (1994) and, in particular, its attack on publicly funded systems.

Bolivia, and Hong Kong. Since Chile's funds are invested, its system has given 'a boost' to the fund management industry (see, e.g., *Economist*, 1997, p. 12). The Canadian government, persuaded by the report of the World Bank, set up a board of directors to invest the CPP Reserve Fund.

Yet these systems may not provide universal coverage for people in retirement. Only 40 per cent of Chilean workers belong to their national plan: the unemployed, self-employed, and agricultural labourers are excluded. Of those in the plan, an estimated 70 per cent will end up with few benefits (Fazio and Riesco, 1997).

Interestingly enough, other pension systems (e.g., those that public sector employers provide for their own employees) receive cursory attention from the World Bank, even though there are staggering amounts of money in public sector pension funds worldwide. For example, *Benefits Canada* reported that assets of the top 100 pension funds in Canada total approximately $480 billion (Press, 2000). Of these, fifty-three are public sector, occupational, 'privately managed' pension funds, which earn much higher returns than 'publicly managed pension funds and reserves' (World Bank, 1994, p. 174).

Furthermore, the World Bank maintains that these occupational or workplace funds have also contributed to financial innovation through their use of investment vehicles that increase liquidity and therefore enable faster and cheaper trading on the stock markets (ibid., p. 177). This is particularly interesting because a study of the top pension funds in Canada shows that there is a distinct trend among unions towards control over their pension funds (Carmichael, 1998). The argument made by these unions, consistently, through campaigns with their membership, is that these funds constitute members' deferred wages, and as such their unions should have some control over their use.

Pension plans have also traditionally been used as a means of ensuring loyalty and punishing dissent: Those loyal to the employer would receive their pensions, those not in good favour would be fired without any stipend. Although this historical inequity has been outstripped by pension laws and regulation of employers (as will be described in the following chapters), it has also ensured that pension issues remain at the top of the agenda for many Canadian unionized workers, particularly in the public sector. Their plans are often contributory. Therefore, the lack of trust in future political regimes to act as guardians of their funds has driven the unions' struggle for control. Deferred wages have been viewed as a means for employers to control their workforces, but many public sector workers have now taken over the language as a call for greater control over their pensions (Benjamin et al., 1998).

Not all unions are seeking greater control over their pension funds. Lack of trust in the employer has led the Canadian Auto Workers (CAW) to resist becoming more actively involved in their pension fund investment. With pension plans that are negotiable and not dependent on worker contributions, the CAW has historically negotiated 'flat' pension benefits for its members and disregarded any further role in the administration of pension funds.

Fundamental to this debate between the CAW and the rest of the trade union movement is the role of the trade union movement in the Canadian economy. Peter Drucker (1976) predicted a pension revolution, where by means of their pension funds unions and their workers would take control of financial markets and national economies. He assumed that workers and their unions would lead a pension revolution, which, presumably, would overturn existing relationships in the economy and create an economy driven by a quite different set of values. The CAW argues that because the economy is antithetical to workers' interests, pension fund investment must work against these interests in order to provide the returns necessary for workers' retirements (Stanford, 1999a). I argue, on the contrary, that pension fund investment is a vehicle for promoting values in addition to the rate of return. These values can transform the economy as well as provide good benefits.

This debate was reflected in Gord Wilson's closing speech to the Ontario Federation of Labour (OFL) in November, 1997, prior to his stepping down from the presidency. Industrial strikes, he said, are no longer effective; we have to use new levers, such as pension funds, to hold accountable the bankers and investment managers who increasingly have more power over the economy than does the nation state. However, Wilson said, workers need to gain control of their deferred wages in the funds (Urquhart, 1997).

On the other hand, Sam Gindin (1992) of the CAW has argued that creating pools of capital, as well as worker ownership, are 'secondary' in that such strategies 'do not confront the real issue' of changing the structure of our economy. This debate within the trade union movement is discussed in greater detail in Chapter 5.

Focus of the Study

Academic research attempting to build a theoretical underpinning for productive investment practice for pension funds has only just begun. In Canada, Jack Quarter (1995, p. 213) has suggested that 'it is possible to have investment policies that take into account a broader range of criteria than the rate of return'; he notes that pension funds can be invested to provide social housing, jobs for members of the fund, and additional contributions to the fund.

In the United States, Barber and Ghilarducci (1993) have proposed the 'whole participant' approach, which recognizes that pension funds rely on a strong economy to keep fund members at work so that they can pay their pension contributions. Also in the United States, the Heartland Project – a group of union pension leaders and researchers – has produced research on the collateral benefits of pension fund investment. The term 'collateral' is used to denote social benefits that can be accrued by investment once the financial needs of the plan are met (Baker and Fung, 2000).

In the United Kingdom, Zadek et al. (1997) have suggested approaches to monitor the evolution of social and ethical accounting, auditing, and reporting. This work is broader than pension fund investment and deals with corporate accountability and its measurement.

More attention needs to be paid to union involvement in pension fund investment for a number of reasons. First, as public sector unions in Canada take greater control of occupational pension funds through joint trusteeship and more control of investment decisions (Carmichael and Quarter, 2003), they are in dire need of leadership training in pension fund investment – from a union perspective. Rudd and Spalding (1997) have shown that the education of union trustees is critical to the informed and productive use of pension funds. Trustees need models of alternative investment strategies that will promote economic growth to benefit their communities, their jobs, and their pension funds. Invariably, trustee education is delivered by representatives of the financial industry, who stress the high levels of accountability expected of union trustees compared with that expected of employer trustees.

Undermining union trustees is not unusual, where fund managers stress their own professionalism and objectivity, in contrast to the lack of expertise and supposed bias of most 'lay' or union trustees. For example, William Dimma, chairperson of several Canadian companies, in a brief presented to the Senate's Standing Committee on Banking, Trade, and Commerce (1998, p. 6) said that 'while many plans are managed professionally, their boards are sometimes stocked with persons whose principal merit is that they are members ... [who] have been elected by their fellow employees. While this is laudably democratic, it does not always produce the quality of direction and oversight necessary in today's bewildering world.' Union trustees are expected to set aside the interests of their members and communities to employment security, pension protection, environmental safety, and workplace standards in the interests of the 'maximum rate of return.' This generally means investment in large transnational corporations that are already highly capitalized.

Second, although pension funds move their assets to the stock markets, new economic research documents the irrationality of the stock markets. The same research analyses the psychological as well as structural factors influencing the tripling of the Dow Jones industrial average between 1994 and 1997 (Shiller, 2000). I critique prevailing investment practices of pension funds as a move towards more irrational, speculative investment. More productive investment practices can take into account the interests of beneficiaries, workers, government, and the broader community. Underlying this direction is an assumption that pension funds through wiser investment may provide for 'good' rather than 'bad' jobs, thus increasing productivity (Barber and Ghilarducci, 1993).

Finally, I call for a greater level of accountability for pension fund investment, given the foregone taxes 'invested' in pension funds. Greater accountability can be achieved through a social accounting of pension fund investment that may show fiscal returns to government and returns to the broader community in increased productivity. This inevitably requires a higher standard of reporting on the part of pension funds in Canada.

We need greater accountability and transparency of pension funds in Canada. One way of achieving these goals is to have more diverse governance on pension boards of trustees. Both Air Canada and Stelco have company plans where the board of directors of the company is also the board of trustees of the pension plan. I contend that, inevitably, this has led to a conflict of interest between the interests of the company and the interests of beneficiaries. Both companies, when in trouble, have turned to their pension funds as available sources of capital to help bail them out of bankruptcy. Nowhere was this seen more clearly than in the collapse of Enron, an American company that espoused corporate social responsibility as a cover for the 'greed, hubris and criminality' of its executives (Bakan, 2004).

Chapters in Part 1 of this book describe the competing interests of government, employers, and workers that have shaped the development of Canada's pension system. These competing interests form the barriers to worker control and, ultimately, social investment of pension funds. Chapters in Part 2 describe the findings of a study of Concert, a real estate company, and Mortgage Fund One, a mortgage trust, both funded by pension assets. Part 3 offers an analysis and discussion of the findings and proposes a new definition of social investment, as well as providing an analysis of the social accounting models presented in the earlier chapters and suggesting two models for union control of pension funds. Furthermore, Part 3 discusses the implications for labour education and concludes with comments on further research needed on pension fund investment.

Part 1

chapter 1

The Development of Unions and Workplace Pension Plans

Workplace pension plans have existed in Canada for 140 years. They developed largely in response to labour unrest, the rise of unionism, and demands from working people for a national social security pension for the elderly (Morton and Copp, 1981; Stafford, 1987a, 1987b; Palmer, 1992; Heron, 1996). Pension plans were originally introduced in the late 1800s by the banks, railroad companies, and the federal and later the provincial governments to provide for their large workforces and, incidentally, as a means of workplace control. Pensions were used as a form of patronage by government employers and by other employers as a reward for 'good service.' This could obviously be interpreted arbitrarily. Unionizing and community organizing often would not be considered good service; nor was illness, pregnancy, or getting older and slowing down. Workers and their unions consequently inherited some suspicion of employer-sponsored pension plans, and this helped fuel campaigns for a national, universal pension system.

By 1906, in response to the introduction of pension plans by large employers, Canadian trade unions were organizing for a public pension system. They were strongly influenced by labour success in the United Kingdom, as well as in other parts of the world. Germany had established a contributory pension plan in 1889. Denmark and New Zealand had passed means-tested plans in 1891 and 1898, respectively for people in financial need only. France passed a pension law in 1905, Austria did so in 1907, the United Kingdom in 1908, Luxembourg in 1911, Romania in 1912, and Sweden in 1913 (Bryden, 1974).

The Canadian government was pressured not only by the unions but also by the corporate sector (Bryden, 1974; Deaton, 1989). In response, the government introduced a voluntary plan, in 1908, to encourage young people to purchase annuities repayable upon retirement. The annuities were purchased by the middle classes, mostly teachers and clergymen, rather than the working class who were in most need of benefits but could not afford to buy them (Stafford, 1987a).

The general public was also suspicious of workplace pensions. In 1920, the Ontario government introduced a pension plan for its employees; however, the plan was controversial enough to be a factor in the downfall of the government in the next election. The plan was introduced after discussions with the newly formed Civil Service Association of Ontario, which was the precursor of the Ontario Public Service Employees Union (OPSEU). It provided benefits to men over seventy years of age in exchange for 'good and faithful service.' This was widely viewed as patronage. The electorate wanted the government to introduce a pension system for everyone, not just a few people.

The federal government was eventually forced to introduce a universal benefit in 1927. The Old Age Pensions Act provided for a means-tested benefit that was hopelessly inadequate to meet the needs of the elderly. Known as the 'old age security,' it was designed as a subsistence benefit for those in need, so that the program would not become a universal savings plan which would draw capital away from the market. In this way, it allowed the private sector to maintain its share of the market and protect its profits (Deaton, 1989).

Workplace Pensions and Taxation

Meanwhile, from 1919 to 1937, workplace pension plans proliferated across Canada in the form of employer allowances for good service (Canada, Dominion Bureau of Statistics, 1947). The introduction of income tax in 1917 to raise funds for the war effort had, incidentally given employers tax exemption for pension fund capital. Pension funds were likely an important source of additional capital from employers, since benefit payments were voluntary and there was at the time no system of financial accountability. However, in the early 1930s, after the onset of the Great Depression, employers were short of capital. Government, therefore, made pension contributions tax deductible and extended employers' tax exemption retroactively by ten years. This was an astonishing boon to employers, underlying the point that pension funds had already become an important source of investment capital (Greenough and King, 1976).

During the Second World War, taxation became the primary regulatory tool to raise funds for the war effort. In 1938, the yield from the corporate income tax was only $85 million, but within five years this sum had increased to $740 million (O'Grady, 1991). Because of the government's need for greater income to finance the cost of the war, the tax-exempt status of pension funds came under closer scrutiny. In 1942, the federal Department of National Revenue decreed that employer contributions to a plan would only be tax deductible if they were supported by an actuarial statement attesting that a pension fund was in place. This was primarily intended to prevent tax evasion; however, it also had the effect of making both employer and employee contributions into deferred income, as opposed to an allowance for good service which could be revoked (ibid.). By 1949, employee contributions were also tax deductible, and the federal Income Tax Division was considering 'broadening its approval of plans, to include plans in which the employer's contributions [would vary] to some extent on the basis of his profits' (Canada, Department of Labour, 1949, p. 696).

A survey conducted in 1947 by the Department of Labour recorded that over 70 per cent of all of the Canadian pension plans existing at the time had been introduced during the period from 1938 to 1947 (Canada, Dominion Bureau of Statistics, 1947). Because of government need for extra capital during the Second World War, there were few restrictions placed on the corporate sector's accumulation of private capital through pension funds. On the contrary, federal encouragement and support of employer accumulation of capital through pension funds continued. Today, in most industrialized countries, pension fund capital remains tax exempt. Contributions are also exempt but benefits are taxed (Davis, 1995).

Bargaining Pension Plans

In the immediate postwar period, the government of Prime Minister Mackenzie King introduced the Industrial Relations and Disputes Investigation Act. This law pulled together much of the ad hoc industrial relations regime that had been in effect during the war. Moreover, it provided unions with a permanent collective bargaining framework for industrial relations. Union members now turned to their unions to negotiate pension plans. Given the inadequacies of the federal old age benefits benefit, unions continued their agenda of lobbying for better universal security for the elderly, but decided reluctantly to bargain for workplace pension plans and for improvements in benefits, instead. At this point, less than 3 per cent of pension plans covering fewer than 20,000 workers were actually part of collective agreements (Canada, Department of Labour, 1949).

In 1948, the Canadian Congress of Labour (CLC) adopted a resolution encouraging its affiliates to bargain pension benefits. This resolution was based on a grudging acceptance that many of the more obvious abuses by employers were now prevented through state intervention, and it had become difficult, if not impossible to oppose workplace pension plans.

The new reality was that, in a collective bargaining environment, employers would push to minimize benefits and maximize productivity by pushing such issues as mandatory retirement (Mosher, 1952). The first pension plans to be bargained in Canada were in 1950; they were between the United Auto Workers (UAW) and Ford Motor Company, and General Motors (Yates, 1993). Private sector unions had no choice but to go to the table. Furthermore, the absence of a universal pension plan put pressure back on unions to beef up the benefits in private plans. Unions of the day emphasized bargaining plan improvements to the exclusion of joint administration of pension funds, a policy maintained by the CAW to the present day.

In 1952, lobbying by the trade union movement and by social reformers resulted in the long overdue reform of the national pension system. Parliament passed the Old Age Security Act (OAS), providing the first universal pension plan in Canada. A means test applied was only to people over 65 and under 70; those who could prove destitution could then receive a maximum of $40 a month. Everyone over seventy received $40 a month as a right. The mandatory retirement age was reduced to sixty years of age for women and sixty-five for men. The new program was to be funded through general tax revenues set aside in an old age security fund.

In 1951, under the 1927 law, 308,825 people received pensions from the federal government of Canada. Under the new law, this number doubled immediately to nearly 700,000 (Finlayson, 1988). However, within five years, inflation had eroded the new benefits, and lobbying began again to increase them.

One million Canadians were drawing OAS benefits by 1964, and a further two and a half million adults had incomes that were so low that they paid no income tax. Together, this amounted to a large proportion of the Canadian electorate (ibid.). Enormous pressure was put on the federal government to bring in more increases in OAS benefits – in the absence of inflation protection – and, at the same time, to bring in a contributory, universal pension plan. Both the corporate sector and government were alarmed at the proportion of federal revenues going to the non-contributory OAS; the idea of a contributory plan therefore appealed across the board. The federal government entered into negotiations with the provinces, and by 1966 there was agreement on a plan for Quebec and on the CPP for the rest of the country. The CPP had a contribution rate of 3.6 per cent of pensionable earnings, to be shared equally between employer and employee. Benefits would be partially indexed, and a ten-year transition period ensured that older Canadians could get help from the plan in the near future.

Under strong pressure from Ontario, which was threatening to set up its own provincial plan (as Quebec had), Ottawa agreed that it would administer the plan, but provinces could 'borrow' surpluses from the 'fund' at advantageous interest rates. Started as a pay-as-you-go scheme, the CPP was soon transformed into a partially funded plan. What followed was predictable. In the four years prior to 31 March 1974, the CPP provided the provinces with $4.67 billion, or 38 per cent of all provincial borrowing, at favourable rates of interest. More money was coming in as contributions, but less was going out in benefits, thus encouraging the provinces to view the CPP as a convenient 'slush fund' for provincial initiatives (Calvert, 1977).

The Canada Pension Plan was enacted much later than national plans in many other industrialized countries. The Canadian government had managed to avoid providing a mandatory, universal, publicly funded pension plan up until this point, despite almost a hundred years of organizing by workers and their unions. Both systems, the OAS and the CPP, became outdated fairly quickly. They were not indexed and simply could not keep up with inflation.

Meanwhile on the provincial front, pressure continued for legislative reform of private pension plans. Until 1963, there were no statues that dealt directly with the regulation of occupational pension plans. That year the Pension Benefits Act was enacted by the Robart's government in Ontario. It marked a watershed in pension policy and provided a model for other provinces. The Ontario pension act established the principle of vesting, whereby workers accrued a right to their pensions during their period of employment, although the vesting was modest; it did, however, provide for minimum standards to ensure that pension funds remained solvent.

Canada's Retirement Systems Today

In sixty years, the gains in pension reform for Canada's workers had been modest. National standards were established in principle, through the OAS and the CPP, but the actual benefits that both acts provided to workers were inadequate. Workplace pension plans were still heavily controlled by employers, and they remained a vehicle for investment purposes. They also covered a relatively small sector of the population. In the early twentieth century it was already clear that trade unions were the only way for workers to make gains in pension reform. Resistance from the corporate sector, individual employers, and all levels of government was strong. Federal and provincial governments responded with commissions, task forces, and committees.

Peter Drucker had coined the term 'pension socialism' as early as 1976. In fact, by 1980, employer-sponsored pension plans still accounted for only 14 per cent of the total income of Canadians over the age of sixty-five. More than 53 per cent of retired Canadians lived in poverty (Finlayson, 1988). Nevertheless, private sector employers continued to lobby the federal government strenuously against raises in benefit levels for the state plans, while at the same time resisting reform of the private pension system. Government programs for the elderly were in trouble; benefit levels were too low, and the plans – OAS and CPP – were going broke. Benefits were too low for the 'average man,' and for women they were nearly non-existent. As Ann Finlayson (1988) points out, pension plans, public or private, still described the average worker as male, working full-time from age eighteen till sixty-five, working for one employer after thirty-five, receiving steady salary increases (and pension entitlements) until age sixty-five. Workplace pension plans were weak because of low coverage rates, mismanagement of pension funds, employer contribution holidays, discriminatory impacts on women, lack of inflation protection, and the paternalism of employers.

The Report of the Royal Commission on the Status of Pensions in Ontario (Ontario, 1982), concluded that an expanded CPP should replace the private pension system. At the same time, Monique Begin, federal minister of health and welfare delivered an ultimatum to employers: reform private pension plans, or face either an expanded CPP or mandated private pension plan coverage. Under Prime Minister Trudeau, the federal government set up a Parliamentary Task Force on Pensions, chaired by Douglas Frith (Canada, 1983). Its report, insisted on keeping universal benefits safe from political tampering. Provincial governments were warned not to use CPP funds to pay down deficits. Workplace pension plans under federal jurisdiction were to provide vesting after two years and be extended to cover part-time workers. This task force came under heavy pressure from the business sector and insurance companies and backed away from a recommendation on protection against inflation.

In the 1980s, surplus grabs were popular with employers because there was double-digit inflation and stock markets were overheated. Pension funds were a ready source of capital for investment purposes. Meanwhile pensioners were in despair, as their pension benefits shrank in value without the advantage of indexing. Pensioners with defined contribution plans were doubly affected without the protection of either a guaranteed benefit or indexing. While employers took contribution holidays, and used surplus funds for their own purposes, retirees sank into poverty.

Pension funds were being used to transfer wealth from workers to employers, and this was completely legal. Furthermore, employers were arguing that because the assets and liabilities of pension plans were now comparable 'in size [to] those of the main-line businesses of the sponsor corporations,' they should be managed for the benefit of the corporation and its shareholders (Ambachtsheer, 2003).

Public sector pension plans faced the opposite problem. Because governments had borrowed from their employees' pension funds at extremely low rates of interest, the funds were not showing adequate growth, they were not keeping up with inflation, and they were unable to keep benefits in step with inflation. It was sometimes impossible to tell whether government employers were actually meeting their obligations to contribute. Unfunded liabilities were therefore growing, and there were predictions that, like the CPP, public sector plans such as that of the Ontario Teachers were in trouble.

The defeat of the provincial Conservatives in Ontario in 1985, and the accord between David Peterson's Liberals and the New Democratic Party (NDP), put pensions at the top of the agenda in that province. This resulted in amendments to the Pension Benefits Act similar to amendments to the federal legislation. A moratorium was declared on surplus withdrawals until a decision was made on inflation protection. But how could inflation protection be introduced without upsetting the corporate sector? A landslide election victory for the Ontario Liberals followed in 1987, with still no action on indexing of pensions. By the beginning of 1996, 76 per cent of public sector workers had won indexing, compared with only 14 per cent in the private sector (Canada, Statistics Canada, 1996b).

Table 1.1   Pension plan wind-ups, 1985–1996

Year	Active plans	Individuals covered
1985	9,215	1,727,688
1987	10,926	1,867,571
1989	9,589	1,927,756
1992	8,043	1,931,972
1993	7,666	1,891,827
1996	7,032	1,827,114

Source: Ontario Pension Commission, personal
communication (1996).

Nevertheless, there was enough regulatory change to discourage employers. Employers in Ontario were no longer willing to set up plans at the same rate as they had in the past, and increasingly plans were wound up, or discontinued. (O'Grady, 1991). Table 1.1 shows 1987 as a turning point in the growth of workplace plans in Ontario. From then on, the number of plans in Ontario began to decrease. The number of members covered by plans, however, does not fluctuate as greatly because of the greater proportion of members in fewer, and larger, public sector plans. Workers without benefit of pension plans are employed in smaller workplaces in both the private and public sectors.

The trend towards wind-ups of pension plans has policy implications for the retirement system in Canada. The accumulated assets of the three retirement income programs (OAS, CPP, and QPP) in Canada in 2000 amounted to $935 billion. The assets of workplace pension funds, at an estimated $644 billion, still outweighed the assets of either the CPP and QPP or the Registered Retirement Savings Program (RRSP), established in 1957. CPP and QPP assets were $49 billion, and RRSP assets totalled $241 billion (Canada, Statistics Canada, 2001).

In the ten years from 1983 to 1993, the largest growth – at 327 per cent – was seen in RRSP assets, compared with 158 per cent for the assets of workplace pension plans. Contributors to RRSPs have almost doubled in these ten years. By 1993, just under 35 per cent of the labour force contributed to RRSPs, up from 18 per cent a decade earlier (Canada, Statistics Canada, 1996b).

Nevertheless, workplace pension funds are still the largest source of retirement income for Canadians, although they are growing at a slower rate than RRSPs. Only 42 per cent of workers are covered by workplace plans, and the number of workplace is plans decreasing. Furthermore, the numbers of paid workers not covered by workplace plans is increasing. Altogether, it appears that the RRSP system is replacing workplace pension plans as the predominant retirement income system in Canada. Moreover, since employers of smaller workplaces are winding up pension plans, and with mass reductions of workers in both the public and private sectors, as well as the shift towards a lower wage, 'bad job' economy (Townson, 1997), the trend towards jobs without workplace pension plans will likely continue.

The public policy implications are disturbing. First, it is becoming less likely that workers in lower waged jobs will be able to buy RRSPs. The reverse is also true: the more money workers make, the more likely workers are to be in a pension plan or to buy RRSPs. This holds in spite of age. However, women, minorities, and younger people are disproportionately affected in that they do not invest in RRSPs very much, because they have lower incomes (Maser, 1995).

Second, the RRSP program is very similar to the first voluntary, individual, contributory plan set up in 1908, although with an important exception. The latter was managed by the government. It limped along for fifty years, despite being under relentless attack from the insurance industry and Canada's growing financial sector – for taking capital out of the market and charging lower fees than the market. Eventually, it was starved out of existence. The RRSP industry is, for the most part, controlled by the financial sector (through the mutual fund industry and the banks). Both lobby strenuously against any form of state regulation of their practices and for market control of pension capital. However, both argue equally strenuously for changes in tax policy which would increase the incentive of Canadians to save money and thereby increase their access to capital.

The history and development of workplace pension systems in Canada has been about the accumulation of capital by employers and the corporate sector. Government has encouraged this access to capital through workplace pension plans. Large, private sector employers introduced pension plans for their employees to increase productivity and margins of profit. Public sector employers used pensions as allowances to be dispensed as a form of patronage.

The need to raise capital, however, during the First World War incidentally acted as an incentive to the development of workplace pension systems, because pension funds were made tax exempt. The value of pension funds as sources of capital became more apparent, and with the tacit support of the state, the number of workplace pension systems increased dramatically. The shortage of industrial capital after the Great Depression encouraged employers to make systems contributory, and this provided them with a new source of capital, that is, workers' deferred wages. However, government prevented employers from denying pension benefits as a method of inhibiting union activity, and this prohibition limited worker resistance to contributory pension plans. The development of collective bargaining after the Second World War persuaded trade unions, under pressure from their membership and in the absence of a national pension system, to negotiate pension plans and benefits. This provoked another surge in the growth of pension plans.

Trade unions reluctantly took pension benefits to the bargaining table under pressure from their members. This was deemed a concession in face of the intransigence of the federal government in providing a decent and universal pension system for Canadians. To the present day, this background has affected the approach of some private sector unions – in particular the Canadian Auto Workers – towards issues of pension fund control.

In fact, and in law, workers in Canada and their unions were guaranteed that their pension money would be safe and secure because their funds were 'in trust' for their retirement. The philosophy underlying pension investment policy and trusteeship of capital is based on 'fiduciary responsibility' or the so-called prudent man rule. The next chapter analyses the history and development of this rule and examines further the ways in which this rule has continued to enable the accumulation of capital by employers and the financial industry.

chapter 2

The 'Prudent Man' Rule
and Maximum Rate of Return

The prudence rule is a central concept of trust law and a legal requirement of the management of pension fund assets in the United Kingdom,
the United States, Canada, and most other industrialized countries. The
trust concept has its origins in the Middle Ages, and has a history of juris-
prudence and litigation covering several centuries. The concept of the
'prudent man' is central to the accumulation of private capital through
the protection of family wealth. The roots of trust law are patriarchal,
lying in the remnants of feudal society where wealth was passed on
through the male heads of households. In the absence of the male head
of the family, the prudent man was essential in keeping the wealth of the
family secure for the benefit of the male heirs (Longstreth, 1986). The
trust ensured that the trustees would act only in the interests of the family, that is, the male heirs, and not in their own interests. Trustees, in
effect, control the wealth on behalf of the family, but cannot access it for
their own use. Therefore, trusteeship embraces the responsibility of ownership, without the ownership itself. Trustees must not act out of self-
interest or personal bias (Longstreth, 1986; Mercer Ltd. 1997; Minsky,
1988; Scott, 1987; Waitzer, 1990).

Prudence is the antithesis of speculation. According to the prudence
rule careful investments are characterized as low-risk ones. With the
development of stock exchanges, lists of investments were published for
trustees as well as other cautious investors. Everything else was classified
as speculation. However, the stock market crash of 1929 and the Great
Depression of the 1930s brought a re-examination of lists. Nevertheless,
lists persisted as a prescription for investment until the 1970s.

In the United States, trust law originates from an 1830 case in Massa-
chusetts, *Harvard College* v *Amory*. That ruling states that the trustee's duty

is to 'conduct *himself* faithfully and exercise a sound discretion, observe how *men* of prudence, discretion and intelligence manage their own affairs, not in regard to speculation, but in regard to the permanent disposition of their funds, considering the probable income as well as the probable safety of the capital to be invested' (26 Mass (9 Pick) 446, 1830; emphasis added).

In a similar manner, in a decision of the Supreme Court of Canada, a century and a half later, it is stated that 'where ... one party has an obligation to act for the benefit of another and that obligation carries with it a discretionary power, the party thus empowered becomes a fiduciary. Equity will then supervise the relationship by holding him to the fiduciary's strict standard of conduct' (*Guerin* v *The Queen*, 1984). The Supreme Court has identified the following criteria for a fiduciary relationship (in *Frame* v *Smith*, 1987):

1 The fiduciary has scope for the exercise of discretion or power.
2 The fiduciary can unilaterally exercise that power or discretion so as to affect the beneficiary's legal or practical interests.
3 The beneficiary is peculiarly vulnerable to, or at the mercy of, the fiduciary holding the discretion or power.

American and British Case Law to Date

No decision has been made in a Canadian court addressing the issue of social investment, although there have been several in American and British courts. A summary of the key cases follows. U.S. case law supports several points. First, union trustees cannot act as union officers in the interests of the union. They must act clearly as trustees responsible for the fund, and in the interests of the fund members. Otherwise they are in a conflict of interest. Second, the long-term interest of the fund and its members is a legitimate investment concern, even where the rate of return may be lower and risk to the investment may be higher. Third, the investment decision itself must be based on independent financial advice. If the trustees are fully informed, then they are not liable for a lower rate of return. Finally, trustees do not violate their duties of prudence by considering the social consequences of investment, providing the costs of considering such consequences are minimal; in fact, they are encouraged to do so given the power of pension funds (see, e.g., *Blankenship* v *Boyle* [1971]; *Withers* v *The Teachers' Retirement System of the City of New York* [1978]; *Donovan* v *Walton* [1985]; *Board of Trustees* v *City of Baltimore* [1989]).

Blankenship v *Boyle* (1971) has been cited as the case most opposed to social investment. Sir Robert Megarry, Master in Chancery, referred to *Blankenship* in his decision in *Cowan* v *Scargill* (1984) in the British Chancery Division. In this case, the United Mineworkers of America Welfare and Retirement Fund had invested in electrical utilities stock as a way of encouraging the utilities to use union-mined coal in order to maintain and increase the number of jobs in the coal industry. This was part of a larger union campaign. The utilities' shares subsequently decreased in value. The court judged that these investments were in the interests of the union rather than the beneficiaries and noted the close relationship between the trustees and the union. Some commentators have interpreted *Blankenship* as a warning to trustees that they may not invest according to non-financial criteria (Langbein and Posner, 1980). In fact, the court required both employer and union to refrain from conflict of interest. The decision enjoined 'the trustees from operating the fund in a manner designed in whole or in part to afford collateral advantages to the union or the employers' (*Blankenship* v *Boyle* (1971), p. 1113). One finding of the court was that the union conspired to benefit from the breach of trust. The case was really about conflict of interest – self-dealing – and breach of trust rather than social investment. Given that investments did decline, it is notable that the decision rested on breach of trust rather than prudence. Furthermore, the court recognized that 'in the longer view of matters, the union's strength protects the interests of beneficiaries, past and prospective' (ibid., p. 1112; in Hutchinson and Cole, 1980). A B.C. lawyer and one-time director of research at the B.C. Federation of Labour, Patricia Lane (1991) also observes that the union campaigns in *Blankenship* were for the benefit of union members.

In *Withers* v *The Teachers' Retirement System of the City of New York* (1978), a group of retired teachers sued their pension fund after the trustees, having sought independent advice, invested $860 million in New York municipal bonds to prevent the city's bankruptcy. The trustees took this extreme action to secure the assets of the fund (which were employer contributions from the City of New York) and protect the interests of all beneficiaries, given that the fund was not fully funded. This case corroborates and relies on *Blankenship* in finding that the duty of trustees is to act in the best interests of all beneficiaries, even if it may mean making investment decisions that may appear on the face of it to be imprudent. The court went so far as to endorse *Blankenship* because 'neither the protection of the jobs of the city's teachers nor the general public welfare were factors which motivated the trustees in their investment decision' (*Withers* (1978), p. 1256). Furthermore, the court said: 'The extension of aid to the city was simply a means – the only means, in their assessment – to the legitimate end of preventing the exhaustion of the assets of the [Teachers' Retirement System] in the interests of all the beneficiaries. Notably, the importance of the solvency of the city to fund lay not only in its role as the major contributor of funds but also as the ultimate guarantor of the payment of pension benefits to participants' (ibid.). *Withers* – like *Blankenship* – addresses the intentions of the trustees in making an investment and the process by which they make that investment.

In *Donovan* v *Walton* (1985), trustees financed, built, and leased out an office building with the union as principal tenant. They based the project on close research and analysis, aided by independent consultants at every step of the way. This project benefited the union because of the reasonable leasing costs, and it clearly took the interests of the union into account. The court, however, decided that the investment decisions of the trustees were made with the interests of the beneficiaries paramount. Most clearly articulated in *Donovan* v *Bierwirth* (1982), and known as the *exclusive benefit rule* under the U.S. Employee Retirement Income Security Act (ERISA), the rule requires trustees never to put themselves in a position of divided loyalty and always to act solely in the interests of beneficiaries, whether or not others benefit. This, of course, allows for the notion of collateral benefit so long as there is no divided loyalty.

Board of Trustees v *City of Baltimore* (1989) is the most significant of U.S. cases regarding social investment. Trustees opposed a City of Baltimore ordinance supporting a South African boycott on the grounds that it would trustee activities of the impair and performance of the funds. The ordinances – which dealt directly with the issue of rates of return of the pension funds and divestiture – were declared to be valid in not impinging on the trustees' responsibilities of prudence. Furthermore, the obligation of trustees to consider social factors did not violate case law standards. Finally, standards of prudence were deemed not to be threatened as long as the costs of considering social consequences are minimal; in fact, the court commented that, given the power of pension funds, trustees should be encouraged to consider social consequences.

These decisions leave open a broad conception of prudent investment, encompassing the job security of pension plan members and the health of their union and communities, as long as the (union) trustees are informed, responsible, and hold the interests of beneficiaries paramount. Indeed, social criteria for investment should be encouraged in the general good as long as the costs are minimal.

These decisions are supported by legal commentary from Professor A.W. Scott, a leading American scholar on trust law, who says: 'Trustees in deciding whether to invest in, or to retain, the securities of a corporation may properly consider the social performance of a corporation. They may decline to invest in, or to retain, the securities of corporations whose activities or some of them are contrary to fundamental and generally accepted ethical principles. They may consider such matters as pollution, race discrimination, fair employment, and consumer responsibility ... a trustee of funds for others, is entitled to consider the welfare of community and refrain from allowing the use of funds in a manner detrimental to society' (1987, p. 277).

During this same period in the United Kingdom, however, one case in particular was not supportive of social investment issues. In *Cowan* v *Scargill* (1984), the British Chancery Division Court had to decide whether the union trustees of the Mineworkers Pension Scheme were in breach of their fiduciary duty in seeking to prohibit overseas investments and any investments supporting an industry in competition with the coal industry. The five trustees for the National Coal Board (the employer) successfully opposed union policy. Master in Chancery Megarry held that the best interests of the beneficiaries were the best financial interests: 'The power [of investment] must be exercised so as to yield the best return for the beneficiaries, judged in relation to the risks of the investment in question; and the prospects of the yield of the income and capital appreciation both have to be considered in judging the return from the investment' (p. 760). However, Master Megarry also said that non-financial criteria could be used if alternative investments were equally beneficial to beneficiaries. In subsequent commentary, Megarry maintained that it was Arthur Scargill's uncompromising prohibition on certain types of investment and his ideological approach that made a more balanced decision difficult. It may not have been helped by Scargill's insistence on representing himself, although Megarry says in the decision that Scargill represented himself 'with courtesy and competence.' This may be just one of the many confusing and contradictory details of this decision. Other commentators have also found this decision unnecessarily confusing and incomplete (Yaron, 2000; Lane, 1991; Farrar and Maxton, 1986), although the majority of U.S. commentators pay it little attention, having a very extensive case law and detailed laws and regulations themselves.

Cowan v *Scargill* has retained an undeserved influence with trustees in Canada and Britain that is out of proportion to its place in case law. The ideology in *Cowan* is fundamental to the characterization of the prudent man. This case has been maintained in some academic and legal commentaries even in the United States, however, in spite of the progress in legal decisions and the practical realities of the law (see Hutchinson and Cole, 1980; Langbein and Posner, 1980; Manitoba Law Reform Commission, 1993; Palmer, 1986; Romano, 1993; Scane, 1993). It has also been promoted heavily by the financial industry, as well as by trustees who oppose social investment and union involvement in investment criteria.

Other legal commentators disagree with this characterization and argue that, within the context of prudent decision-making, and considering the balance of decisions, there is a right to make investment decisions based on social and political criteria (Campbell and Josephson, 1983; Farrar and Maxton, 1986; Lane, 1991; Pearce and Samuels, 1985; Ravikoff and Curzan, 1980; Scott, 1987; Waitzer, 1990; Yaron, 2000).

Decisions in the United Kingdom subsequent to *Cowan* have moderated Megarry's decision. In *Martin* v *City of Edinburgh District Council* (1998), the court held that trustees may have a policy on ethical investment that is consistent with general standards of prudence and pursue it 'so long as they treat the interests of the beneficiaries as paramount' (Trades Union Congress, 1996, p. 86). *Martin* v *Edinburgh* brings British case law on trusts more into line with the American cases to date. It also echoes the standard set by the Goode Committee, which was established in 1992 by the British government to make recommendations on legal frameworks for pension funds, in view of the huge losses suffered by pension funds under the control of newspaper owner Robert Maxwell. The committee found: 'this means trustees are free to avoid certain kinds of prudent investment which they would regard as objectionable, so long as they make equally advantageous investments elsewhere, and that they are entitled to put funds into investments which they believe members would regard as desirable, so long as these are proper investments on other grounds. What trustees are not entitled to do is subordinate the interests of beneficiaries to ethical or social demands and thereby deprive the beneficiaries of investment income opportunities they would otherwise have enjoyed' (ibid.).

Underlying *Cowan* v *Scargill* is an outright rejection of a union's right to represent its members, as well as a denial of the relevance of workers' lives to investment practice. According to this ruling, even though the membership of the union and the union trustees may be in agreement on utilizing social criteria in making investment decisions, union trustees should not represent their members' desires. Furthermore, Megarry denies any connection between the general prosperity of the coal industry and financial benefit to the fund, calling it 'speculative and remote' (ibid., p. 751). This opinion was in spite of union arguments that members of the pension plan were dependent on the coal industry for their own job security as well as for ensuring the prosperity of their communities. (Similar arguments were put forward successfully in the *Withers* case, where the welfare of New York teachers as well as the viability of the pension fund depended on the welfare of New York City.) In the *Cowan* v *Scargill* ruling, the general prosperity of the coal industry is characterized as the 'personal interests and views' of the trustees (p. 761). Based on these arguments, *Cowan* v *Scargill* establishes the concept of the maximum rate of return as *the* principle for investment.

American case law broadens the concept of fiduciary responsibility to take into account who makes the investment decision, how it is made, and in whose interests, as opposed to evaluating the decision solely according to the rate of return. It also attempts to align workers' interests with the investment, so that the investment can actually support rather than undermine their livelihoods. Furthermore, it exhibits tolerance of a strong role for union trustees, as long as the union is not directly represented at the trustee table and as long as the trustees seek independent advice.

Union and Employer Accountability

Trustee law has set a high level of accountability for union trustees, but standards for employer trustees are substantially weaker. It is fully accepted that some level of (self-interested) investment of pension assets in an employer's enterprise must be permitted so that employers are not discouraged from continuing to have workplace pension plans (Scane, 1993). A pension fund may be a source of economic advantage to a sponsoring employer, in which case 'the opportunity to earn exceptional returns may itself be a part of the sponsor's purpose' (Ambachtsheer and Ezra, 1998, p. 37). Employers wishing to invest fund capital in their own business have not been viewed as using personal bias, as long as they proceed under self-imposed guidelines. Furthermore, investments which would otherwise violate the duty of loyalty can be permitted in a trust. If an investment is made in an enterprise where a trustee is an officer of the company, or has some conflict of interest (or dual loyalties), a trustee's 'independent investigation' into the basis for the investment must be 'both intensive and scrupulous.' In Ontario, investment in an employer's securities is lawful, where the securities are publicly traded (Scane, 1993). Pension fund capital does not belong to the employer. Nevertheless, many employers view it as their own, and the judiciary have tended to accept this appropriation as legitimate.

Maximum Rate of Return and Diversification

Cowan v *Scargill* has been responsible for promulgating the myth of the maximum rate of return. Many commentators have noted the irrationality of this notion in the context of portfolio diversification. An underlying issue is how, and over what period of time, investment returns should be measured. Asset management requires that trustees understand how asset classes behave in relation to the liabilities of pension funds. Interestingly, there is no industry agreement on the rate of return of a fund. In answer to this point, Tom Gunn, chief of investment for the Ontario Municipal Employees Retirement System (OMERS), makes this comment: 'We see our first role as fiduciary for our beneficiaries. Social investment or any other form of investment or economic-directed activity must be subordinate to the long-term interest of the plan' (Canada, Senate Standing Committee on Banking, Trade, and Commerce, 1998, p. 8). In Canada, the Ontario Teachers Pension Plan board of trustees has as its goal to maximize rates of return. In the United Kingdom, the Trades Union Congress (TUC) – clearly cowed by *Cowan* v *Scargill* – concedes that the ultimate responsibility of the trustee is to maximize return and that prudence attaches to each investment (TUC, 1996, p. 51). However, trustees can invest ethically and still meet their legal duties.

The maximum rate of return is not the standard for all plans. The OPSEU Pension Trust (OPT), for example, has an investment policy to achieve 'reasonable rates of return' (OPT, 1997). Nor is this standard of the maximum rate of return reflected in U.S. case law. *Cowan* v *Scargill* reflects the tail end of a trend in British case law that was based on the old investment practice of lists, where the financial rate of return was the standard by which the individual investment remained on the list. One can only assume that this was – or could be – regardless of risk. Because modern investment practice is based on the diversification of assets in terms of their asset class benchmark and risk-to-return ratios, a maximum rate of return for each investment clearly does not make sense. It may even encourage imprudent investment to maximize return, as well as more short-term investment strategies, thereby threatening the long-term viability of a fund.

The Department of Labor, the regulatory body for pension law in the

United States, does address the issue of portfolio diversification and returns. It stipulates that trustees must consider:

- The composition of the portfolio with regard to diversification
- The liquidity and current return of the portfolio relative to the anticipated cash flow requirements of the plan
- The projected return of the portfolio relative to the funding objective of the plan.

A fourth standard compels trustees to consider expected returns. The U.S. Department of Labor also states that 'because every investment necessarily causes a plan to forego other investment opportunities, an investment will not be prudent if it would be expected to provide a plan with a lower rate of return than available alternative investments with commensurate rates of return' (U.S. Department of Labor, 1994).

As Zanglein (2000) points out, this addresses the issue of investments within an asset class – and not the level of risk. It is, therefore, neither an exhortation to be conservative, nor a duty to maximize benefits. The first is not in the interests of portfolio diversification. The second would be too onerous on trustees and is not supported by American courts. Rather, it says that trustees may not select an investment with collateral benefit but lower returns than can be found with another investment in the same asset class with similar risk-to-return ratios. Benchmarks are therefore critical.

An often overlooked fact of *Cowan* v *Scargill* is that the National Union of Mineworkers and the union trustees of its pension fund were also seeking to promote a union policy of investing only in Britain to the exclusion of overseas investment: 'Pension funds have enormous assets. If all, or nearly all of these assets were invested in Britain, and none, or few, were invested overseas, this would do much to revive this country's economy and so benefit all workers, especially if the investments were in the form not of purchasing established stocks and shares but of "real" investment in physical assets and new ventures. For the mineworkers' scheme, the prosperity of the coal industry would aid the prosperity of the scheme and so lead to benefits for beneficiaries under the scheme' (p. 755).

Sir Robert Megarry Master in Chancery, decided that this evidence on economic and investment strategy was too remote from the interests of beneficiaries and, instead, relied on the British Trustee Investments Act (1961), which said simply that trustees should have regard for the need for diversification of investments. Furthermore, Megarry screened out the possibility that international investment might harm the fund, particularly in a downturn of the British economy (even though he had acknowledged that the pension plan was fully funded). This was notwithstanding his earlier comments that if (adult) beneficiaries had strict moral or social views about alcohol or tobacco, then trustees would be justified in not investing in these corporate sectors even if returns were thereby lowered. Interestingly, Megarry was thrown back on a law – predating major changes in the economy and investment practice – which actually was unclear about levels of diversification, as well as being forced to speculate about the specific interest of beneficiaries of the pension fund. This may be the fundamental weakness of Megarry's decision.

Impact of the Prudence Rule on Union Trustees

Based on the case law, trustees should be mindful of the overall investment strategy and asset allocation, rather than individual investments. Broadening portfolios through the addition of more asset classes, some of which might be riskier than others is permitted. In other words, trustees are not required to be conservative investors (whatever, that may mean in the days of Bre-X, Nortel, and Enron). Indeed, there is a growing interest in private equity as reported in *Benefits Canada* (Falconer, 1999).

The interests of beneficiaries are paramount. What would beneficiaries want if they were investing this money themselves and they knew what informed trustees know? Trustees must always seek independent advice and their process (and progress) should reflect whose interests are being considered and pursued. The interests of the union may be considered and may even be integral to the investment project, but these must not dominate the interests of beneficiaries and thereby cause a conflict of interest.

Divestment, essential to union boycott campaigns, must be handled carefully. This is because of the greater potential for lower rates of return from untimely and, therefore, potentially costly withdrawal of investments. (It needs to be handled as carefully as coming into the market.) However, divestment can be planned with alternative investments designed to minimize costs.

This all speaks to a greater transparency on the part of union trustees so that beneficiaries gain a greater understanding of investment choices and decision points.

There are several significant legal commentators from a Canadian perspective. The prevailing and more conservative legal view in Canada is possibly reflected by Edward Waitzer, a former chief commissioner of the Ontario Securities Commission (OSC) and lawyer practising in both Canada and the United States: 'If ethical choices do not lower investment returns, the practical (and legal) reality is that trustees are unlikely to face judicial interdiction, regardless of their motivation. If investment returns are lowered, trustees are in trouble' (1990, pp. 10–11).

Patricia Lane, while reflecting the undue influence of the British case, argues that, first, social investment can be defended even if its sole concern is not to maximize the rate of return; second, using financial criteria alone hurts the growth of fund assets because there is evidence that the rate of return is not damaged and may be increased by investing according to non-financial criteria; finally, unions may make the decisions about which guidelines to apply in the investment of their members' funds. Lane advises union trustees to amend trust documents to encourage engagement in socially responsible investment. If this is not possible, she recommends:

> [Union trustees] should consider how they may be able to show that the decision they took was in the best interests of the beneficiaries. To this end, it would be wise to seek and rely on independent advice. At least one of the large investment houses in Vancouver now offers advice to clients interested in this investment concept. More will follow as the market grows. There is no need to lose money simply because of the application of some ethical guidelines to one's investment portfolio. If the decision does require a short-term loss: for example, the sale of shares at a poor level because of the desire to honour a boycott or to divest from a country with a repressive regime, or to apply leverage to assist another union in a dispute, it would be a good idea to canvass the beneficiaries and potential living beneficiaries in some way. Finally, there is growing indication that all trustees should establish ethical guidelines because of the performance of these funds. (1991, pp. 181–2)

Finally, Gil Yaron, director of law and policy for the Shareholder Association for Research and Education (SHARE) has published an extensive legal commentary where he finds that 'in the context of socially responsible investment, consideration of non-financial investment criteria does not violate the principles of prudence and loyalty provided that the investment decision adheres to the pension plans' investment policy and independent expert advice' (2000, p. 36).

This view, Yaron points out, is supported by the Pension Commission of Ontario (now subsumed under the Financial Services Commission). Yaron makes points similar to Lane's with respect to trustee knowledge of corporate social and environmental behaviour and its impact on the bottom line, the favourable rates of return associated with social investment, and finally, consideration of beneficiaries as members of communities that rely on corporate investment and good behaviour.

Few union pension funds have social investment in their statements of investment policy (Quarter et al., 2001; Yaron, 2002). The Hospitals of Ontario Pension Plan (HOOPP, 1994), (with union joint trustee representation from the Ontario Public Service Employees Union (OPSEU), the Canadian Union of Public Employees (CUPE), and the Service Employees International Union) and OPSEU's Staff Pension Plan are two of the few that do cite social investment in their policy statements. The presence of unions as sponsors or trustees is, therefore, no guarantee of socially responsible investment policies (Quarter et al., 2001). The SHARE in British Columbia sponsored by the Canadian Labour Congress (CLC), has recently undertaken a study of pension fund investment policies to educate trustees on models of investment policy guidelines.

In the United States the American Federation of Labor and Congress of Industrial Organizations (AFL-CIO) has taken an interestingly progressive stance towards the use of independent advisers: 'Process prudence assumes there is a set of objective criteria against which to measure a particular investment option; the most common and effective being historical data on risk and return ... foreign securities as a class should not be ruled out as an acceptable investment under the Employee Retirement Income Security Act (ERISA) on the basis that fiduciaries engaging in international investing are somehow acting in a different manner than their peers in the community, or that there is a lack of expert independent assistance to pursue such investing' (1993, p. 4).

Many trustees still maintain that there is a scarcity of investment managers with appropriate expertise in various types of alternative investment strategies. A recent survey of pension officials in Canada, sponsored by the Canadian Labour and Business Centre (CLBC) and the Pension Investment Association of Canada (PIAC), reported that 73 per cent complained of the shortage and cost of investment specialists. A further 69 per cent said that there was too little expertise in private capital markets to enable economically targeted investment (see Falconer, 1998).

Union trustees frequently complain of the lack of union-sympathetic, progressive fund managers with experience in socially responsible investment strategies (Carmichael, 1998). Rather than a shortage, this may reflect a need for more coordination and networking between trustees and their unions as well as for education for trustees on how to deal with their fund managers (Carmichael et al., 2001). The CUPE (2003) has recently published an impressive fact sheet for trustees: *Questions for Money Managers.*

Union trustees, therefore, should begin to develop investment strategies more in line with the interests of their members and the general community. This approach is being facilitated by the trade union movement. Unions, union activists, and trustees now have networks through a number of union educational opportunities: conferences being held by the CLC and the Canadian Labour and Business Centre; publications from SHARE and individual unions; and academic research as a basis for educational strategies being pursued by the Ontario Institute for Studies in Education (OISE) of the University of Toronto, and Carleton University in Ottawa.

The prudence rule and fiduciary responsibility have enabled the corporate sector to maintain its control over pension funds, originally through individual employers and subsequently through the financial industry. This rule supposedly protects workers' pensions by keeping assets safe and secure against speculation through prudent trusteeship. However, the high level of accountability to which union trustees are held, in contrast to the lack of accountability for employer trustees, disguises the capital accumulation function of this rule: 'Safety is a pseudo policy. Preservation of revenue and profitability are the genuine ones. In practice, the goal of safety ... has served as a protection and ... mystification for the status quo' (Orren, 1974, in Deaton, 1989, p. 302).

This rule has blocked union trustees from alternative investment strategies on the grounds that these decisions would represent subjective or ideological viewpoints and that they would lower the rate of return. Although the prudent man rule does not prevent trustees from taking social criteria into account, it assumes that these criteria are likely to reduce the rate of return and, thus, violate the trustee's responsibility. Objectivity of investment, and therefore prudence, are supposedly ensured when trustees follow prescribed investment procedures.

American and British case law has become less stringent on the issue of non-financial criteria for investment. There is also a trend among public sector unions in Canada to seek more control over their pension funds. Yet the prudent man ideology still retains its power with many trustees. Social or political investment strategies remain cast as moral views, or views lacking in objectivity, that would otherwise be obtained through a purely financial strategy or process. If objective, financially sound procedures are followed for investment, it is assumed that the rate of return will be maximized. However, as the new economy and globalization factors play a growing role, the behaviour of markets appears less predictable and more irrational. Faith in 'financially sound procedures' is beginning to be shaken, and trustees may be willing to look for longer-term investment that is less irrational and speculative.

This chapter has summarized the significant cases in the United States and the United Kingdom available as guides to union trustees. It has assessed the legal opportunities presented union trustees to develop social investment strategies as part of their portfolio management. In the absence of significant social investment initiatives in Canada, it highlights recent Canadian legal opinion which encourages trustees to work on statements of investment policy as a first step in making investment practice more in line with progressive trade union policy on economic development. This chapter also speaks to a much stronger role for unions in working with their trustees on education initiatives, investment policy, and even joint economic development projects for the benefit of members of pension plans.

chapter 3

The Expansion of Capital Markets

During the 1960s and 1970s, as the courts attempted to come to grips with the impact of the prudence rule and trust law on pension fund investment decisions, pension fund assets continued to expand. In 1980, pension fund assets in Canada were $65.5 billion, having grown from $4.8 billion in 1960. Their growth exceeded that of any other financial institution (Deaton, 1989, p. 234). By 1985, they had outstripped most other financial institutions to become second only to the chartered banks in Canada (ibid., p. 237). Pension funds had also become a major source of capital in financing government expansion through the purchase of government debt. Between 1970 and 1982, Canadian pension funds purchased 20 per cent of all net, new, marketable government bonds placed in Canada (ibid.).

There was no doubt that pension funds were eyed as an invaluable source of wealth for the private capital markets. Given the downturn in the economy, Canadian companies were increasingly dependent on sources of capital and, in particular, pension funds. Deaton reports that 'as one study [in 1976] concluded, pension funds are now so important as a source of funds that any marked diminution ... would have very serious consequences for the future financing patterns and growth ... of Canadian industry' (Grant, 1976).

In Canada, pension funds held 24.2 per cent of corporate securities in 1964. This proportion had risen to 49.8 per cent by 1980 (Deaton, 1989). In the United States, this increased reliance on pension fund investment by the corporate sector was encouraged by the deregulation of brokers' fees and commissions in 1975. Average fees fell from 26 cents to 7.5 cents per share per trade (Lorie et al., 1985; Ghilarducci, 1994). However, the financial markets were adjusting to a major downturn in the economy and a loss of faith by investors in the equity markets. The loss of faith could not be attributed to the economy alone. James Vertin, a financial management expert, comments: 'The business badly needs to replace its cottage industry operating methods – and the rationale underlying these methods – by the development of a better understanding of the workings of the marketplace, by the application of new technology, and by the introduction of new forms of management conduct' (1974, p. 10).

Crucial to modernization of the financial industry was the management of institutional portfolios such as pension funds. Modern portfolio theory became the major influence in stock market practice in the 1960s and 1970s and provided the vehicle for equity investment by pension funds. Rather than a listing of securities in order of their individual expected returns, investments were now to be evaluated as a group according to their average risks and returns (Lorie, 1985). Risk, rather than being the possibility of loss, was defined as the likelihood of deviance from an expected norm (Sharpe, 1963; Vertin, 1974; LeBaron, 1974; Elton, 1981; Lorie, 1985; Harrington, 1987). Risk and return were to be the only variables in assessing investment. The role of the financial industry would be to assemble portfolios, manage ongoing assessments of risk and return, and practise 'market timing' through the purchase and sale of stock to maximize the rate of return (Woolverton, 1998). The role of the corporation was to yield the maximum rate of return to its shareholders. Modern portfolio theory (MPT) built modern financial management practice and effectively supplanted the need for the prudent man rule as a control mechanism over pension capital by the capital markets (Gordon, 1986). Through the MPT's promise of technical assessment of asset allocation and rates of return, the entry of pension funds into the capital markets was ensured.

Pioneered by Harry Markowitz (1952), modern portfolio theory identified the two critical variables as risk and expected return. An efficient portfolio offers the maximum return for a given average level of risk. This is expressed in the capital asset pricing model, where the portfolio return is calculated as the average expected return for all the assets. The risk is the variance of an asset's expected return around a norm in comparison with a low-risk benchmark like cash or treasury bills (Sharpe, 1963; Vertin, 1974; LeBaron, 1974; Elton, 1981; Lorie, 1985; Harrington, 1987). The relationship of risk and return for the portfolio results in a line – the security market line – where the return rises with the risk. The key to the pricing of stock is therefore its level of risk.

The security market line – the expression of the capital asset pricing model (CAPM) – is thus the prime tool used by portfolio managers to restrict evaluation of investments to the two variables of risk and return. It provides the technical enforcement process for fiduciary responsibility and, therefore, is critical in preventing other criteria from being used in investment such as options that either:

- Have strong social yields such as the creation of good jobs or housing, or
- Support innovative industry with no demonstrated history of rates of return and – therefore – the possibility of higher risks.

The assumptions of modern portfolio theory prevent social investment and economic innovation (Blair, 1995; O'Sullivan, 1999). Conversely, investments with serious social risks cannot be opposed on social grounds.

Portfolio Management and the Efficient Market Theory

Modern portfolio theory makes assumptions about the market in general that are summarized in efficient market theory (EMT). The purpose of EMT is to prove that markets are fair, in that investment decisions are made only on the basis of readily available information, and speculators cannot make unreasonable profits (Fama 1970, 1991). EMT is designed to reassure shareholders that they should be the central group to generate wealth, since their wealth is not guaranteed through compensation, unlike the case for corporate managers or employees. Investors all operate on the basis of the same – publicly available – advice, and the market price reflects the fundamental value of the company. The implication is that the market is inherently efficient, when the underlying worth of a company is correctly assessed and investors have decided on the right mix of risk and return. If a company receives a low evaluation, it is characterized as a poor investment because of its risk-to-return profile (Lorie, 1985; Ghilarducci, 1994). There are three hypotheses, ranging from weak to strong, that follow from efficient market theory (Fama, 1991):

1 Rates of return cannot be predicted; past stock behaviour cannot indicate future prices. (weak).
2 Stock prices adjust immediately to significant news or events. (medium).

3 There should be no privileged access to information; therefore, the price reflects all available information. (strong).

Each version of EMT, if correct, has practical implications for pension trustees in relation to the maximum rate of return.[1]

If the weak version of the efficient market theory holds true, then presumably fund managers cannot 'beat' the market, and they may have a poorer investment performance than the market average (Zeikel, 1974; Barber, 1982). Called the 'random walk theory,' the assumption here is that 'a random guess will enable you to predict the next market move with the same (or higher) degree of accuracy than the estimate provided through either technical or fundamental analysis (Zeikel, 1974, p. 20). The random walk theory was confirmed by Rorke and Ianet (1976), in the Canadian equity markets, on the basis of a sampling of the monthly returns of 133 stocks listed on the Toronto Stock Exchange (TSE) and the Montreal Stock Exchange (MSE) over a ten-year period.

This thinking led to the development of indexed funds, which are lists of stocks benchmarked against the local market. The indexed portfolio was pioneered in the United States by the Samsonite Pension fund in 1971. Canada's first commercial TSE 300 index fund was introduced in 1978 by National Trust (Ilkiw, 1997). Indexed funds were developed as a reaction to the poor investment performance of managers in relation to the market averages: 'Since it has been shown that throwing darts at the stock quotations is as effective as spending millions of dollars for in-depth research in terms of investment performance, pension funds are increasingly opting for these much less expensive vehicles which are designed to perform as well, or as poorly, as the market' (Barber, 1982, p. 36).

In spite of this evidence, active investment has continued where fund managers are given money to – essentially – beat the market with their own choice of investment. Therefore, all equity investment, as well as the performance of fund managers, has come to be measured against benchmarks of the markets, such as the TSE 300 (Woolverton, 1998).

Fund managers may continue to sell active investment because it is good for business. But there is also a large body of research pointing to evidence of the predictability of stock prices and future market perfor-

---

1 In spite of my criticisms, I rely on Doug Henwood's (1997, pp. 137–86) admirable account of market models.

mance (Fama and French, 1988; French et al., 1987; Campbell, 1987; Fama, 1981; Fama and Schwert, 1977; Bodie, 1976; Jaffe and Mandelker, 1976; Nelson, 1976). This research poses a serious challenge to the capital asset pricing model, since it is the CAPM that has enabled the massive investment of pension funds into capital markets. Although most of these studies show a small level of predictability on the variation of returns over a shorter period of time, Fama and French (1988), in their study of stock prices from 1926 to 1985, estimate that 25 to 45 per cent of the variation is predictable from past returns. Using the same set of data, they also show that the variation in stock and bond prices is related to economic cycles. Moreover, they demonstrate that firm size and market value are better predictors of return than is level of risk, thus further calling into question the CAPM, as well as the supposed efficiency of the markets (and the EMT). This debate, characterized as a 'battle' by the *Economist* (1997, p. 87), has spawned many studies, with financial economists rushing to the defence of the CAPM (Amihud et al., 1992; Breen and Korajczyk, 1993; Jagannathan and Wang, 1993; Kothari et al., 1995). However, the results of these studies are highly dependent on the choice of data and evidence used (Jagannathan and McGrathan, 1995). There are obvious advantages to using the same set of data, consistently, over a long period of time, as Fama and French were able to do. Henwood comments: 'The message seems to be that, yes, the more volatile an asset, the higher its likely return *over the very long term*, but the relation escapes precise quantification of the sort most conventional economists crave. Since CAPM is not only used to analyse financial markets, but is also used by corporate managers, to decide on real investments, the model's fate is of more than technical interest' (1997, p. 168; emphasis added).

One can only imagine the scrambling to pin together the CAPM, as it has enabled the massive investment of pension funds in the capital markets, supplanting the 'prudent man' rule, and putting into practice the principle of diversification of assets. CAPM has given portfolio managers the tool to evaluate assets by risk and return. In short, the CAPM has propped up the financial industry since the 1970s. However, it is more surprising that Henwood (a Marxist commentator and founding contributor to *Monthly Review*), cannot let go of efficient market theory at this point. On the face of it, rates of return appear to be random over time. Yet there is increasing evidence that stock market returns are influenced by upturns and downturns in the economy; corporate mergers, acquisitions, and takeovers; size of corporation; government monetary policies; and events – as well as by the unbridled behaviour of fund managers (Johnson and Jensen, 1998). Shiller (2000) argues that an unprecedented confluence of events is influencing stock prices. These events include an explosion in day trading, increased access to the Internet (enabling day trading), the ageing of the baby-boomers, the size of pension funds on international stock markets, and 'herd' behaviour. Shiller's work reflects a broader, less insular perspective on the financial world, and – dare it be said? – common sense.

Maximum Rate of Return and Fund Manager Performance

Henwood allows efficient market theory to stand. He bases this position on his assumption that most traders (or the corporations they work for) are unable to exercise more responsibility, insight, and sober second thought in their work: 'Things that seem "predictable" in retrospect aren't easy to see in real time. Mortal traders who have to worry about commissions, taxes, and other worldly complications, can't easily translate an anomaly announced in the *Journal of Finance* into a profitable trading system ... once discovered, anomalies can be self-unfulfilling prophesies' (1997, p. 170).

The weak version of market efficiency, then, is often agreed to hold, inasmuch as abnormal returns are not made by investors on the basis of prediction of market movements. The exceptions are corporate insiders and stock exchange specialists, who have access to privileged information, which, of course, should not happen according to the strong version of EMT. For example, in a study of large industrial companies listed on the Toronto Stock Exchange, Baesel and Stein (1979) found that over a four-year period bank directors and other insiders achieved consistently high, abnormal rates of return on their investments. Similar results have been found over a ten-year period (Fowler and Rorke, 1988; Suret and Cormier, 1990). Therefore, the 'fairness' or efficiency of the Canadian markets does not extend to financial industry insiders.

Fund managers, who advise pension funds, appear not to be on the 'inside track.' Rates of return are no higher when stocks are actively managed by fund managers. This is confirmed by Schmitz, in a synthesis of forty-five studies dating from 1962 to 1995: 'In fact, the average gross performance of the average active manager at best equals the performance of standard passive benchmarks, and is most likely marginally below these benchmarks. In achieving this relatively poor performance, the average active manager possesses marginally positive stock selection ability, but also perverse market timing ability (Schmitz, 1995, p. 3). This conclusion is corroborated by research in the United States that, on balance, indicates that professional investment managers do not have access to private information (Brinson et al., 1986; Elton et al., 1991, cited in Fama, 1991, p. 1603).

Complementary evidence shows that pension fund equity returns, on average, fall below market indices – and, incidentally, below mutual funds. Lakonishok et al. (1991) undertook an analysis of 769 corporate pension funds in the United States. They find that representative funds underperformed the Standard and Poor (S&P) 500 Index by 1.3 per cent per year before accounting for management fees; over an average three-year period, which is the typical evaluation period for fund managers, the underperformance was 1 per cent. Patry and Poitevin (1995) observe that the latter findings are consistent with those of other major studies, for example, Beebower and Bergstrom (1977) for 1966–75, Brinson et al. (1986) for 1974–83, and Malkiel (1995) for 1975–89. They also point out that, in Canada, Taylor concludes that 'for periods ranging from one to eight years, the annualized return of the index has outperformed the median manager by between 0.10 per cent and 3.10 per cent, before management fees' (1995, p. 25). Lakonishok and colleagues (1991) note that the average pension fund in the United States tends to buy more stock that has performed poorly and sell a disproportionate amount that has performed well. Most damaging, perhaps, Lakonishok's group (1992) 'froze' pension portfolios to see the impact of trading by fund managers – trading proved to be counter-productive, and not working to increase value. However, it may be pointed out here, as Bruyn suggests (1987, p. 113), that the pension trustees could have done better by investing in union-built housing for the poor at low interest rates.

The final irony is evidence that over the long term, bonds perform better than stocks (Hodges et al., 1997). Pension funds, which by their nature should be invested for long periods of time and which were primarily invested in bonds until the 1980s (as described at the beginning of this chapter), are now predominantly invested short term and, unfortunately, at their own expense.

Damaging criticism of the fallaciousness of efficient market theory is emerging. EMT is criticized for its dependence on a narrow view of rate of return based on financial criteria only, the centrality of a disembodied (or supposedly objective) view of 'information,' its insistence on the corporation as an isolated entity accountable only to its own shareholders, and its dependence on the values of the shareholder (or corporation) based, again, on narrow, financial criteria to the exclusion of the more dynamic assets of a corporation such as its research and development capabilities and its human resources (Glickman, 1994; O'Sullivan, 1999; Low, 1999). Efficient market theory depends on a view of the economy as an essentially unregulated arena operating under natural, rather than state-imposed laws, which, as we have seen, suits the self-interest of the financial industry.

It is fitting that financial 'guru' Peter Drucker should have the final say: 'Global bankers ... have introduced not "a single major innovation in 30 years," he said. Rather, the financial industry has turned inward to perfecting "supposedly scientific derivatives" in a shortsighted hope of wringing the risk out of financial speculation, like Las Vegas gamblers futilely trying to devise "systems" to beat the house' (cited in Andrews, 1999, p. B19).

Pension Funds and Asset Allocation

Pension funds, ideally suited to long-term investment, measure rates of return on a quarterly and yearly basis. Fund managers, selected for their different 'styles' or approaches, are required to provide both quarterly and annual reports to investors on portfolio rates of return. Research shows that fund managers may 'dress up' their portfolios either at the end of the quarter or at the end of the year, to persuade pension trustees of the acceptability of their investments: 'Nobody wants to be caught showing last quarter's disasters ... You throw out the duds because you don't want to have to apologize for and defend a stock's presence to clients even though your investment judgement may be to hold' (Jansson, 1983, p. 139). These patterns are found in Canada (Athanassakos, 1997).

Furthermore, in the fourth quarter of the year, pension funds accelerate their sales of 'losers,' and buy into more acceptable stocks even if the rate of return is lowered as a result (Lakonishok et al., 1991).

All this is evidence that investments are evaluated by factors other than the rate of return and that fund managers are evaluated for factors other than performance. This practice also involves more trading than necessary, indicating an extremely short-term approach to investment, fund management performance, and rate of return when it comes to pension funds: 'Pension funds suffer from earnings shortsightedness, but they are more victims than perpetrators ... money managers hired by pension funds want to maximize the fund's short-term gain; there are dozens of candidates for every manager's job and the incumbent tries to stay in place by showing the best performance' (*Financial Post* 1 July 1997, editorial). Larger funds, in particular, diversify asset allocation across styles of active managers, as this is deemed to be a more sophisticated strategy, drawing attention away from the benchmark rate of return. Evidence suggests that time spent in lengthy interviews with fund managers on the details of the portfolio selection process fails to produce better results: 'Money managers who can provide a good story about their strategy have a comparative advantage. In fact, the product sold by the professional money managers is not just good performance but *schmoozing*, frequent discussions of investment strategies, and other forms of hand holding' (Lakonishok et al., 1992, p. 375).

The financial industry, to keep pension fund business, has developed new indices to persuade pension trustees that they can outperform their portfolio style, while underperforming the market. To appear to be ahead of the market, another trick is to 'lock-in' to an index when close to reporting back to the pension fund (ibid.).

Based on the evidence, the performance of fund managers leaves a lot to be desired. The question is whether there are alternative options for pension fund trustees.

Canadian Capital Markets Structure

The top 100 pension funds in Canada continue to have over $78 billion invested in active management where fund managers attempt to 'beat the market,' in spite of evidence questioning this approach (Bak, 1998). However, there is a trend towards indexed funds or passive fund management. Bak (1997) identifies passive investment management companies as the fastest-growing, with lower fees, reduced risk, and good rates of return as the key factors in their growth. Citing the same reasons, *Greenwood* (1998) reports that indexed mutual funds are the fastest-growing funds: 'Once derided as the "no-brainers" of the mutual fund business, index funds are attracting a torrent of new money – and embarrassing a lot of hands-on money managers with their superior returns' (p. 1). To explain this continued adherence to active investment strategies by pension funds, we need to examine more closely some additional features of the Canadian capital markets.

First, Canadian corporations are more tightly controlled than American corporations. In 1994, of the *Financial Post* 500 largest Canadian non-financial corporations, 60 per cent were wholly owned or effectively controlled by a single shareholder and only 16 per cent were widely held. This is in stark contrast to the United States, where 63 per cent of

Fortune 500 firms are, by the same standard, widely held (Patry and Poitevin, 1995; Daniels and MacIntosh, 1991). Second, in Canada, there is a strong network of cross-ownership and shared directorships (Clement, 1975; Deaton, 1989). This interconnectedness occurs to a lesser extent in the United States Third, in comparison with the United States, there is very little liquidity in the Canadian markets, and this is partly as a result of the interconnectedness of corporations (Patry and Poitevin, 1995). Only 5.3 per cent of Canadian stocks are widely traded, and these predominantly by institutional investors. Furthermore, these are stocks of larger companies as opposed to smaller companies, whose stocks tend not to be traded to any great extent (Fowler and Rorke, 1988). Thus, Canadian pension funds trade in small and thin equity markets, where 'an excessive amount of capital chases too few investment opportunities' in a limited number of large corporations (Daniels and MacIntosh, 1991). The cost of exit is high, because the withdrawal of large investments can lower stock value. Corporate and fund managers tend to be well entrenched. The control of companies by a few major players can be repressive, leading to a context where fund managers and pension fund officials are careful 'not to rock the boat': 'The extensive control and power yielded by a few large groups or families increases the severity of the penalty that a disgruntled management could impose on an unsettling institutional investor' (Patry and Poitevin, 1995).

As a result, the larger, publicly traded companies are overcapitalized. Moreover, an investment strategy that concentrates on passive investment in equity markets merely compounds the problem of overinvestment in a small market. Canada is an example of a country with high capital accumulation but lower productivity because of the failure of fund managers to invest in new and small companies (Canadian Labour and Business Centre, 1993).

Pension funds, given the size of their investments and the critical part they play in the markets, appear to have little control over their level of influence in the corporate sector and, hence, their rates of return. Can these investment strategies continue, and yet allow pension funds to be more influential in the capital markets? Several points can be made:

1 The structure of Canadian capital markets is inefficient, in that investment often fails to provide support to new, developing business.
2 Canadian capital markets are also inefficient, because they are heavily controlled by a few corporate players who keep a tight rein on publicly available information.

3 Increased concentration has caused the ownership of larger blocks of shares by institutional investors. Less liquidity is the result, since the buying and selling of shares disrupts the market.
4 Pension fund officials and fund managers are reluctant to rock the boat.' Exit is costly. Therefore, shareholder activism is limited and difficult if the issues raised challenge the corporate structure and prevailing ideology.
5 Despite protestations to the contrary, equity investment decisions are made by criteria other than rate of return.
6 Pension funds tend not to be economically productive. They often do not create value in the marketplace, and they may provide far less support for their members' livelihoods or their communities than would otherwise be the case.
7 The markets, by their own standards, are in need of overhaul, so they too can be productive with their more-than-adequate resources. Less investment under active management and more in passive indices is not the answer. It compounds the problem of oversaturated markets.
8 There are alternatives. Appropriately diversified, real estate, mortgages, and pooled vehicles are all means of investment that may be shaped in such a way as to have collateral benefits such as creating jobs. Venture capital is a way of investing in new, emerging, developing, and restructuring industries to save and create jobs and to provide regional development. All require a longer term commitment of funds, similar costs to active equity investment, and expertise which is available but not so familiar to many pension fund officials.

Pension funds across Canada have substantial resources and experience to bring a broader perspective to investment and at the same time deal with some of the inefficiencies of the Canadian markets. They need not be restricted to liquid investment, since pension funds take in more than they have to pay out in expenses and benefits. They can therefore be invested long term and drive a new industrial policy through more strategic investment. This is possible, because there is room in the larger funds for experimentation (or research and development), as the Caisse de Depot et Placement du Quebec has done in supporting regional and industrial development, by using 'non-material' – or financially insignificant – amounts of money which, by policy, do not need to be accounted for. All can pursue new directions to set a pattern of Canadian market productivity, corporate accountability, and innovative industrial development.

chapter 4

Shareholder Activism

This chapter examines the feasibility of pension funds becoming more active as shareholders, given the barriers (cited in the previous chapter) of capital concentration and a lack of market liquidity, and the centrality of shareholder theory in corporate law. Since, in Canada, the cost of selling shares can be high, is it possible for a pension fund to be active in improving the value of its shares or even the behaviour of the company, without the effective threat of withdrawing funds?

This chapter is included in this study for two reasons: (1) It addresses the issue of pension fund power in the capital markets. If pension funds have power, can they affect change? If so, what kind of change? (2) Shareholder activism, or corporate governance, is often viewed as a form of social investment. It is, therefore, important to address what value there is in being a shareholder activist and, in particular, whether shareholder action enhances or reduces the rate of return.

Definition and Description

Some would argue that shareholder activism is impossible when shares cannot be withdrawn from the company by pension funds without loss to the fund, as is the case in Canada. The American Federation of Labor and Congress of Industrial Organizations (AFL-CIO), for example, has a company boycott program whereby it notifies all affiliated unions of companies that either are operating in bad faith or are struck. Affiliated unions who have pension investments in the company are encouraged to write to the company, threatening withdrawal of funds unless the company mends its relationship with the in-house union. Is this kind of campaign possible in Canada?

I use 'shareholder activism' to describe a whole range of actions up to and including the pulling out of shares to force corporate accountability. This term may have more resonance with trade union and community activists. Actions that have been taken, to be described later, include meeting with corporate players, writing letters, and stacking annual meetings. These actions are directed at bringing about social change in the corporation's relationship with its shareholders, employees, or community (local or global).

'Corporate governance' is a term coined by the corporate sector itself and is defined by the Toronto Stock Exchange (TSE) as
'the process and structure used to direct and manage the business and affairs of the corporation with the objective of enhancing shareholder value, which includes ensuring the financial viability of the business' (TSE, 1994, p. 7). In line with this definition, pension funds in Canada universally use 'corporate governance' to mean the exercise of their rights as responsible shareholders and fiduciaries to engage in the affairs of the corporation. When I wish to refer to shareholder behaviour in general, I use the term 'shareholder action.'

Corporate governance as an issue is a relatively recent phenomenon for pension funds in Canada, but has a somewhat stronger tradition in the United States. It makes sense to some pension funds that if pulling out shares is to be avoided because of the high cost, then perhaps they can make their presence felt and 'bring value' to their investments through becoming active share owners. It is argued that the effect of liquidity on corporate governance is profound; the more essential is active governance, the higher the cost of exit (Coffee, 1991). An alternative position, however, is that institutional investors must have liquidity to back up 'voice' (Black, 1992). Given the size of their investments and the limited range of their alternatives, Canadian pension funds have little choice but to maintain and improve their corporate investment.

Influencing corporate policy can cover a variety of variables such as compensation for the chief executive officer (CEO), representation and rotation of board members, management pay, as well as takeovers and mergers. It is less likely that it will also cover issues of corporate performance such as human rights, employee working conditions, and environmental impact. However, taking action as shareholder activists on this latter set of issues could refashion the link between ownership and control and provide a way of monitoring corporate conduct (Waitzer, 1991). As can be seen, the critical difference in these terms is the dependence of corporate governance on shareholder theory.

Figure 4.1   Basic black box model of the corporation.

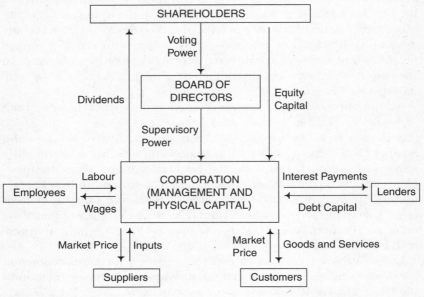

Source: Blair (1995, p. 21).

Shareholder Theory

The theory of corporate governance asserts that shareholders are the central figures in the corporation. Illustrating the basic model of the corporation, called the 'black box' model (BBM), Figure 4.1 shows all the stakeholders in a corporation and their relationship to each other and the corporation itself. If the business makes money after employees, lenders, and creditors have been paid, shareholders can claim the residue. For this reason, it is argued that shareholders take the greatest risk – through their investment in the company – and, therefore, they should reap the greatest reward when the company is profitable. For this reason also, it is argued, they have the right to elect the board of directors (Roe, 1991; Blair, 1995).

But is this control by shareholders real, when shares are as widely dispersed as they are in the United States? It has been argued (Manne, 1965), that shareholder control is real, since managers who work against shareholders' interests will discourage new investment in their company and will lose existing shareholder investment. Managers will then be vulnerable to a takeover (ibid.). The argument, therefore, is made that shareholder theory is a theory of the market, in that when shareholders' interests are primary and central to the running of the corporation, the economy is functioning as it should, with the least level of regulation. Furthermore, taking into account other criteria of corporate performance such as environmental or community standards, social productivity, or innovation would detract from the maximization of shareholder value and should be avoided.

The parallels to pension plan governance cannot be avoided where, as we have seen, the maximum return on the investment is seen as automatically excluding any other criteria than financial ones. A vice-president of the teachers' pension plan in Ontario is quoted as saying: 'When we buy shares in a company, we treat it as though we're the owners of the company. We believe the board of directors is representing us as owners and they have a duty to maximize the share value for us. If it's not going to be looking after our interests first and foremost, then we will invest elsewhere' (Ip, 1996, p. B1). Furthermore, 'companies aren't put together to create jobs. The number one priority is creating shareholder wealth' (ibid.). In contrast, in the same article, John Manley, industry minister in the federal government of Canada at the time, expresses concern that 'business ... reinvest a good portion of its earnings into expansion, growth and the creation of jobs' (ibid., p. B4). Surprisingly, however, Peter Godsoe, chairman of the Bank of Nova Scotia, confesses: 'Scratch me deeply and I believe the mandate of business to only maximize shareholder value is wrong. It ignores too many other realities' (ibid.).

In the United States, both shareholder activism and corporate governance have flourished more easily, because of larger capital markets and more widely held corporations. In such a context, smaller shareholders can have a greater influence on some decisions that affect the corporation. However, as Daniels and Waitzer (1994) argue, each structure brings with it a different set of governance problems. Accountability of management is an issue where shares are broadly held. This is a problem that tends not to be encountered in Canada where, as they say, a telephone call from the majority shareholder will suffice. The problem encountered in Canadian corporations is accountability between majority and minority shareholders to prevent 'bloated compensation arrangements, unfair self-dealing transactions or unanticipated changes in shareholder risk-taking' (ibid., p. 27). Regardless, the prevailing model for pension funds in the United States and Canada is based on increasing the financial value of the corporation and, as such, the return to investors. However, in recent years it has come to be argued that corporations, from a market perspective, have a social function and responsibility in providing leadership in new ventures (O'Sullivan, 1999) and, from a societal perspective, in creating wealth and resources for society (Blair, 1995). Following are some examples of corporate governance and shareholder activism that expect a broader accountability from corporations.

California Public Employees' Retirement System (CalPERS)

The California Public Employees' Retirement System (CalPERS) is the founding leader in the field of shareholder activism, and the largest pension plan in the United States, with U.S. $80 billion in assets. It is the third largest pension fund in the world. CalPERS serves more than one million members and beneficiaries, and its membership includes state, local government, and school district employees. Organized as an 'entity of state government,' it has a central office and eight field offices; its system includes health coverage, a variety of retirement-related programs, and health retirement plans for state judges, legislators, and other state officials. Its thirteen-member board represents public employee and employer interests, in 'careful balance.' The board's composition is set in statute and protected from political influence by the state constitution. Six of the board members are elected by various employee groups (active and retired), two serve by virtue of office, and five are appointed by the governor or the legislature (CalPERS, 1995).

Prior to 1986, CalPERS had a commitment to a passive investment strategy; it did not vote its proxies. Furthermore, its investment approach tended towards a long-term commitment of funds, with a high level of diversification. In 1986, alarmed at a downturn in stock that seemed to be caused by inept corporate management, CalPERS demanded corporate accountability but was routinely ignored by corporate management. The combination of a long-term investment horizon and a passive investment approach began to look like a recipe for disaster. As a result, CalPERS launched its first corporate governance campaign by targeting ten of the poorest-performing companies in its domestic stock portfolio for improvement.

The issues raised by CalPERS include effective shareholder involvement in the election of corporate directors shareholder communication on votes, eliminating staggered boards, and working towards the independence of directors, and confidentiality of voting. Despite pressure from its union representatives, CalPERS, however, is cautious about incorporating social values into its corporate governance approach on the grounds of compromising the fiduciary responsibility of its trustees. But it has incorporated a workplace practices screen in its program since 1994, on the grounds that it will add value to its investments (McCritchie, 1996).

The Interfaith Center on Corporate Responsibility

Counterposed to CalPERS is the Interfaith Center on Corporate Responsibility (ICCR), a coalition of 275 institutional investors from a variety of religious communities, pension funds, healthcare corporations, foundations, and dioceses. The ICCR's combined portfolios are worth an estimated U.S. $90 billion. The ICCR is the leading organization in the United States that is in the shareholder resolution process, and it is instrumental in coordinating resolutions co-filed by different investors. Members of the ICCR hold corporations accountable using arguments backed by economic pressure from consumers and investors. They sponsor resolutions, meet with management, screen their investments, divest stock, conduct public hearings and investigations, publish special reports, and sponsor actions such as prayer vigils, letter-writing campaigns, and consumer boycotts (ICCR, 1998). The centre has contributed research to the Domini Social Index (to be described in Chapter 5), which publishes a newsletter, the *Corporate Examiner,* as well as an annual tracking of all shareholder resolutions dealing with social issues. It has worked with sister organizations in Great Britain and Canada to publish principles spelling out a new business philosophy to govern a corporation's behaviour in a global economy: 'Economic decisions have profound human and moral consequences. Faith communities measure corporate performance not only by what a corporation produces and its profitability, but also by how it impacts the environment, touches human life and whether it protects or undermines the dignity of the human person. Protection of human rights – civil, political, social and economic – are minimum standards for corporations seeking to act responsibly' (ICCR, 1995, p. 1).

Taskforce on the Churches and Corporate Responsibility

Canada's history of shareholder activism has been led by the Taskforce on the Churches and Corporate Responsibility (TCCR), an organization similar in focus to the ICCR. Issues raised by the churches go beyond corporate governance to concerns related to the environment, labour relations, and human rights. The churches collectively funnel their strategies through the task force, as it is set up to research and imple-ment shareholder strategies of social investment. The TCCR has the advantage of being able to build expertise and work exclusively on social policy relating to investment: 'Shareholders have responsibilities and opportunities to help reshape corporate priorities so that the way our money is used reflects our priorities' (Hutchinson, 1996, p. 69). The separate structure of the task force has provided the resources to allow the churches to both safeguard their investments and to have them reflect their organizational values.

In 1984, the churches submitted a shareholder proposal to the Cana-dian Imperial Bank of Commerce (CIBC) asking for a secret ballot policy for voting on shareholder proposals. The issue had arisen the year before, when the churches had forwarded in advance a proposal for a dis-closure on foreign loans above a certain level. After the proposal had been submitted, the bank contacted shareholders in support of the pro-posal to ensure that they knew that this was a vote for the churches and against management. The churches, therefore, brought the secret ballot proposal forward again the following year, and it was promptly opposed by management. Only 7 per cent voted in favour. Nevertheless, the CIBC then agreed to support the churches' proposal and instituted a secret bal-lot: 'What must be clear ... is that we've never actually *won* a vote on a shareholder proposal. But even 10–15% ... given the ownership structure of modern corporations is often taken by the company as indication that an issue is one it can't ignore' (Hutchinson, 1990, p. 67).

To attempt to effect a change in corporate behaviour without raising the issue at an annual meeting, the churches use an incremental approach in raising issues with corporations, starting with a letter and then moving to meetings. But the threat of a proposal to the annual general meeting is always in the background, with accompanying publicity.

Pension Funds and Shareholder Action

For several years, Yves Michaud, a former Quebec politician, Canadian diplomat, and small shareholder, raised shareholder proposals at annual meetings of Canadian banks, and this brought considerable public atten-tion to shareholder action. He has also lobbied pension funds to support his proposals. Although he met with but limited success in his lobbying, during the 1990s, he brought attention to the potential for shareholder action by pension funds.

Among Michaud's successes, is an acknowledgment by the Royal Bank of Canada (RBC) that it would 'give serious consideration to a new way of electing directors that would hand more clout to ordinary shareholders' (Whittington, 1998, p. D1). This came after a very close vote on Michaud's proposal to discard the RBC's system of voting for a slate of directors.

Shareholder experience on the part of union trustees of pension funds is mixed. In a study of union trustees in the top twenty-three Canadian pension funds, unionists were 'unclear about what proxy voting entailed, whether their fund had a policy and who, if anyone, would exercise votes' (Carmichael, 1998, p. 20). Kathryn Montgomery, in her 1995 study of institutional investors, reported an increased interest in corporate governance matters because of abuse of power by management. In a *Globe and Mail* article it was reported that issues of institutional investor governance will gain 'much more attention': 'Institutional shareholders were once called the sleeping giants of capitalism because of their size and traditional docility. In truth, the real sleeping giants are the plan members and beneficiaries: teachers and municipal employees and the employees of companies like Canadian National Railways and Bell Canada, whose pension funds hold billions of dollars in corporate investment' (Finlay, 1997, p. B2).

A significant barrier to institutional investor governance is the control of funds by the financial industry. As has been noted already, fund managers have considerable control over investment of pension funds, particularly where assets are pooled into larger funds. For example, the Carpentry Workers' Pension Plan of British Columbia (CWPP) was unable to join in the shareholder action on child labour, organized by the B.C. Federation of Labour, because its equity is in pooled funds and, hence, under the control of the fund managers (Wayne Stone, interview, 1999). Fund managers actively seek to influence the behaviour of corporations in which they invest pension funds. Douglas Grant, chairman of Sceptre Investments, which is the fifth largest pension fund manager in Canada, explains: 'We have private meetings with companies ... These meetings are valuable to us, in part, because we control the agenda and, in part, because it is important to us to know the character of the people managing the companies that we invest in. It is important to the companies, and they agreed to do it because they need to keep in touch with their shareholders and we are, typically, a big shareholder' (Canada, Senate, 1998, p. 8).

The Pension Trust of the Ontario Public Service Employees Union (OPSEU) has taken an unequivocal position on using its proxy votes where possible. Colleen Parrish, manager of the plan, describes the process for instructing fund managers on how to vote proxies: 'We instruct all our investment managers and our custodian to bring forward issues that we then screen for those that should receive the attention of the Board of Trustees ... Well, when a lot of pension plans do that, then there's a real sense out there that corporate governance matters. Slowly you start to have an impact because it changes the way the capital markets work' (Parrish, cited in Carmichael, 1996, p. 108).

Following the CalPERS model, the Ontario Municipal Employees Retirement System (OMERS) has registered its interest in actually pursuing active corporate governance strategies beyond proxy voting: 'OMERS approach is to work with companies privately to resolve concerns. If that doesn't work, the fund will introduce a resolution at a shareholders' meeting. That has never happened, [OMERS] said because the fund has been successful in resolving issues' privately (Waldie, 1998, p. B7).

The Ontario Teachers Pension Plan (OTPP) board of trustees also has face-to-face meetings with management. The board considers these meetings as 'an integral part of our due diligence in selecting companies for major investment and managing those investments in the long-term' (Canada, Senate, 1998, p. 9).

William Dimma, a director of several public companies, believes that the preferred way is the 'quiet and private' way. Indeed, he maintains that this is the 'Canadian way ... the way to get things done' (ibid.).

The OPSEU Pension Trust, OMERS, and the OTPPB have all developed proxy voting guidelines, which includes social criteria, and they publish these on their Web sites.

CalPERS chooses ten companies yearly and publishes the list, ranking the companies by relative and absolute performance and identifying shareholder returns over both five- and ten-year averages. CalPERS, therefore, is monitoring its index on a regular basis through mechanical screens and analysis. The cost of corporate governance is the cost of the regular screening of its index. Since 1992, CalPERS has included international security markets, arguing that these strategies should be effective in any country. It has also developed the corporate governance strategy to pick issues that have industry-wide significance, in the hopes that improved performance will be initiated throughout the industry, and not restricted to one corporation.

OMERS is considering publishing an annual ranking of companies, based on their corporate governance (and, presumably, their financial performance). In other words, OMERS would comment on changes that would be needed to improve these companies' financial performance.

Barriers to Shareholder Action

Corporate governance assumes that taking a more proactive role in a corporation by exercising proxy votes will raise the financial value of the shares of a corporation and, hence, the rate of return. American law, through the U.S. Department of Labor, has confirmed that voting rights are, in fact, pension plan assets; therefore, it is the duty of fiduciaries to ensure that such assets are voted solely in the interests of the plan members (McCritchie, 1996). Canadian law, it can be argued, also supports trustees as active shareholders. Trustees must, under the standard of prudence, be informed in making investment decisions and seek out information that allows them to assess the financial performance of the company in which they have invested; furthermore, they should oppose mismanagement or other inefficiencies (Waitzer, 1990).

This legal perspective has been extended to decisions based on social concerns about corporate performance. A company may be inefficient, less productive, and therefore, less profitable because of its labour relations, hiring practices, poor environmental standards, or negative relationships to communities. One legal view suggests that trustees are obliged to pursue change in these areas where it is likely that such policies would not harm the investment, or may lead to increased economic return (ibid.). Montgomery (1995) found in a study of institutional shareholders that fiduciary responsibility to clients ranked as the second most important incentive to becoming active.

Nevertheless, it is difficult for a shareholder to put forward proposals relating to corporate social performance in Canada. The Canada Business Corporations Act was originally reformed in 1975 to enshrine shareholders' information on votes and the right to communicate with other shareholders. This reform, however, provided little substance to shareholder rights. (More effective shareholder rights were introduced in the United States in 1942.) Management, prior to 1975, was able to control sparsely attended shareholder meetings by holding enough proxy votes to outvote any challenges.

This Canadian reform was intended to enable shareholders to have similar rights, whether or not they attended meetings. Shareholders were to receive basic information through a proxy circular produced by management, and they were to have the right to include resolutions in the circular (Iler, 1990). The right to circulate resolutions was hedged with qualifications. One of these was the right of corporations to exclude a proposal from the management's proxy circular, if such a proposal was submitted purely to promote 'general economic, political, racial, religious, social or similar causes.' Furthermore, if 'substantially the same' proposal had been submitted and defeated within the previous two years, management could refuse to circulate the proposal.

The effect of such restrictions was mitigated through further changes to the Canada Business Corporations Act. As of November 2001, corporations may not refuse to circulate proposals to shareholders when the proposal promotes 'general economic, political, racial, religious, social or similar cause,' and they must circulate proposals as long as they relate 'in a significant way to the business or affairs of the corporation.' Shareholders can now communicate with one another about shareholder proposals, as long as they do not solicit proxy votes (Yaron and Kodar, 2003).

Implicitly, these changes in law recognize that shareholder activism may not only affect the interests of beneficiaries but also the long-term performance of the company. They therefore raise the question of the connection between corporate social behaviour and financial returns.

In 2000, a shareholder proposal, submitted by Working Enterprises Limited, a company owned by seven unions in British Columbia, asked Placer Dome 'to provide independent public assessments of environmental risk at each of its operations and to disclose detailed information to shareholders about insurers and levels of insurance that the company has in place to protect shareholders from liability' (*Mining Watch Canada*, 2000, p. 1). This proposal reflects concern arose from the increased costs of a spill at Placer Dome's Marcopper operations. Shareholder concern arose because Placer Dome did not have enough insurance to cover the disaster. This proposal addresses the social and economic behaviour of a corporation and is grounded in financial concerns about corporate performance. In effect, this proposal calls for a social accounting by Placer Dome. (This, and other cases, will be discussed further in Chapter 6.)

In 1997, Fairvest Securities reported that, in their survey, a 'significant minority' of shareholders voted against management proposals at twenty-seven out of 405 companies. In one case, shareholders defeated a management proposal. The Fairvest Securities survey was the first of its kind in Canada, even though 'the outcome of proxy votes must be disclosed in public filings in the United States but aside from a short verbal report at annual meetings, in Canada, voting results are rarely disclosed' (Westell, 1997b, p. 12).

The B.C. Carpenters' Union was successful in a shareholder proposal to account for stock options in a campaign for greater transparency in corporate accounting (CBC, 2002).

American law is far more lenient to shareholders, in that a proposal may only be excluded if the subject matter is not sufficiently related to the affairs of the corporation. Needless to say, this has offered more encouragement to the shareholder movement.

Canadian institutional shareholder action, while on the rise, remains largely uncoordinated, with little communication between institutional investors. It is also largely reactive to proposals generating from management. Pension funds in Canada do not put resources into research or analysis of proposals, nor into negotiating activity with corporations whose shares they own. Some have viewed this uncoordinated approach to shareholder action as economically wasteful activity, which if changed can lead to greater control over corporate performance and add to shareholder value (e.g., Daniels and Waitzer, 1994).

The Shareholder Association for Research and Education (SHARE) issue a key proxy vote survey to help pension trustees monitor the performance of their fund managers. SHARE surveyed twenty-seven shareholder proposals in 2003, selected for their 'long-term, worker-owner view of shareholder value that emphasizes management accountability, good corporate governance, international labour standards and corporate social responsibility.' SHARE (2004) notes that 60 per cent of firms contacted declined to participate or did not respond.

Shareholder Action and Rate of Return

CalPERS reports that corporate governance strategies improve share values dramatically. A study that it commissioned (published by Wilshire and Associates of Santa Monica in 1994) examined the performance of companies targeted by CalPERS between 1987 and 1992. The stock price of these companies trailed the Standard and Poor 500 index by 66 per cent for the five years prior to the campaign, and outperformed the index by 41 per cent in the following five years.

Another study of CalPERS (Smith, 1996) reports that when shareholder action is successful in changing governance structure, it also results in added shareholder value. However, when the shareholder action is directed at improved operating performance, there is no statistically significant change in value. (Overall, during the 1987–93 period, shareholder action resulted in a net increase of U.S.$19 million.) The latter finding is not corroborated by either Romano (1993) or Wahal (1996). In his study of the activism of six funds (including CalPERS) for the same period (1987–93), Wahal (ibid.) concludes that although pension funds are successful in changing the governance structure of targeted firms, their activism does not change the rate of return on investment.

Even though the evidence is inconclusive as to whether shareholder activism actually increases the rate of return, there is no evidence of declining returns. Therefore, as a social investment practice, pension funds may engage in shareholder action and maintain fiduciary responsibility.

In spite of the barriers posed by corporate law, pension funds could decide to base their shareholder action on a broader view of corporate performance beyond governance issues, encompassing indicators of social economic performance. This would involve submitting, and not just responding, to shareholder resolutions. Unions in British Columbia have been successful in circulating shareholder resolutions on child labour, in that the corporate sector has agreed to fund and participate in an agency to research child labour issues. Collaborative work between union pension funds and unions themselves can clearly overcome the barriers of corporate law, since the accompanying publicity forces the corporate sector to respond.

Pension fund activism could also take a more proactive approach to corporate governance by representing the pension fund on the board of directors of the company and, thereby, working with a company on a long-term basis. Rather than 'schmoozing,' this could be a productive practice providing expertise to a new company or renovating an older one. As we have seen, rarely do pension funds engage in this sort of enterprise. However, labour-sponsored investment funds do. The Crocus Fund in Manitoba, for example, invests in regional, new and older private placements with a view to providing support to an investment through board representation (Kreiner, 2003).

Through traditional proxy voting mechanisms, as well as through more proactive shareholder campaigns, it has been shown that pension funds may be successful in changing corporate behaviour without reducing their rates of return. However, in the event that rates of return fall, pension funds tend not to withdraw. In Canada this is an even more likely scenero than in the United States because the higher cost of exit is caused by an oversaturated market. Both active and passive investment suffer from the same problem. Pension funds can be more effective shareholders if they apply more resources to become more informed and less reactive, and if they work collectively with other pension funds. But shareholder action is not a substitute for finding alternative forms

of investment. It can, however, complement alternative forms of investment, and shareholder involvement in the daily life of the corporation
can be used to target economic investment to social objectives (i.e., economically targeted investment). Shareholder action, or corporate governance, is often viewed as one form of social investment, because it goes
beyond the 'hands-off' measurement of corporate behaviour by risk and
return only. The next chapter examines definitions and approaches to
social investment and ways of measuring corporate accountability using
models of social accounting.

chapter 5

Unions, Social Investment, and Corporate Accountability

This chapter offers a definition and framework for examining several types of social investment. This framework has two key elements. The first is that the framework itself is a model for social change, and the second is that it calls for corporate accountability in terms of the corporation's social and economic benefit to the community. The debate within trade unions on involvement in investment and social investment, in particular, is illuminated. This chapter also reviews the literature on corporate social performance (CSP), including the measures that have been used to assess corporate behaviour. A further question is whether investment returns can be measured and, thus, evaluated on criteria broader than financial ones only.

Definition and Framework for Social Investment

'Social investment' is usually defined as the inclusion of various social standards in investment decision-making to accompany financial standards (Kinder et al. (KLD), 1998; Ellmen, 1996; Bruyn, 1987). This definition allows for the inclusion of right-wing criteria, for example, anti-gay criteria for investing in companies. Such funds do exist in the United States and could easily develop in Canada. Therefore, 'social investment' is further defined to include its purpose as a tool to challenge conventional corporate behaviour (Bruyn, 1987; Lowry, 1991; Zadek et al., 1997), often because such a challenge arises in an arena of contested control (CUPE, 1992; Lane, 1991; Carmichael, 1998). Corporations are therefore put under scrutiny to assess their impact on their communities. Such scrutiny is a necessary condition for pension funds to undertake social investment. However, I also propose that the collective action of pension funds is necessary for effective social investment, yielding value for beneficiaries. It has been shown in the previous chapter that shareholder action may be less reactive and more informed through collaboration with other institutional investors, pension funds in particular.

Control over investment for unions is only a reality once trusteeship of pension plans is won, according to Carmichael (1998). Out of the top twenty-three funds in Canada, eighteen (representing total assets of approximately $250 billion) are in the process of winning, or have won, joint trusteeship. All of these unions are in the public sector. There are also unions in the private sector which are active in various forms of social investment. Most of these appear to have sole trusteeship of their pension funds (in other words, in the past, in the absence of employer support, the employees have had to set up their own pension funds). However, as was mentioned earlier, one major union, the Canadian Auto Workers (CAW), remains vehement in its opposition to the social investment of pension funds and, furthermore, to union involvement in pension fund administration (Stanford, 1999a, 1999b).

Unions and Social Investment

The CAW argues against social investment on the grounds that social investment will lower the rate of return on investments. This, they say, is inherent in the workings of the market. Pension funds must make tradeoffs between the interests of their members and the broader interests of social investment (Stanford, 1999a).

I am arguing that unions can and should become more directly involved in the administration of pension funds and, furthermore, that different forms of social investment are in the interests of both workers and communities. Not all forms of social investment, *on their own*, however, have the potential to redress the power imbalance in the capital markets. Shareholder action may be less effective than it could be unless pension funds work together and pool their active shareholder involvement, the cost of exit notwithstanding. Similarly, ethical screens used alone (as discussed later in this chapter) are simply a first step in gaining some control over the investment of pension funds. The previous chapter has shown that shareholder action does not reduce the rate of return, and this chapter will show that ethical screens also do not lower rates of return. The CAW position that social investment damages the interests of beneficiaries through lower rates of return is, therefore, incorrect.

More fundamentally, the CAW has advanced two further arguments. The first is that involvement in the market through investment in pension funds or labour-sponsored investment funds 'muddies' the 'traditional understanding' (Stanford, 1999a, p. 372) between unions and employers, and undermines the role of unions in representing their members through collective bargaining. As described in Chapter 1, unions and workers have not, historically, played a significant role in shaping the practices of pension fund investment or the capital markets and, thus, have not had a legitimate role in shaping national industrial and economic policy. In fact, such a role for itself has been resisted by the CAW since the end of the Second World War. Historically, the focus of pension activism has been on lobbying for a universal pension system, rather than on bargaining for workplace pension plans.

Traditional forms of collective bargaining based on adversarial relationships may be of limited benefit to workers. Among industrialized countries, Canada is noted for its rigid model of labour relations that no longer effectively serves the interests of unions or employers (Adams, 1995). In spite of being in decline since the 1960s, collective bargaining has remained the prevailing arena for union activity, influence, or struggle. All residual rights, including control of capital, have remained with the employer (Drache and Glasbeek, 1992).

One assumption that has enabled this cloistered approach to the capital markets is the supposed bifurcation of the economy into a public and a private sector. Investment is seen as a private sector concern of the capital markets, with no social foundation. Concerns about social value are relegated to the public sector, where a non-profit, rather than a profit orientation, is paramount. Because it is assumed that social value is a cost, it follows that the public sector is an ongoing financial liability. (This question is dealt with more fully in Chapter 6.)

Pension funds have been treated as private entities in relation to their investment practice, their tax-exempt status notwithstanding. This is misleading for several reasons. First, the administration of a pension fund is a matter of public policy. Apart from the deferred wages, which are tax deductible, the investment of returns on investment is also tax exempt. For these reasons pension funds should be held accountable. Accountability, in particular, should be directed at their investment practices. (This question is examined further in Chapter 7.)

Second, public sector unions pension activists in (most of whom are associated with the largest pension funds) are driven to gain control over investment decisions because, in many cases, they have seen the potential for investment to be in the public interest (through public infrastructure projects such as hospitals, highways, and educational institutions). They have also seen the abuse of their funds through use of poor methods of accounting and reporting.

Measures for assessing social investment and corporate social performance (which will be described later in this chapter), once again, confuse the artificial distinction between public and private sectors. In using these measures, the assumption that these sectors are distinctly separable is replaced with an expectation that corporations, as an interdependent sector of the economy, are accountable to their employees, shareholders, local communities, and broader society. This means that corporations are accountable to all levels of government, as well.

Social investment can hold the corporation accountable on an operational level. Recognizing the social and economic nature of investment can enable better information on equity value and, thus, a more efficient market (Sethi, 1995; Bruyn, 1987). Social investment can also provide a 'real' return on investment through benefits beyond those to the direct investors. As Roy Adams (1995) makes clear, it is not just labour that benefits. Countries such as Germany, where unions are more engaged in shaping economic policy, are more productive than those that depend exclusively on the adversarial model of collective bargaining.

The second argument from the CAW is that, in the struggle to democratize the economy, there are strategic imperatives to be addressed by the labour movement. These need to 'carry a dynamic with a potential to build and politicize the movement' (Gindin, 1997). Some strategies are primary and some secondary. Secondary strategies are distant and often global (ibid.). For example, lobbying international institutions such as the World Bank or the International Monetary Fund (IMF) are secondary, and as such, Gindin argues, these institutions cannot be influenced.

History has outstripped this argument. Labour and community groups from across the world gathered in Seattle (1999) and Quebec City (2001) to protest World Trade Organization policies and in Washington (2000) to challenge the IMF. Nevertheless, can organizing for joint trusteeship by unions be considered secondary or distant? The evidence is to the contrary. In my study of union pension funds across Canada, it became clear that activists welcome the opportunity to challenge the unilateral and sometimes self-interested decision-making of the employer; to train other union members in how to administer pension funds; and to challenge the power of financial institutions by applying mechanisms set up through collective bargaining (Carmichael, 2004). Rather than weaken the union, it appears that pension fund activism could strengthen its role (ibid.).

Union involvement on an equal basis is critical. New forums for union activism are needed. Legal rules, theoretical frameworks, and the practices of the financial industry have not only limited the role of workers and unions in the social investment in pension funds, but have also prevented workers and unions from playing a more meaningful role in the economy. Redressing the balance of power calls for a shift in the balance between unions and the corporate sector, as well as accountability measures for corporate behaviour. Measures of corporate social performance can be used to hold companies to account.

Corporate Social Performance

Research and debate continues about the measurement of CSP and, hence, the nature of corporate accountability in the United States, Canada, and the United Kingdom, as well as in international development circles. The first question is how other values have been measured in relation to financial value. A second question is whether other values relating to performance of necessity detract from profits and, thus, reduce the rate of return to an investor (i.e., the pension fund). A third question is the extent to which indicators of CSP contribute to productivity.

In the United States, twenty-five years of research in the management literature was sparked by free-market economist Milton Friedman, who said: 'Few trends could so thoroughly undermine the very foundation of our free society as the acceptance by corporate officials of a social responsibility other than to make as much money for their shareholders as possible' (1970, p. 123). Friedman maintains this position, recognizing its contradictory nature. In Joel Bakan's interview with him, Friedman says: 'It's true..that this purely strategic view of social responsibility reduces lofty ideals to "hypocritical window dressing." But hypocrisy is virtuous when it serves the bottom line. Moral virtue is immoral when it does not' (2004, p. 34). Implicit in Friedman's argument is a conflict between profit maximization and social objectives.

A number of studies find a negative relationship between corporate social performance and corporate financial performance (CFP; see, e.g., Bromiley and Marcus, 1989; Aupperle et al., 1985; Ullman, 1985; Vance, 1975; Bragdon and Marlin, 1972). These studies examine corporate illegalities, product recalls, and situations incurring immediate and often unforeseen costs; however, they were undertaken prior to any significant development of CSP research. Other studies show that the additional costs of being socially responsible can be offset by added efficiency, resulting in a neutral effect on profit maximization (Parker and Eilbert, 1975; Moskowitz, 1972). Griffin and Mahon (1997) conclude that the larger number of researchers find a positive relationship between CSP and CFP, although the studies vary substantially in the definitions and methodologies that they follow. These studies use many variables of financial performance (including profitability, growth, asset utilization, and market measures) in contrast to but a few measures of social accountability.

The theoretical basis for the selection of social indicators as a measure of corporate performance remains unclear. This has led to confusion over which standards 'should' be used as measures of social responsibility and, therefore, the relationship of social to financial performance. The lack of clarity also serves to maintain the notion that these standards are a matter of ethical choice, or even of benevolence on the part of the corporation, rather than a matter of normal business operation. Early efforts at a definition of CSP produced a methodology based on corporate response and involvement in social issues. The interdependence of social institutions was stressed, but theoretically there was no reason why a corporation would get involved in a social issue beyond a vague prescription (Preston and Post, 1975). This approach shaped the first empirical study of corporate social performance undertaken in Canada, (by the Royal Commission on Corporate Concentration in Canada, in 1977 (see Clarkson, 1995). Archie Carroll (1979) has attempted to provide a theoretical and operational link between social and economic objectives, using the concept of social responsiveness as the basis for his model; however, his attempt ultimately failed for the same reasons that others' did. What needed to be measured was CSP, rather than the level of social response of a corporation (Clarkson, 1995). Wartick and Cochrane (1985) built on Carroll's model, incorporating the notion of 'economic responsibility' in an attempt to bridge the gap between social and economic expectations. According to Donna Wood: 'the entire CSP concept has taken on subtle "good" and binary connotations, as though corporate social performance is something that responsible companies do, but irresponsible companies do not do. Even though such connotations are common in the literature, they are misrepresentations of CSP. Every firm can be evaluated on its social performance, and a firm's social performance can be negatively or positively evaluated' (1991, p. 693).

Wood identifies the notion that CSP should measure the extent to which business is accountable to society through its responsiveness to its stakeholders. She relies on Freeman's definition of 'stakeholders' as 'those groups who can affect or are affected by the achievement of an organization's purpose' (Freeman, 1984, cited in Wood, 1991, p. 697). The outcomes of corporate behaviour – social impacts, programs, and policies – become the measure of understanding the relationship between the organization in all its parts and society. This framework allows for measures of accountability between managers, employees, shareholders, and community (Clarkson, 1995; Wood, 1991). It also breaks down the separation of economic and social value, and incorporates the two evaluations into the daily operations of an organization. Finally, this approach to CSP also breaks down the bifurcation between the private and public sectors, so that measures of corporate social performance can also, theoretically, apply to public as well as private sector organizations.

This redefinition has enabled significant new directions in research, as Wood predicted (1991). For example, in the United States, in their study of large manufacturing companies during the period 1982–7, Herremans et al. (1993) report that a good reputation for CSP and higher reported profitability are strongly related, as is CSP and lower total risk to the firm. Furthermore, investors in industries with social conflict tend to be aware of differences in reputation and invest accordingly. This may have encouraged the corporate trend towards 'window-dressing,' reported by Bakan (2004) and others. Waddock and Graves (1996) conclude that the quality of management, treatment of shareholders, employee relations, and customer relations are strongly and consistently related.

Measures of Social Performance

Social performance has been measured in many studies primarily by using either the yearly *Fortune* survey of 'the most admired corporations' or the Domini Social Index, developed in 1990 by Kinder, Lydenberg, Domini (1998). The *Fortune* survey has been criticized for being simply a tool to assess the perceptions of CEOs about the ethics of their own industry (see Fryxell and Wang, 1994; Brown and Perry, 1995; Wood, 1995; Baucus, 1995). The *Report on Business* magazine has a similar survey report on Canada's 'best and brightest.' This has been challenged more substantially by the Social Investment Organization (SIO) on the 'reputational' basis of the data, the 'unspecified biases of the CEOs and the lack of comprehensive and systematically-collected data available to them' (Walker and Hylton, 1998, p. 1). These survey reports have been criticized for being, in fact, disguised measures of corporate financial performance (Graves and Waddock, 1994).

The Domini Social Index assesses companies on seven indicators of corporate social performance. These are community relations, employee relations, environment, product, treatment of women and minorities, military contracts, and nuclear power. A five-point scale is used to rate a company from 'major strength' to 'major weakness' (KLD, 1998). The advantages of the Domini indicators are that all Standard and Poor (S&P) 500 companies are rated consistently and independently (Graves and Waddock, 1994).

Typical measures of CSP are shown in Table 5.1. Data such as job category earnings, health and safety violations, numbers of union certifications and de-certifications, grievances and strikes, collective agreements, employee benefits, records of layoffs, product safety and environmental violations tend to be available through government departments (Bruyn, 1987; Clarkson, 1995).

Additional data on performance such as employee involvement, internal rates of pay by job category, and gender and race breakdown by job classification can be obtained through the corporations themselves. These data, or 'bellwethers' (Kinder and Domini, 1997), are indicators of corporate behaviour. They establish 'best practice' standards within an industry and, on a national level, may form the basis for industrial policy. These measures, then, are far from 'subjective.'

In Canada, the work of assembling corporate data has been led by the Social Investment Organization and by one of its board members, Michael Jantzi of Michael Jantzi Research Associates. At this time, the organization's social performance and accountability indicators are (see SIO, 1996):

1 Community indicators of charitable donations and donations policy.
2 Corporate governance indicators such as reasonable compensation and severance policies for senior management and directors as well as proxy voting procedures.
3 Diversity indicators such as the number of women and visible minorities in senior positions, employment equity programs, and policies.
4 Labour relations indicators such as good relations with in-house unions, (no) layoff policies, worker participation policies, and favourable employee benefits.
5 Environmental indicators such as exceptional commitment to envi-

Table 5.1 Typical corporate and stakeholder issues

1.	Company	2.20	Other employee or human resource issues
1.1	Company history		
1.2	Industry background		
1.3	Organization structure	3.	Shareholders
1.4	Economic performance	3.1	General policy
1.5	Competitive performance	3.2	Shareholder communications and complaints
1.6	Mission or purpose		
1.7	Corporate codes	3.3	Shareholder advocacy
1.8	Stakeholder and social issues management systems	3.4	Shareholder rights
		3.5	Other shareholder issues
2.	Employees	4.	Customers
2.1	General policy	4.1	General policy
2.2	Benefits	4.2	Customer communications
2.3	Compensation and rewards	4.3	Product safety
2.4	Training and development	4.4	Customer complaints
2.5	Career planning	4.5	Special customer services
2.6	Employee assistance program	4.6	Other customer issues
2.7	Health promotion		
2.8	Absenteeism and turnover	5.	Suppliers
2.9	Leaves of absence	5.1	General policy
2.10	Relationships with unions	5.2	Relative power
2.11	Dismissal and appeal	5.3	Other supplier issues
2.12	Termination, layoff, and redundancy		
2.13	Retirement and termination counselling	6.	Public Stakeholders
		6.1	Public health, safety, and protection
2.14	Employment equity and discrimination	6.2	Conservation of energy and materials
2.15	Women in management and on the board		
		6.3	Environmental assessment of capital projects
2.16	Day care and family accommodation		
2.17	Employee communication	6.4	Other environmental issues
2.18	Occupational health and safety	6.5	Public policy involvement
2.19	Part-time, temporary or contract employees	6.6	Community relations
		6.7	Social investment and donations

Source: Clarkson (1995, p. 101).

ronmental management, use of recycling materials, superior preventive maintenance of property and equipment, and development of products with environmental advantages.

6 International indicators such as good treatment of employees and good environmental practices in developing countries (this would now include the absence of child labour).

7 Product and practice indicators of high quality relative to others in the industry, superior research and development, and written codes of conduct.
8 Military and nuclear power indicators.

These measures can be used voluntarily by an organization to measure its own performance through a 'social audit.' They may also be used in ethical screens by pension funds, either to screen out a corporation from an investment portfolio or to screen it in. They can also have various uses in economically targeted investment vehicles. Pension funds and other investors need publicly available information on companies. However, establishing indicators of social performance is an emerging field in its application, and caution is therefore warranted. Standards, for example, of legal infractions of environmental or health and safety laws are still fairly crude measures of unhealthy work environments. Standards also may not be very rigorous. In the absence of pressure from constituencies or labour negotiation of standards, standards will remain low.

Social Audits

There are some examples of social auditing in Canada, but there is a stronger academic history of doing so in the United States and Britain (see Zadek et al., 1997). There are two distinct trends of thinking on this topic. The first recorded uses of social audit were in the United States. In the 1930s, as a result of the Great Depression, economist Theodore Kreps (1936) called for a greater social accountability on the part of corporations and argued that corporations had to assume a greater social responsibility. Kreps defined a *social audit* as a mechanism to provide greater transparency of corporations. In the 1950s, Howard, Bowen (1953), an adult educator and evaluator, argued that corporations should hire social auditors to better understand their social impact. Bowen saw a social audit to be essentially an internal management tool. George Goyder (1961), a British academic, presented social auditing and reporting as an alternative form of accountability to nationalizing industry. Customers, suppliers, and community are stakeholders and have a right to know how companies operate. Goyder established a broad base of stakeholder accountability, using a voluntary management tool (ibid.). Both Bowen and Goyder emphasized the importance of corporate social reporting in acknowledgment of a broader social responsibility.

In Canada, there are a number of examples of organizations using social auditing, the Metro Credit Union (1996) and VanCity Credit Union (Brisbois, 1997), among others. The *Financial Post* has reported that 'within ten years, some companies will give shareholders an "ethics audit" at annual meetings ... an independently prepared assessment of a company's ethical performance, [to] join the financial audit' (Westell, 1997a). They all appear to follow the stakeholder accountability model, viewing social auditing as a public reporting or transparency mechanism. However, VanCity had signalled its intention to 'have discussions with the Society of Management Accountants of Canada regarding quantifiable social information' (Brisbois, 1997, p. 199). Models for quantifying the social value of the company through an accounting procedure alongside its financial value have been proposed for labour-sponsored investment funds (Quarter, 1995) and for non-profit agencies (Quarter et al., 2003).

Ethical Screens

Ethical screens are used primarily in mutual funds whose investors are institutions or individuals, or both. However, pension funds may develop ethical screens as well. Ethical screens may be negative or positive. A negative screen (e.g., directed at nuclear power corporations or tobacco and alcohol manufacturers) prohibits a fund from particular investments. A positive screen (e.g., directed at labour-friendly corporations) encourages particular investments. A study of pension funds in Canada shows that there are few examples of pension funds with ethical screens to screen out or screen in investment in Canada (Quarter et al., 2001). The pension plans of the United Church of Canada and the Ontario Public Service Employees Union (OPSEU) Staff Union Pension Plan both have comprehensive screens. Nevertheless, screens are under consideration in several other union pension plans and, in general, they seem to be gaining in popularity with unionists across the country. There are indications that union pension trustees are beginning to view ethical screens as one of several strategies in social investment.

One pension fund that has implemented ethical screens over a period of time in Canada is the OPSEU Staff Union Pension Plan, a small fund for approximately 250 union staff. The barriers to social investment are real, and apprehensions by trustees have been exacerbated by the highly publicized *Cowan* v *Scargill* ruling of the British Chancery Division. In a previous study, I reported the comments of Terry Moore, a trustee of this fund: 'We read *Cowan* v *Scargill* and were so alarmed that we knew that we had to do this right. First of all, we went to the membership at an

AGM; we wanted their consent and we got a vote on screening out investments to South African and anti-union companies with 95% of members in favour. Then, under our duty to be prudent, we asked for an ongoing tracking of our screen to measure the economic impact on our plan. It was usually favourable, in the range of 46% rate of return. We were actually doing really well. Social investment seemed to make good financial sense' (Carmichael, 1996, p. 102). The other variables in the ethical screen are downsizing beyond the sectoral average, poor labour relations, ongoing employment equity programs, and the proportion of women in upper management.

The advantages of ethical screens for pension funds are that they can be applied to all investments, so that there is a minimum acceptable social standard. Screens are usually established around one issue such as child labour, but they can also involve a range of issues on labour relations, environmental concerns, or national policies such as apartheid, genocide, or murderous oppression. They can be introduced and monitored carefully to track rates of return over the long term. Screens can be responsive to the concerns of pension plan members. Heather Gavin, another trustee for the OPSEU staff plan had these concerns: 'Do we want to invest in companies that exploit child labour? Is it in our members' interests to invest in companies that make their business bidding on public sector work? Why would it be in our members' interests to invest in an area that erodes their interest? We need to screen these companies out; but we need members participating in these decisions. We need their informed consent; it can't be the interests of the trustees; we need members' opinions, their wishes' (Carmichael, 1996, p. 103).

There are some disadvantages to ethical screens. For one, the 'power of the purse' is not necessarily felt by the companies that are screened out. Screens are not boycotts unless done collectively. They have been used, for example, as part of a successful boycott strategy to bring apartheid to an end in South Africa, before the African National Congress (ANC) took power. Nevertheless, one pension plan alone rarely has enough clout to make its lack of investment felt. Moreover, pension laws prevent investments in one company that are greater than 10 per cent of the value of the company.

Boycott strategies are not out of the question. Given the concentration of workers' pension assets in a small number of plans, it is conceivable that pension plans could coalesce around ethical investment strategies or establish a pooled ethical fund. Ethical investment may be a first step towards a social investment program. But, in the absence of collective pension power muscle, ethical investment is not sufficient to ensure that workers are making full use of their investment power.

Trustees and others are critical of the seemingly minimal standards set through ethical screens. Ethical investment portfolios can include, for example, banks and less-than-perfect representatives of the mining industry. For these reasons, ethical investment has attracted controversy in the United States and Canada, on the grounds that claims of principled investment are a 'hoax' (Stanford, 1999a; Ellmen, 1997; Hayden, 1998). Furthermore, the summation of negative and positive factors necessarily leads to negatives being cancelled out by positives. A company that has points against it for serious environmental violations can neutralize its score for numbers of women on its board of directors. Also, rigorous trade union or environmental values incorporated into an ethical screen tend to leave little room to invest in the smaller Canadian markets. Finally, screens often do not accommodate portfolio diversification.

Perhaps the most interesting example of positive screening has been developed by the California Public Employees' Retirement System (CalPERS). It may address some of this criticism. With assets of about U.S. $170 billion, CalPERS instituted a comprehensive screen for international investment (emerging markets) based on the Global Sullivan Principles (see Sullivan, 1999) and the ILO Declaration on Fundamental Principles and Rights at Work (1998) principles. An underlying sentiment is that these principles contribute to economic growth (although economic growth is equated with high returns). Considerable interest in this screen has developed because it may provide a complementary strategy to global activism in challenging corporate behaviour and setting labour standards. The screen is actually an evaluation framework using country and market factors to assess emerging markets.

In the CalPERS screen, all factors are weighted. Country and market factors each account for 50 per cent of the total score. Country factors are political stability (17 per cent), transparency of government (16 per cent) and productive labour practices (17 per cent). Market factors are market liquidity and volatility (10 per cent), market regulation and/or legal system and/or investor protection (15 per cent), capital market openness (10 per cent), settlement proficiency (10 per cent), and transaction costs (5 per cent). Each factor is defined and has subfactors which are also scored. Productive labour practices are defined as ratification and adherence to the ILO principles. Countries are then assessed as 'permissible' countries for investment. Active rather than passive investment is used, and fund managers are expected to refer to the Global Sullivan Principles and the ILO Declaration on Fundamental Principles and Rights at Work (1998) in the process of solicitation and in annual reporting. As of February 2002, plans were being made to assess and mitigate the transaction costs by 'transitioning the assets' over a period of time. Implementation of the CaLPERS screen will provide more information on the efficacy of ethical screens, particularly with respect to labour standards. One question that is not dealt with is how the level of acceptance is set. Is the cut-off line for permissible countries set by the standards of what is acceptable, or is it set by the demands of asset allocation in the emerging markets class?

Another example of screening was developed by the Social Investment Organization. SIO uses what is called a 'best-of-sector' approach. The SIO screen was developed to protect diversification so that corporations get compared only within their sector. So, for example, an environmental screen grades within the mining industry or the financial sector for the best company within its respective sector. In summary, 'once you have screened your investment portfolio, you will still have investments in companies that will not and cannot be expected to be forever perfect. You have a responsibility to monitor how these companies are using your investments and try to persuade them to change practices which don't meet your criteria for responsible behaviour' (Ellmen, 1997, p. 3).

The best-of-sector approach is gaining ground among labour-sponsored investment funds in Canada. This is in the belief that it can raise standards in a sector by increasing the market share of companies that are maintaining the preferable standards. Decisions using the best-of-sector approach have been difficult and controversial for trade unionists and community activists alike, as the case of the Crocus Fund in Manitoba (Kreiner, 2003) may indicate. The Crocus Fund used the best-of-sector approach in a social audit to evaluate potential investee companies in the hog industry. Manitoba had experienced a dramatic increase in hog production from one million to nine million hogs in six years. A number of hog producers had approached the fund for investment. The fund's social audit suggested that if the environmental practices being utilized by many of the companies that produced hogs were maintained, the industry would not be environmentally sustainable. But one company, Dynamic Pork, reflected a different approach to environmental compliance by committing to the construction of new facilities, immediate compliance with and constant monitoring of environmental regulations – to be implemented by the province four years hence – as well as subcontractor compliance. Crocus believed that if these practices were implemented across the hog industry, growth could be sustained at the anticipated levels without creating permanent long-term environmental damage. The fund decided to invest in Dynamic Pork as the best-of-sector operator and to try to increase Dynamic Pork's market share, which has, of course, put increasing pressure on competitors to raise their performance to the environmental bar set by the fund's investee company.

Impact on Rate of Return

Ethical screens have borne the brunt of the debate on the impact of social investment on the rate of return. In particular, attention has focused on the development and investment returns of ethical mutual funds. Ethical funds have been in existence in the United States since the 1970s. Only in 1986, however, was Canada's first ethical mutual fund started, by Vancouver City Savings Credit Union. This fund attracted attention for weathering the 1987 stock market crash, with 40 per cent of its funds in cash and ending the year with an 8 per cent return (Won, 1997). As of 1997, Canada had twelve ethical (including green) funds: eight were managed by Ethical Funds Incorporated from Vancouver, Investors Group's Summa Fund from Winnipeg, and the Desjardins Environment fund; the other four were managed by Clean Environment Mutual Funds Limited from Toronto (Press, 1997). The SIO reported that, in April 1998, $2.1 billion was invested in ethical funds in Canada and that this amount was growing rapidly (Walker and Hylton, 1998). However, this figure is very small in comparison with the approximately $300 billion invested in mutual funds in Canada.

The situation is very different in the United States, where in 1998 social investment funds – including screened investments, funds protected by shareholder advocacy, and money invested in community development banks, loan funds, and economically targeted investments – were very roughly estimated to be at $1.185 trillion (ibid.). Walker and Hylton report that social investment has a much broader connotation in the United States Funds implement their own belief systems through their investment practice. 'Sin' screens, such as tobacco, gambling, and alcohol, are more widely used than in Canada. Thus, a progressive social and political agenda is far less focused in the United States, where funds are established and ethical screens are used to support right-wing as well as left-wing values.

The creation of the Domini Social Index (DSI) in 1990 by Kinder, Lydenberg, and Domini (KDL) provided a standard for the performance of socially responsible investment (SRI) portfolios. KLD now releases regular statistical reviews of their index, and reports that the DSI has outperformed the S&P 500 on a total return basis and on a risk-adjusted basis since its inception in 1990 (Kinder et al., 1998). This database plays a critical role in research on social investment and in case law.

Given the prevalence of ethical investing in the United States, the issue of the rate of return on ethical funds' has attracted more systematic studies there than in Canada. These studies do not provide strong evidence that ethical funds outperform unscreened funds, but they also present no evidence that screened investments hamper performance. For example, in one of the earliest studies, Grossman and colleagues (1986) compare the returns of an unscreened New York Stock Exchange (NYSE) portfolio that included South African stocks with the returns of a portfolio with South African investments screened out. The unscreened portfolio did not outperform investments free of South African holdings; doing business in South Africa was found not to pay (ibid.). For the 1986–1990 period, Hamilton et al. (1993) find that seventeen socially responsible mutual funds, which were established prior to 1985, marginally outperformed traditional mutual funds of similar risk, but the outperformance was not statistically significant. In the Hamilton group's study, mutual fund data (ethical and otherwise) are unidentified, as are the social criteria for the ethical mutual funds. Luck and Pilotte (1993), using the Domini Social Index performance measures, report that the social index outperformed the S&P 500 index during the period May 1990 to September 1992. However, as they point out, this period was characterized by the outperformance generally in the market of smaller stocks over larger stocks, and the DSI has a larger proportion of smaller stocks. Nevertheless, active returns of 9 basis points per month over and above the S&P 500 remained unexplained. This was the first study to show an unexplained benefit. Kurtz and DiBartolomeo (1996), for the period May 1990 to September 1993, find that the DSI outperformed the S&P 500 by 19 points per month, which they attribute to the higher price of the DSI stock and their higher price-to-book ratios. In his review of 159 securities, using social data from the Council on Economic Priorities, Diltz (1995) observes no statistically significant difference during the 1989–91 period between the returns of two sets of fourteen screened and unscreened portfolios, with the exception of the environmental and military business screens, which had a positive impact on portfolio returns. Finally, Guerard (1997), for the period 1987–94, finds no statistically significant difference between screened and unscreened portfolios, and also that during some subperiods screened portfolios may have yielded higher returns.

The one Canadian study, done over a five-year and a ten-year period, is by Asmundson and Foerster (2001). They compare Canadian equity funds and the TSE 300 total return index (the 'benchmark'). They consider two different timeframes, a five-year period (January 1995 to December 1999) and a ten-year period (January 1990 to December 1999). Their results indicate underperformance of most of the SRI mutual funds relative to the benchmark, but lower exposure to risk. However, in all cases, any underperformance is not statistically significant at the 95 per cent confidence level. The performance exception is the Investors Summa fund, which all statistics indicate outperformed the benchmark.

During the period January 1990 to December 1999, the annualized compound returns for the two Canadian SRI mutual funds were 9.45 per cent for Ethical Growth and 13.26 per cent for Investors Summa, with the composite earning a return of 11.34 per cent. Over the same time period, the annualized compound return for the benchmark was 11.74 per cent and, for ninety-one-day Government of Canada treasury-bills, it was 6.43 per cent. Of the two funds with ten-year histories, Investors Summa outperformed and the Ethical Growth underperformed the benchmark, on the basis of mean excess return, although for both funds the results were not statistically significant.

The results suggest that those who engage in SRI through investing in Canadian SRI mutual funds, on average, are neither giving up anything nor gaining anything in terms of financial returns. However, it appears that the screens may actually decrease exposure to risk, although such a conclusion depends on the extent to which the funds are fully invested in equities.

Productive investment of pension funds depends on a view of the economy that goes beyond a practical interest in alternative ways of investing in the markets. It relies on a concept of the economy which is socially constructed, composed of peopled institutions, and governed by a mixture of social regulation and human values. This conception of the economy presupposes a complex mix of values and regulation in both the private and the public sectors (Bruyn, 1987). In this view, there is no fundamental distinction between the public and private sector with respect to the inclusion of social and financial values in investment. It is simply that the social values of exclusion practised by the financial industry are usually unacknowledged.

Measures of corporate social performance may provide a useful tool to account for the social value of investments. These measures, although still fairly crude, can provide the beginnings of a social accounting system. As a framework they can set up a system of accountability between an organization, its shareholders, employees, and broader community. CSP measures are used in social audits and ethical screens for investment.

While ethical screens are new for pension funds, they have been used more in mutual funds, and have proven that they do not damage the rate of return. However, their implementation in investment portfolios is problematic. Diversification tends to require that all sectors be represented in portfolios. Therefore, a best-of-sector approach requires different standards for different industries. On the other hand, using the same indicators for all sectors means that some sectors may slip completely through the screen because of poor standards throughout the sector.

As a first step in screening investment, ethical screens are important in exercising some control over investment. There are but few examples of pension funds with ethical screens. Yet indications are that pension trustees view ethical screens as one of several strategies in social investment (Carmichael, 1998).

chapter 6

Value, Capital Accumulation, and Radical Accounting

The financial industry and the corporate sector, in general, do not acknowledge the social values implicit in their policies and practices. This approach promotes profit at the expense of social concerns. Furthermore, the social investment and corporate performance literature offers little in the way of tools that assess social value in financial terms. This chapter surveys the literature of radical accounting for a framework of value, and assesses studies from various disciplines that can assist in building models of social accounting for pension fund investment.

Accounting and Capital Accumulation

Accounting is taught as the process of 'recording, measuring, classifying, summarizing, communicating, and interpreting economic activity' (Meigs et al., 1988, p. 4). It is represented as a neutral, technical representation of fact. Accounts are prepared in accordance with generally accepted accounting principles (GAAP), which in Canada are the recommendations of the Canadian Institute of Chartered Accountants (CICA), as published in its handbook. These principles are often reinforced through statute. For example, a regulation made under the Canada Business Corporations Act states: 'The financial statements referred to ... in this Act shall ... be prepared in accordance with the standards, as they exist from time to time, of the Canadian Institute of Chartered Accountants, set out in the *CICA Handbook*' (Business Corporations Regulation 402/81, in Beechy, 1990).

Resting on a bedrock of positivist theory, financial decisions must satisfy a series of criteria or 'qualitative characteristics' (CICA, 1999). These characteristics are supposed to ensure the objectivity, neutrality, and accuracy of accounting. Yet, a growing literature asserts that accounting not only describes or reflects but also affects institutions in the social, corporate, financial, and global arenas through its interpretative role in recreating reality (Tinker, 1985; Hopwood, 1985; Lehman and Tinker, 1987; Hines, 1988; Lehman, 1992). Tony Tinker, an accounting theorist, defines *accounting practice* as 'a means for resolving social conflict, a device for appraising the terms of exchange between social constituencies, and an institutional mechanism for arbitrating, evaluating and adjudicating social choices' (1985, p. 81).

Rather than being an objective, technical exercise reporting financials, accounting is infused with politics. Managers, owners, the financial industry, and government interests all have used accounting practices and procedures to control investment on their own behalf (Tinker and Lowe, 1984; Cooper and Sherer, 1984; Tinker, 1985; Neimark and Tinker, 1986; Hopwood and Miller, 1994). This approach to accounting implicitly challenges the claim that any social concern necessarily inhibits maximization of profit. It exposes the narrow self-interest of the corporate sector which has used accounting for its own ends. Claims of technically objective approaches to investment have disguised a system that works against the broader interests of the members of pension funds and of society.

Traditional accounting has been used as a mechanism for appropriating surplus value, legitimating the social control of one group over another, and enabling the accumulation of wealth (Tinker, 1985; Hopper and Armstrong, 1991). Traditional accounting has been the mechanism used to demonstrate that efficient markets work perfectly through equal access to information, if in fact market forces require accounting at all (Fama and Laffer, 1971). Finally, traditional accounting has bolstered the power of the corporation through financial reporting by reinforcing hierarchical control, controlling workers, and acquiescing to shareholder interests (Hopper and Armstrong, 1991; Cooper and Sherer, 1984; Neimark and Tinker, 1986).

Transformative Accounting

Accounting can be transformative, as Tinker explains:

Accounting rules supply one of the most fundamental ingredients of economic and social choices: the valuation of alternatives. Unions, hospitals, banks, taxpayers, investors ... all share one thing in common: the problem of deciding, of economizing, of discovering needs and ways to fulfil them ... accounting rules may distribute widespread benefit and damage between different members of the community. Alternative rules may, for the individual citizen, mean the difference between employment and unemployment, reliable products and dangerous ones, enriching experiences and oppressive ones, stimulating work environments and dehumanizing ones, care and compassion for the old and the sick versus tolerance and resentment. (1985, p. xx)

Miller (1994) contends that, through quantification, accounting can make activities and processes visible. This, in turn, allows us to think in different ways, unveils new perspectives, and creates knowledge. Quantification sets up a new reference point for action. Accounting, therefore, can be used to describe the social benefits of investments so that what was previously separate from the financial returns – and incidental to the investment – can now be examined from a comparative and more central point of view.

Accounting can recognize a broader social interest in corporate reporting both within and outside the organization. First, it can illuminate internal, lateral processes, and involve workers in planning and budgetary programs. Second, recognizing the interdependence of organizations, accounting can provide information links between organizations and their communities (Hopwood and Miller, 1994). In so doing, organizations can move from being agents of control to being agents of change. In this way, accounting becomes an instrument of social change.

Some arguments against social accounting put forward by pension fund trustees are concerned with the measurement of 'externalities' or factors external to companies and 'intangibles' like research and development capabilities. They say that such measurement is irrelevant to shareholders (and pension fund trustees), except on purely altruistic grounds; furthermore, these measurements can be confusing when compared with the rate of return which is directly linked to the financial benefit of the investment to the shareholder.

There are several responses to such arguments. First, there is considerable debate over how to go about valuing the corporations themselves. Intangibles, for example, such as research and development (or workers and training) are valued. However, in traditional accounting methods, they are expensed against current earnings, unlike 'tangibles,' such as equipment and buildings, which are recognized as investments in the future and depreciated over years. Consequently, intangibles bring down the reported earnings of companies that otherwise may be doing extremely well through the rising value of their stocks (Low, 1999; Ip, 1999). Intangibles therefore are viewed as a present expense that damages shareholder return. Similarly, in mainstream economics, human capital theory (HCT) regards investment in human capital as a present expense, or cost, for expected future benefits (McDonald, 1997). Any investment in the future value of workers' to the company is essentially viewed as a liability.

The accounting profession, through its regulatory framework and its practices, controls the structure of the balance sheet and what counts as an asset or a liability, a cost or a benefit. Some research casts suspicion on the current practice of double entry accounting said to have been generated in medieval Europe as a rhetorical device designed to justify accounting, since the practice was viewed with considerable suspicion as a tool of usurers; (see, e.g., Aho, 1985). Accounting can be designed to provide more or less relevant information, depending on one's perspective.

Understanding the social context for an investment provides a better perspective on the value of the investment (Sethi, 1995; Bruyn, 1987), and there are competing uses of accounting. The lack of 'accessibility, translatability and acceptability' of accounts of a governmental waste management department allowed a community movement to challenge, and win, an environmental campaign to close down an incinerator (Hanninen, 1995). A transformation by government of its own accounting procedures to reflect costs and profits enabled the privatization of water services in Great Britain (Ogden, 1995). Better reporting methods on plan for risk management and their associated costs, could lead to the prevention of oil spills (Rubenstein, 1989).

A shareholder proposal submitted in British Columbia by Working Enterprises Limited to Placer Dome calls for stronger accountability to shareholders, in the event of disasters, through better reporting. Placer Dome had already been engaged in clean-up of a spill that had happened four years earlier, with costs steadily accumulating. It had become clear soon after the 1996 spill occurred that there was inadequate insurance to cover the damage. *MiningWatch Canada* (2000) reports that studies suggest that the disaster could have been avoided had proper risk management plans been in place.

Accounting does tend to serve dominant, corporate interests in ideological conflict rather than the interests of social movements. Arnold and Hammond 1994 find this to be so in their study of the debates on South African divestment in the 1970s in the United States.

According to Herman Daly (1996), denial of the interdependence of the corporation and its environment leads to short-sighted investment. Daly calls this interdependence 'throughput' or locating the economic subsystem within its own ecosystem. Rather than a mechanistic and reversible flow of exchange, production is 'entropic' or evolutionary. Qualitative change feeds the economic interdependence of a company and its community. The company therefore cannot grow more than its ecosystem – or community – can sustain. In Daly's view, the limits of sustainability occur when the physical 'barriers' of pollution, resource depletion, and environmental degradation have been reached. Production also involves use of human resources. Far from being inefficient, as traditional economists have maintained, decent wages and worker involvement in decision-making improves productivity (Gregg et al., 1994). Sustainability, for example, could depend on decent wages and the right to unionization. The limits of sustainability would be reached when wages are lowered, training is cut back, or workers laid off (or 'downsized') to allow for continued production.

Sustainability can be maintained in the long run. When companies value all their stakeholders over the long run, when they value their workers as well as their shareholders, and communities as well as consumers, there are short-term payoffs reflected in improved company behaviour and long-term increases in share value (Hebb, 1998, p. 42).

Value Added Accounting

Value added accounting was used fairly widely in the United Kingdom in the late 1960s and the 1970s, in the annual reports of many major companies (Morley, 1979). The intent of this accounting practice met several requirements of the time. In contrast to a profit and loss statement (or statement of income), the value added statement (VAS) represents the wealth used and created by a company, as an expression of a 'collective effort of capital, management and employees' (Accounting Standards Steering Committee, 1975, cited in Hopwood et al., 1994, p. 212). This form of accounting practice was instituted in response to a broader view of the organization, where employees joined shareholders as stakeholders and, as such, had a right to receive information about the company. It was also, under a Labour government, in response to trade union demands for better financial information for bargaining purposes. Cooperation in increased productivity was to be expected through increased disclosure of information.

The VAS provides government and the public with a productivity and efficiency statement of the company, a statement of performance that includes capital support with items such as corporate taxes set off as 'returns' to society (Meek and Gray, 1988). The practice suddenly declined in the early 1980s, with the election of the Thatcher government and, thus, the beginning of a fundamentally different era of economic management and industrial relations. In the United States, there has been a call for instituting a value added statement as a supplement to the income statement 'consistent with calls for increased co-operation between management and labor' (ibid., p. 75), and for wider use of the VAS by agencies in the public sector (Quarter eat al., 2003).

The VAS (see Table 6.1) balances sources of income against disposal of 'total value added,' on the assumption that income generated should equal income disposed of. The intent is to define income in a broader way by including rewards to all stakeholders, not just the shareholders (Morley, 1979). Presumably, the interest of all stakeholders is held because creating wealth will sustain and improve payments of wages, taxes, and dividends. In its third column, the value added statement gives a measure of the company's sustainability, as a percentage gain or loss since the prior accounting period. This column, in particular, flags the interdependence of all the stakeholders and demonstrates either greater cooperation or worsened antagonism (Meek and Gray, 1988, p. 78).

The VAS can be compared with an income statement (see Table 6.2) whose descriptive ability is limited to profits and losses. For example, in the income statement, dividends to shareholders are described as a loss to the gross profit, as are taxes (or government gains). Workers' pay is invisible in 'operating costs.' The value added statement not only provides more information and is a far more effective measure of wealth than is the income statement. By employing a broader concept of company wealth to include government gains in taxation and workers' pay, the VAS recognizes the concept of sustainability in relation to the long-term health of a company. I am proposing that the value added statement could also accommodate the following:

- Expenses for a risk management plan to prevent or pay for pollution damage, in the section for reinvestment in the business
- Research and development investment, in the same section
- Worker training, also in the same section (since an investment in workers is a reinvestment in the business) or under 'employees' (indicating that it is viewed as an employee benefit).

Table 6.1　Imperial Chemical Industries – Sources and disposal of value added

	1985 (£m)	1984 (£m)	Change (%)
Sources of income			
Sales turnover	10,725	9,909	+8
Royalties and other trading income	142	116	+22
Less: materials and services used	(7,560)	(6,845)	+10
Value added by manufacturing and trading activities	3,307	3,180	+45
Share of profits less losses of related companies and amounts written off investments	56	71	–21
Total value added	3,363	3,251	+3
Disposal of total value added			
Employees[a]			
Pay, plus pension and national insurance contributions, and severance costs	1,835	1,647	
Profit-sharing bonus[b]	48	58	
	1,883	1,705	+10
Governments[c]			
Corporate taxes	308	373	
Less: grants	(28)	(28)	
	280	345	–19
Providers of capital			
Interest cost of net borrowings	122	100	
Dividends to stockholders	214	186	
Minority shareholders in subsidiaries	52	56	
	388	342	+13
Reinvestment in business			
Depreciation and provisions in respect of extraordinary items	514	460	
Profit retained	298	399	
	812	859	–5
Total disposal	3,363	3,251	

Notes

This table which is used for calculating the bonus under the Employees Profit-Sharing Scheme, is based on the audited historical accounts; it shows the total value added to the cost of materials and services purchased from outside the Group and indicates how the increase in value has been disposed of.

[a] The average number of employees in the group worldwide increased by 3%. The number employed in the U.K. decreased by 2%.

[b] 1985 U.K. bonus rate 8.1p per £1 remuneration (1984, 10.1p).

[c] Does not include tax deducted from the pay of employees. Income tax deducted from the pay of U.K. employees under Pay amounted to £157m in 1985 (1984 £148m).

Source: Meek and Gray (1988, p. 76).

Table 6.2   Imperial Chemical Industries – 1985 income statement

Group Profit and Loss Statement
For the year ended 31 December 1985

	1985 (£m)	1984 (£m)
Turnover	10,725	9,909
Operating costs	(9,917)	(8,990)
Other operating income	170	144
Trading Profit (after providing for depreciation 1985 £474m, 1984 £440m)	978	1,063
Share of profits less losses of related companies and amounts written off investments	56	71
Net interest payable	(122)	(100)
Profit on ordinary activities before taxation	912	1,034
Tax on profit on ordinary activities	(308)	(373)
Profit on ordinary activities after taxation	604	661
Attributable to minorities	(52)	(56)
Net profit attributable to parent company	552	605
Extraordinary items	(40)	(20)
Net profit for the financial year	512	585
Dividends	(214)	(186)
Profit retained for year	298	399
Earnings before extraordinary items per £1 ordinary stock	86.4p	98.2p

Source: Meek and Gray (1988, p. 77).

This last point illustrates the values inherent in financial statements. All these investments could be spread or 'appreciated' over several years. The VAS can, therefore, accommodate 'intangibles' very well because it recognizes stakeholder interests in corporate growth.

The value added statement is a useful tool in assessing the real stakeholders in an organization, its productivity, and the beneficiaries of its productivity. Some of the following studies illustrate other ways in which the productivity of an organization can be accounted for. They may be able to yield guidelines for reporting on and assessing the value of an investment to pension funds.

Studies Accounting for Social Criteria

Three studies are considered here. The first is *The Benefits and Costs of Good Child Care*, by Gordon Cleveland and Michael Krashinsky (1998).

They assess the cost of a national system of child care centres, 20 per cent of which would be paid for by parents in fees. They use an accounting framework to set off these costs against the financial benefits of such a system. One value to parents would be access to employment by the mothers of the children in child care. This benefit is measured in increased incomes, increased taxes, decreased poverty, decreased social assistance, and reduced likelihood of poverty in old age or after divorce. In effect, this is a measure of increased productivity and revenues for the government. On the basis of their estimates, Clevelandand Krashinsky conclude that the net benefit of a child care program is twice its net cost.

The value of this study on child care is in accounting for productivity and increased revenues to government. The same standards can be set for pension fund investment on the grounds that the investment of government in pension funds (or the costs to government), as described in the previous and following chapters, can be offset against the benefits of investment.

The child care study was set in a narrow economic framework on the assumption that this was the only framework that could assess the profitability, productivity, and efficiency of a national child care system. I hope to build a broader framework for pension fund investment on the assumption that some of the traditional approaches of market analysis, for example, are themselves barriers to change.

The second study is the *Analysis of Fiscal and Economic Benefits of the British Columbia Working Opportunity Fund*, prepared for the fund by Regional Data Corporation (RDC) and Perrin, Thorau, and Associates (1998). This study examines the extent to which the Working Opportunity Fund (WOF) has achieved government objectives as a labour-sponsored investment fund. Although labour-sponsored funds will be considered more extensively in Chapter 8, for the purposes of accounting for social criteria in financial terms, the WOF study deserves consideration here, as well.

The WOF study assesses the public fiscal costs assumed by both the federal and provincial governments through tax credits to purchasers of the investment funds, taking into account that these purchasers may have invested in other RRSPs had it not been for the Working Opportunity Fund. It also assesses the fiscal benefits of 80 per cent of the activity of investee firms, which are the taxes paid by new employees and suppliers of the investee firms. The study concludes that each dollar of fund financing results in 3.7 dollars of capital for the companies invested in. As significant is the balance between fiscal costs and benefits of the labour-sponsored fund. In the early years of the fund, it took three years for the federal government to cover its costs. By 1997, the payback was almost instantaneous. For the provincial government (of British Columbia), payback was slightly slower, because of the province's lower share of income tax revenues.

This WOF study provides a useful model of accountability for pension fund investment also, because here, too, there are fiscal costs and benefits (more fully described in Chapter 8). Contributions are tax deductible and returns on investment are tax exempt, and on these grounds I have argued (in Chapter 6) that pension fund administration is a matter of public policy. Accountability should be directed at investment practices, which also benefits pension funds, in my view, since it will challenge trustees to invest productively. The study of the Working Opportunity Fund raises some other issues relating to the evaluation of economic development initiatives, including the following:

1 A cost-benefit analysis tends to have a built-in assumption that if the benefits outweigh the costs, the economic development is effective. This is not necessarily the case. The benefits may also be produced through other means (Bartik and Bingham, 1997).
2 Conversely, if the costs outweigh the benefits, we should not assume that the project is ineffective. It may be that socially necessary benefits cannot be produced any other way (ibid.).
3 Estimating what would have happened in the absence of a program is imprecise. Surveys asking people's views of 'what-if' can produce different and sometimes conflicting results (Giloth, 1997). Nevertheless, analysis of each situation can yield more information on the options open to the company and the likelihood of expansion, downsizing, or collapse without the venture capital (Persky et al., 1997).

Inevitably, this last question takes on added significance when the economic development is directly and wholly government funded, as many such projects are in the United States. However, given the tax- exempt nature of pension fund investment, this question will be considered in relation to the case study. The same question has been raised by critics of labour-sponsored funds in Canada, who argue that given the benefit of tax credits, the funds should be able to point clearly and incontrovertibly to net job creation. The WOF study, then, is an exercise in accountability.

The third study considered here is *Assessing the Local Economic Impact of the Arts: A Handbook*, prepared by the Ontario Arts Council (OAC, 1997).

The OAC study, through an analysis of the impact of job creation and taxes, povides an impressive educational tool that can be used by arts activists in any size of community to provide an economic assessment of their local theatre. This study offers an often neglected perspective on the economic role of the arts; nevertheless, it issues the important cautionary note that 'government officials, business leaders and consumers should be made to recognize that economic impacts are only some of the benefits provided by the arts' (ibid., 1997, p. 44).

An economic analysis may be a narrow perspective from which to view the benefits of the arts. This kind of perspective, however, would be seen as substantially broader than the norm, as we have seen, in depicting pension fund investments. The OAC study uses basic economic concepts, such as types of economic effects. How it does so is useful for this study in untangling the impact of an investment on a community. Consider the following, for example:

- 'Direct' effects can be used to answer the question, 'What new income can be attributed directly to the organization being assessed for impact?' For the theatre, this includes new revenues brought into the community from outside, such as public funding, private donations, and program revenues. Because income must be new to the community, it does not include revenues that were already within the community previous to the theatre. Economic development specialists have pointed out that assessing direct effects may be problematic (Giloth, 1997).
- 'Indirect' economic effects are those resulting from the economic activity of the organization. For example, local businesses used by the theatre may make purchases of supplies or services from other businesses to support their activity, using their revenues from the theatre.
- 'Leakage' is a useful term to employ in discussing the money that leaves the local community in goods or services purchased by local businesses.
- 'Induced' economic effects are those resulting from the spending of income earned by people employed by the local theatre or by the owners and employees of local businesses who have provided services to the theatre. People spend what they get and, in so doing, 'multiply' the effect of their original earnings on the economy.

I propose that accounting methods be used to assess a social return on pension fund investment accruing to a broader group of stakeholders than beneficiaries of the fund. This group may include the plan itself, workers, government, and the community. This position is similar to that of Bruyn, who argues that there are several groups who have a stake in pension funds and the allocation of capital: 'allocation of capital has a social framework: social factors enter into every economic decision' (1987, p. 14). 'Social accounting' can be taken to mean the assessment of or accounting for the collateral benefits – or benefits other than financial – of investment decisions. (Collateral benefits will be discussed more fully in Chapter 7). This form of accounting provides information on the benefits of the company to stakeholders that hitherto have remained hidden, unaccounted for, and thus devalued.

There is no one specific method to be used for such accounting. However, a number of issues significant for social accounting were raised in the studies considered in this chapter and will be further addressed in the remainder of this book, including:

1 Pension funds have the ability and opportunity to contribute to the economy positively. Models of social accounting provide pension funds with the tools to evaluate the impact of their own investments and guide future investment.
2 Governments 'invest' foregone taxes in pension funds and, therefore, foregone taxes and taxes 'repaid' can be accounted for.
3 Pension funds are not accountable to any funder. Economic development using pension funds is not like the situation of many economic development projects in the United States and the United Kingdom, where accountability to funders for net job creation is often a necessary condition of future funding.
4 Investment in workers is an investment in the future. This includes training; pension, welfare, and benefit payments; and taxes.
5 Sustainability can be characterized as a balance in the interests of or a tension (in the literal sense) between stakeholders. An imbalance will result in the dominant power of one group over another and harm to one or more groups. Social accounting may indicate the long-term health of a company through its ability to sustain a balance among the interests of all its stakeholders. Conversely, they may indicate a trend of long-term damage – to the company through lack of reinvestment of earnings; to the shareholders because of negative returns; to workers through a lack of training, low pay, or downsizing; and to the community through abandonment, pollution, or other long-term harm.

The social accounting model then can be a tool for change.

chapter 7

Venture Capital, Economically Targeted Investment, and Economic Development

The existing investment practices of pension funds mimic the prevailing practices of the capital markets and may be socially unproductive and even speculative. Furthermore, pension funds have little control over their investment and, hence, their rate of return. Finally, pension fund investment is primarily short term, influenced by quarterly reporting by the fund's managers. Some forms of social investment have been described that, on their own, are of limited use to pension funds, but that can nevertheless complement a strategy of productive and socially useful investment. This chapter describes investment practices in emerging markets, as well as investment in companies that are in need of restructuring. It also gives brief descriptions of economically targeted investment, a form of social investment where investors pool their funds to fill gaps in the market. Two Canadian models are described: the Caisse de Dépôt et Placement du Québec and labour-sponsored investment funds. These forms of investment are productive, socially useful, and far less speculative than much pension fund investment practice to date.

Venture Capital

Tessa Hebb, capital market policy consultant, has said that we are engaged in telling a new economic story, where investment in the real economy 'creates long-run value for shareholders through increased productivity. As a by-product, this investment creates jobs which in turn create healthy communities. As a result, productive investment in firms that are not able to easily access capital generates additional collateral benefits' (1998, p. 43). Hebb continues by saying that this is almost instinctive to unionists who already invest in their members' own interests and in the long-term interests of their communities.

Pension funds in Canada need new vehicles of investment. A professor of urban land policy at the University of British Columbia has said that 'an ironic situation exists in Canadian markets: an excess supply of funds chasing an insufficient supply of suitable investments, particularly Canadian equities, and an inadequate supply of innovative financial instruments. [We need] to direct serious efforts to the supply side of the capital markets and to the ways in which new securities can be created to provide additional investment vehicles for the growing number of huge capital pools' (Goldberg, quoted in Vancouver Stock Exchange, 1998). He goes on to say that a 1 per cent allocation of Canada Pension Plan (CPP) funds to venture capital would bring $1.5 billion to fund new and restructuring businesses.

Another, more critical, reason for more productive investment of pension funds, which is rarely mentioned, is that pension funds are subsidized by government. For the fiscal year 1997, the Government of Canada reported 'foregone revenue' for pension funds of just over $12 billion. For registered retirement savings plans (RRSPs), other registered pension plans, and deferred profit-sharing plans, exemptions amounted to over $23 billion. In the United States, tax exemptions for pension funds in the federal budget were U.S. $51 billion in 1992 (Barber and Ghilarducci, 1993). This money could be returned to communities through investment that provides wealth through job creation and spillover effects, rather than being used for the largely private gains of individual and institutional shareholders. This is probably the most compelling single argument for the social investment of pension funds.

The Canadian Labour and Business Centre (CLBC, 1993) reports that publicly traded, smaller companies are not supported by pension funds, since investment is limited to companies that have well-established risk-to-return profiles and are already well-known to the financial industry. Nor is the private market supported to any great extent by pension fund investment. These are the middle markets where companies may be small, medium, or large, and may be in new, emerging, or restructuring industries. The venture capital industry in Canada is growing, but it still constitutes only a very small sector of the market. In 1998, for example, $8.4 billion was invested in venture capital, which was up 18 per cent from the $7.1 billion at the end of 1996 (Vancouver Stock Exchange, 1998); at the same time, in the United States, U.S. $250 billion was invested in venture capital (ibid). It is important to note that labour-sponsored investment funds constitute 47 per cent of venture capital investment in Canada and only 5.1 per cent of pension assets are invested in real estate, with 1.6 per cent in mortgages (Canada, Statistics Canada, 2001).

The trend in ownership of real estate is up since the early 1980s, in spite of the near collapse of the real estate industry. Although the temptation is still to invest in the more liquid stocks of real estate companies, pension funds are slowly being persuaded that 'it's really an issue of diversification ... buy real estate and hold it for the long term' (Helik, 1998).

Pooled funds are used by investment managers to provide economies of scale in transaction and administration costs, as well as custodial and legal costs. Investment by Canadian pension plans in pooled vehicles has increased by 137 per cent since 1992 and has accounted for 39 per cent of the increase in assets of plans (Canada, Statistics Canada, 2001). Investors tend to use pooled funds for investing smaller amounts of money in the international markets.

Pension funds are still dependent on fund managers, equity markets, and liquidity. As one venture capital expert said, 'in Canada ... we still rely on the investment bankers and their analysts to give recommendations on buy and sell' (Vancouver Stock Exchange, 1998). In another critical piece of research, the CLBC notes that pension fund officials cite the barriers to investing in alternative markets: the administrative costs are too high, there are not enough specialists or information, and the risks are too high (Falconer, 1999). None of these objections are supported by the facts. However, as we have seen, pension funds tend to be transfixed by a short-term investment practice, overly influenced by equity fund managers and short-term rates of return. Yet, these are the markets and the asset categories where social investment is possible, and where there could be regional and industrial development and job creation. For example, putting venture capital into larger private market enterprises may finance mergers and layoffs. Venture capital may instead support new companies, innovative technologies, and regional development.

Pooled funds may give investors no control over investment decisions and, therefore, be another useful tool for the consolidation of money under the control of fund managers. Or, pension funds can pool funds into limited partnerships, where they may have full control over shaping a new vehicle for investment, as is the case with Concert Properties and Accès Capital of the Caisse de Depôt et Placement du Québec.

Economically Targeted Investment

Economically targeted investment (ETI) is carefully defined in a report sponsored by the Ford Foundation as 'an investment designed to produce a competitive rate of return commensurate with risk as well as create collateral economic benefits for a targeted geographic area, group of people, or sector of the economy' (Bruyn, 1987, p. 67). 'Economically targeted investment' is a very broad term in the United States. Randy Barber (1997, p. 2) identifies seven broad areas of ETI, or job creation initiatives:

1 'Bricks and mortar' investing, e.g., the AFL-CIO Housing and Building investment trusts; Union Labor Life Insurance Company, Multi-Employer Property Trust
2 Responsible contractor requirements, e.g., public fund service contractor compliance
3 Regional development funds
4 Socially responsible investment (SRI) funds
5 Union-friendly investment vehicles
6 Worker buy-outs
7 Privatization alternatives.

There are a number of regulatory conditions to bear in mind about ETIs in the United States. First, in 1995, the U.S. Department of Labor issued an interpretive bulletin allowing pensions to invest in ETIs with their collateral benefits, as long as the investment 'has been carefully screened and selected to meet the prevailing rate of return.' If after careful selection of investments, the actual returns are low, this is not a failure of fiduciary responsibility, as long as the overall portfolio of the fund is prudent (Watson, 1995, p. 4).

Second, ETIs are typically held in securities that are underwritten by the federal government. Departments of the federal government provide guarantees for investments in housing and other real estate. This lowers the risk of the investment while maintaining a good rate of return. The Institute for Fiduciary Education estimates that almost 64 per cent of ETI funds are in real estate (Ambrose, 1993, cited in Levine, 1997).

Third, ETIs are generally funds pooled by a group of investors and managed by an intermediary who provides the knowledge, expertise, and legal background to invest the funds. Pension fund staff rarely handle ETI investments themselves (removing a major barrier of lack of expertise, which has been cited by pension trustees). The trade union movement, through the American Federation of Labor and Congress of Industrial Organizations (AFL-CIO), has been a key player in providing vehicles for investment in housing, mortgages, and job creation projects.

The term *economically targeted investment* has been 'adopted' in Canada by pension fund and capital market activists to indicate 'Pooled or syndication vehicles which permit pension funds – taking on moderate risk and the expectation of moderate return – to channel a small portion of their assets into community development, affordable housing and small business' (Jackson, 1997, p.2).

Eugene Ellmen, a Canadian leader in the social investment field and executive director of the Social Investment Organization (SIO), uses the term 'alternative investing' to describe 'the desire to create an enterprise which is outside the traditional, for-profit, free market, private sector economy' (1990, p. 60). He distinguishes alternative investing from 'social investment' in that new forms of business are created to provide direct benefit to members, consumers, workers, and community associated with the business. Any definition of social investment must exclude supposedly ETI strategies that undermine workers (members of the pension fund) and their communities. The disturbing trend towards alternative investing (rather than social investment) has been described by the Canadian Union of Public Employees (CUPE) in its newsletter on pension fund investment: 'funds which in the past may have been invested in a low-risk but reasonable rate-of-return provincial bonds are now being sought by private companies looking to take over the ownership and management of public infrastructure and services ... It raises the prospect of one worker's pension fund financing a company which is actively seeking to privatize her job – or that of her neighbour' (CUPE, 2002 p. 1). Most notable is Borealis, a fund management company created by the Ontario Municipal Employees Retirement System (OMERS). It was designed to coordinate investment in public-private partnerships and resulted in the large-scale privatization of public services. Privatization results in loss of jobs and lowers workers' pay with dramatic consequences for the surrounding communities. The real threat of privatization is the loss of unionized jobs, lower wages, and the deterioration in services (Kelsey, 1995).

Under true ETI strategies, the interests of plan members and the community coincide. For example, the pension plans of some construction trades have invested in building projects that employ members of the plan to build moderate-income apartment units and offer mortgage loans for those wishing to live in the apartments. The jobs created, as a result, increase contributions to the pension fund (Barber, 1982; Quarter, 1995).

ETIs and Efficient Market Theory

ETIs have been criticized on the grounds that they allegedly violate standards of prudence and loyalty. Described as 'socially dictated investment policies,' ETIs are 'those investment practices and policies which either (1) permit the sacrifice of safety, return, diversification or marketability; or, (2) are undertaken to serve some objective that cannot be related to the interests of the plan participants and beneficiaries *in their capacity as such*' (Hutchinson and Cole, 1980, p. 1346; emphasis added). This definition is in contrast to 'totally neutral investment policies which focus on the financial aspects of investment alternatives' (ibid., p. 1344). Such definitions assume a continuum from the purely financial to the purely social. In fact, contrary to the expectations of efficient market theory (EMT), an examination of the social factors related to an investment can lead to more effective knowledge about the company's behaviour and, therefore, about possible returns (Bruyn, 1987, p.12).

A related argument levelled against ETIs is that they are a result of too much political involvement in investment: 'Public fund managers must navigate carefully around the shoals of considerable political pressure to temper investment policies with local considerations, such as fostering in-state employment, which are not aimed at maximizing the value of the portfolio's assets' (Romano, 1993, p. 796). The assumption is that social or targeted investment will automatically damage rates of return. Passive investment is regarded as 'neutral.' In other words, the abrogation of decisions to fund managers and the status quo of investment practices is the only effective way to maximize the rate of return.

Nevertheless, public sector unionists might sympathize with the view that governments have used the funds for their own purposes (often to pay off government debt through low-interest bonds). Romano (1993) does suggest that there should be more representation of beneficiaries on pension boards. Joint trusteeship by unions and employers is now recognized as a critical developmental step in ensuring more social investment strategies (Barber and Ghilarducci, 1993; Carmichael, 1998).

Collateral Benefits

Collateral benefits is a legal term taken from the language of investment and now in use by pension activists. Collateral benefits denote the social benefits of investment aside from the benefit to beneficiaries. In other words, the concept of collateral benefits accepts as a given the fiduciary obligation of trustees to members and beneficiaries of the plan; however, use of the term is tactical in that it more accurately denotes alternative practices that can add value to investment.

Underlying this term is the question of whether the pension fund is for the benefit of beneficiaries only or whether collateral benefit can be extended to other stakeholders. Teresa Ghilarducci (1994) argues, in response to attacks on economically targeted investing, that a new pension regulatory framework should recognize the realities of the capital markets. She proposes that, to maximize the returns to beneficiaries, pension funds should rely on 'employment growth' of beneficiaries' jobs, as well as on direct returns on investment. Ghilarducci calls this the 'whole participant' approach, which goes beyond Modern Portfolio Theory, taking into account the feedback effects of investment on continuity of employment and the growth of pension fund contributions. The 'whole participant' approach targets investment and sets up specific expectations with regard to the returns and collateral benefits, as opposed to speculating for the best possible returns in a supposedly free market (1994, p. 4). Quarter (1995) proposes a similar approach in interpreting the investments of the Carpentry Workers Pension Plan of British Columbia (CWPP).

Deaton (1989) argues that social investment strategies where the collateral benefits are restricted to plan members further exacerbate the economic inequalities that have historically prevailed between those who are covered by occupational pension plans and those who are not. Tax benefits for those covered by pension plans already create an inequitable distribution of wealth; further social investment policies that benefit members only increase these inequities (ibid.). Barber and Ghilarducci (1993) argue that, given the tax-exempt status of pension funds and their long-term horizons, there should be strong public policyonpensionfundinvestmentpracticeanditsfunctioninthecapitalmarkets. I have already argued in previous chapters that this public policy should be based in a view of a social return on investment or collateral benefit that extends to all stakeholders – contributors, beneficiaries, the broader community, and government.

Economic Development

The link between union pension plans, their members, and the broader community is the practice of economic development. The AFL-CIO (1998), in an innovative educational publication, distinguishes the high road from the low road of economic development. This distinction is drawn in Table 7.1. The AFL-CIO (ibid.) criticizes Grant Thornton's *Annual Study of General Manufacturing Climates of the Forty-eight Contiguous States of America* (see the 'low road' column in Table 7.1). In contrast, the AFL-CIO (ibid., p. 32) suggests the a counterpart – high road – for each

Table 7.1 Two roads for state and local economic development

	Low road	High road
Goals	1 Create new jobs 2 Retain good jobs	1 Retain existing jobs 2 Create good new jobs
Process	Closed	Open, democratic
Strategies	1 Recruit large employers 2 Improve 'business climate'	2 Renew large and small employers 2 Improve quality of life in the community
Elements		
Wages	'Competitive' (i.e., low) wages	High minimum wage; living wages
Unions	Support right-to-work laws	Partner with unions to move towards high road
Education	Underfunded, low quality	High standards; adequate funding
Employment and training services	Customized training for recruitment. Lack of standards. Business is primary customer.	Broad training accessible to all workers; employment services for all. Both workers and businesses are key customers.
Benefits	Cut unemployment insurance taxes and benefits Cut workers' compensation	Maintain adequate employment benefits to support families temporarily Maintain workers' compensation. Increased safety and health technical assistance
Taxes	Use tax incentives to lure new companies Cut business taxes; increase income and property taxes	Limit tax incentives and require public accountability Equitable, progressive taxes on businesses, individuals
Regulations	Reduce environmental, health, and safety zoning regulations	Regulations to maintain quality of life. Land use planning
Government	Shrink government; cut social programs	Invest in people – adequate health care, education, training, welfare
Infrastructure	Target to new companies as part of industrial recruitment	Invest in infrastructure that helps all companies and workers
Technology and Business Assistance	Deploy technology to eliminate jobs / deskill work	Partner with workers and unions to deploy worker-friendly technology

Source: Adopted from AFL-CIO (1998, p. 24).
OJT = on-the-job training.

of Thornton's proposals. It encourages people who live in a community affected by economic development to ask the following questions:

- What are the jobs?
- What will it cost us?
- What are the benefits?
- What are the environmental impacts?
- What are the tax implications?
- What is the impact on other employers?

Economic development theorists in the United States have contributed to three distinct bodies of literature from the 1930s through to the present (Bingham and Mier, 1993; Mier and Fitzgerald, 1991). The first began in reaction to the 'smokestack chasing' of the 1930s, when U.S. states attempted to attract new business through any means that would reduce the costs of production for their companies. Supporting theorists, leaning heavily on shareholder theory, theories of the firm, and neoclassical economics, attempted to isolate the conditions that should govern corporate relocation. These have become known as 'location' or 'space-based' theories, and they generally rely on profit maximization rather than any benefits to the region or community. The goal must be to minimize the damage (or the costs) to those who are harmed, since an efficient allocation of resources cannot benefit everyone equally (McDonald, 1997). This approach is marked by little or no consultation with the community, but often by extensive partnership between government and the corporate sector. Many regional, community, and local development projects have been initiated from this perspective.

The opposing tradition, which grew out of a community (or international) development perspective, sees economic development from the perspective of the community or region. It generates questions about the equity of economic distribution in development and has produced a second phase of development literature, often Marxist in focus. It argues that economic development happens through a capitalist process, driven by the need for accumulation. Neighbourhoods, therefore, are a function of the capitalist process of production, and communities are the site of resistance and a means of class struggle (Harvey, 1985; Scott, 1980). Using a class analysis, this literature attempts to explain the many examples of neighbourhood development that have been marked by conflict between government, real estate developers, and community activists.

The third phase of this literature holds that economic development should be grounded in local communities, with a goal of local sustainability, and generated by partnerships between the public and private sectors (Bingham and Mier, 1993). This view recognizes the limits (or bankruptcy) of municipal or city governments and looks to the private sector for partnership with government in local development. Inevitably there is some public funding and, therefore, some public accountability. There may or may not be productive relationships with community. This literature tends to document conflict in urban economic development, and in particular 'fights [not] over appropriate strategies, but a fundamental struggle over definition of the local problem' (Mier and Fitzgerald, 1991).

Public-Private Partnerships

In Canada, public-private partnerships – or P3s – are highly controversial. P3s are contractual relationships between the public and private sectors to provide public services and public sector infrastructure. They are promoted as legal arrangements whereby the private sector receives government contracts and the public sector mitigates some of the risk of the project. A government contracts a private company to design, build, finance, and then operate public services and/or a facility, such as a new hospital, school, or water and waste water service. The company generally borrows the money for the project. The company's loan is offset by annual fees paid by the government to the private company under a long-term operating contract. The private sector may have ownership of the project. Alternatively, the government may retain ownership and responsibility for the long-term costs of maintenance and repair but have no control over delivery of services. The workers that build the infrastructure may be non-union, and those that deliver the services end up as employees of the company working in a privatized service.

The argument is made that such contractual arrangements transfer the risk of the project from the public to the private sector. However, it is difficult to avoid government accountability in situations where, for example, water becomes contaminated or hospitals or schools are unable to deliver public services. Furthermore, since private companies are inevitably driven by returns to shareholders, they will pick the most profitable ways of delivering services whether or not these are in the public interest by 'cherry-picking,' contract-stripping, cuts to services, refinancing, low-ball bidding, introducing user fees and two-tier services, and avoiding taxes (OPSEU, 2004).

The Canadian Labour Congress (CLC), the National Union of Public and General Employees (NUPGE), the Ontario Federation of Labour (OFL), the Ontario Public Service Employees Union (OPSEU), and CUPE are among those who have passed policy resolutions opposing P3s. Paul Moist, president of CUPE, has said that 'the cold hard reality is that P3s inflate costs, reduce service and confound accountability' (2004). A simpler and cheaper way to raise funds for public infrastructure would be to issue bonds, rather than raise private sector financing.

There is 'stiffening resistance' from the general public. In an Ipsos-Reid poll held in April 2004, 75 per cent of respondents opposed public-private ventures to rebuild public infrastructure such as hospitals, schools, highways, and water systems (Warson, 2004).

Union Training and Collateral Benefits

It has been estimated that, in the United States, about U.S.$30 billion of pension fund assets are currently placed in ETIs (Jackson, 1997). A case study by Rudd and Spalding (1997) compares the ETI approaches of two pension funds in the United States, both of which used the same investment company, McMorgan.

The first fund had an estimated 8 per cent of net assets in ETIs, amounting to U.S.$17.6 million. These were invested in the AFL-CIO Housing and Building investment trusts, the Union Labor Life Insurance Company (ULLI), and the Multi-Employer Property Trust, as well as a rehabilitation program which enabled loans for home improvement to union members using designated contractors.

This rehabilitation program, designed by the investment company, invested a portion of the fund's assets in a bank, which then gave loans to union members for home improvements. The work was done by union members. The advantages of the program for the pension fund were that its investment in the bank was liquid at a market rate of return, and it also 'funnelled pension money directly back into the community, putting pension plan participants and contractors to work' (Rudd and Spalding, 1997, p. 15). This meant that the fund also received increased contributions from the increased hours of work.

By comparison, the second pension fund invested only a few million dollars in ETIs. For the first fund, trustees considered the collateral benefits of ETIs, whereas in the second fund they did not. For the first fund, union training on investment and its collateral benefits was found to be essential to allow trustees to set a 'more broadly progressive investment agenda' (ibid., p. 24).

Union Involvement in ETIs

The Union Labor Life Insurance Company was created in 1977. It is a pooled real estate mortgage fund that provides jointly trusteed pension funds a vehicle with which to generate union jobs in the construction trades. The ULLI fund, consisting of 108 mortgage and real estate assets, has a market value of approximately $850 million. Through a partnership with the California Public Employees' Retirement System (CalPERS) and the New York State Common Retirement Fund, the ULLI is generating U.S.$600 million in construction of commercial real estate in the California and New York regions. The program claims high annualized returns and millions of hours of work created for the building trades (Watson, 1995, p. 4).

The Multi-Employer Property Trust is a real estate equity fund set up in 1982. It invests in income-producing office buildings, shopping centres, and housing. All are new construction, union-built, and located in regions where the members of participating pension plans live and work. It has assets of U.S.$1.2 billion, 107 pension plans investing in it, and returns that are above average for its sector.

The AFL-CIO Housing and Building Investment Trust is a vehicle for investment in single and multifamily residential projects. It was established in 1965 with 390 pension funds investing in it. The AFL-CIO Housing and Building investment trusts invests in commercial real estate from the construction stage on, and builds and owns industrial, medical, retail and apartment buildings. It has assets of US$514.2 million. Both programs have 'solid track records' and competitive rates of return (ibid.).

Pension Funds, Unions, and Economic Development in Canada

With net assets of $110.9 billion at the end of 2003, the Caisse de Dépôt et Placement du Québec (Caisse) is the largest investment agency in Canada and the repository of Quebec's pension and benefits funds as well as the Quebec Pension Plan (QPP). Originally set up in 1965 by the Quebec government to manage the QPP, the Caisse has provided a model in the management and investment of pension funds. (It has also provided survivor, death, and disability benefits that are more generous than the norm.) In the rest of Canada, provincial governments used pension premiums in excess of pay-outs to beneficiaries to fund budget deficits through low-yield provincial bonds. In Quebec, excess funds were invested back into the Quebec economy with a subsequently higher yield. In the expectation of future returns, funds have also been allocated to finance small knowledge-based companies.

The Caisse describes its objectives as 'high returns, financial soundness and an unwavering commitment to the economic vitality of its milieu ... It has had [since its inception] the objective of achieving optimal financial returns and contributing, by its vitality, to the Quebec economy, while ensuring the safety of the capital under management' (Caisse, 1998, p. 3). It has thus combined social investment initiatives with the other more traditional rate of return objectives of pension funds in the rest of Canada.

The Caisse is most noted for its economic development initiatives in Quebec. Through its private investment subsidiaries, it invested $3 billion in 1997. The total value of its 367 private investments is now $4.6 billion. One subsidiary of the Caisse, the Accès Capital network, provides a regional network of development funds across Quebec. Another subsidiary, Capital d'Amérique CDPQ, invests in small, medium, and large companies in various industries, in the amount of $2.6 billion in 1997. Other subsidiaries specialize in the development of emerging, small- and medium-sized companies in communications, biotechnology, health, and financial services. For example, in 1995 with $500 million of the Caisse's assets, Sofinov was created as a venture capital company specializing in biotechnology; in 1997, another $500 million was infused into Sofinov to make it a leading venture capital company in Canada.

This asset allocation strategy was changed in 2002 following a loss of 9.6 per cent. This was below the benchmark portfolio return by 3.9 per cent. These poor returns were blamed on overexposure in the telecommunications, media, and technology sector, particularly in the private equity asset class. The losses associated with this sector alone totalled $6 billion, representing 45 per cent of the losses incurred in 2001–2.

Finally, the Caisse instigates joint ventures and syndications with other investment players in Quebec like the Solidarity Fund, a labour-sponsored investment fund, as well as the provincial government.

Labour-Sponsored Investment Funds

The idea of a labour-sponsored investment fund was first raised by the Quebec Federation of Labour (QFL) in 1982 at a summit economic conference in Quebec City organized by the Parti Québecois government.

As an economic engine for rebuilding the province, labour-sponsored funds were to provide much-needed capital from workers to fund small- and medium-sized businesses and, consequently, to create jobs in the face of high unemployment. As of 1998, these funds provide just under half of all venture capital in Canada with assets of almost $4 billion.

Founded in 1983, the Solidarity Fund in Quebec is the longest established and most successful of the labour-sponsored funds. Since Solidarity's founding, however, labour-sponsored investment funds have been created in most provinces under the umbrella of the provincial federations of labour. Their mandate as venture capital funds has expanded to include providing capital to companies in the early stages of development, to new technology companies, and companies undergoing restructuring. Investments in labour-sponsored funds provide the investor tax credits of 30 per cent divided equally between the federal and the provincial governments. If shares are purchased as an RRSP, they qualify for further tax deductions. Since these funds are viewed as patient capital, investors are required to invest for a minimum of eight years.

In Ontario, the New Democratic Party (NDP) government attempted to introduce a similar model, but there was no consensus in the labour movement. Some unions were very interested, having already had experience in economic development, for example, the United Steel Workers of America (USWA) and the United Food and Commercial Workers (UFCW). But the Canadian Auto Workers Union (CAW) was vociferous in its opposition, on the grounds that it was unclear whether workers would ever get their money back and that these funds would undermine pension plans. Both arguments have been shown to be without foundation.

The Ontario NDP government did create enabling legislation for labour-sponsored funds, but could not use the Ontario Federation of Labour as the sponsoring body. This has allowed a situation where venture capital companies can literally 'rent-a-union' as a sponsor to gain access to the favourable tax exemptions for the investors and the fund. There are, therefore, two classes of labour-sponsored funds in Ontario, only one of which is genuinely union-sponsored.

Because of this confusion, five funds across Canada have drawn up a statement of principles and defining characteristics of 'true' labour-sponsored funds. They are the Solidarity Fund in Quebec, the Crocus Fund in Manitoba, the Workers Investment Fund in New Brunswick, the First Ontario, Fund in Ontario and the Working Opportunity Fund British Columbia. A true labour-sponsored fund:

- Is promoted, sponsored, and directed by a labour body
- Meets economic and social goals in investment
- Provides an equitable rate of return
- Provides risk capital in a diversified portfolio
- Has the participation of a broad base of working people
- Facilitates cooperation between business and labour

These funds recruit union members who, after training and licensing, sell shares to co-workers. In 1993, the Canadian Labour and Business Centre reported that more than 379,000 Canadians were investors in funds across the country. More than half were union members (CLBC, 1993).

Once a year, the Solidarity Fund conducts educational events for employees in investee firms to encourage both transparency of the firm's books and employee understanding of accounts.

The success in raising funds reflects an enthusiastic investor base. The tax credits on investment have been a powerful incentive, and these credits can be reflected in the returns. In its first ten years, Solidarity reported cumulative average returns of 5.88 per cent. With tax credits taken into account the returns jump to 18 per cent (Quarter, 1995; Ellmen, 1996).

The year 1995 produced a flurry of research and reports to provide favourable interpretations of the first ten years of the Solidarity Fund. This was largely in reaction to a critical study by Suret (1993), which claimed that Solidarity had poor performance together with high management costs and that it was not cost effective in relation to the amount of government subsidization. That study concludes that each dollar invested in Solidarity costs governments between $2.02 and $4.24.

The Suret study uses a cost-benefit analysis which has been criticized by Melissa Moye, a labour economist at the American Federation of State, County, and Municipal Employees Union, in an unpublished study entitled 'A Review of Studies Assessing the Impact of Labour-Sponsored Investment Funds in Canada' (1997). Moye points out that the Suret study is merely a narrow cost-benefit analysis which fails to take into account such indirect and induced factors such as the effects of job creation, taxation from the newly created jobs, and increased consumer spending – all of which address the multiplier effects of investment in businesses.

Jackson and Lamontagne (1995), in their study published by the CLBC, further criticize Suret for counting as a cost the opportunity lost to investors by not investing in mutual funds. Suret claims that for every $10 invested, $7.71 is lost. Jackson and Lamontagne analyse the performance of seven investee firms in the Solidarity Fund and three investee firms in the Working Opportunity Fund (WOF) British Columbia. They proceed, through a cost-benefit analysis that includes indirect effects, to conclude that 'with one-time costs of $37.5 million and annual benefits of $13.8 million, the pay back period for the governments' support of these investment projects is less than three years' (ibid., p. 38). Their study is a careful examination of the fiscal costs to governments of labour-sponsored funds and the benefits of direct, indirect, and induced effects of the work of the investee firms. In spite of these studies, the CAW and the Fraser Institute continue to criticize labour-sponsored funds on the basis of government subsidization (Stanford, 1999b).

Concert Properties (Formerly Greystone)

In the early 1990s, twenty-six pension funds in British Columbia pooled a small proportion of their funds – $30 million – and created a real estate development company to provide rental housing. This project is called Concert Properties. It was initiated by the then president of the Telecommunications Workers of Canada (TWC), Bill Clark, and supported by a number of other unions. It was to use union labour only. Concert Properties is now the largest developer of rental housing in Western Canada. Guided by criteria including self-sustaining community development, as well as rate of return, Concert, works together with communities on joint massive neighbourhood redevelopment projects. Concert Properties now has a $450 million asset base, and it uses union labour only.

This chapter has shown that Canada has a small but growing venture capital market. However, about half of the money invested comes from labour-controlled investment funds. This low investment in venture capital is reflected in the lack of money available for the development of new industry and the low levels of productivity in the economy. Pension funds are an ideal source of investment in venture capital because they are 'patient capital,' that is, they have a long-term orientation.

Economically targeted investments are generally funds that are pooled by several pension funds and independently managed. They can be invested in mortgage trusts, affordable housing, commercial building, regional development, or real estate. They are designed to provide job creation, community development, and a reasonable rate of return for the pension fund.

The Rudd and Spalding (1997) study shows that trustees can be encouraged to invest pension funds in economically targeted investment if they have received appropriate education. If they do not receive education, it is unlikely that they will access the full benefits of the investment for pension plan members. This study has extensive implications for trustee training in social investment.

Unions now recognize that standards must be set for economically targeted investment. There can be collateral damage as well as collateral benefit. Private public partnerships (P3s) are an example of how collateral damage can befall workers and their communities when pension funds are invested in contractual arrangements that disguise powerful privatization initiatives. However, asset allocation strategies cannot be abandoned; over-exposure in a sector may lead to higher risk and lower rates of return.

There are few examples of economically targeted investments (ETIs) in Canada. One is Concert Properties, a real estate development company, and it will be examined in detail in the following chapters.

Part 2

chapter 8

A Case Study of Concert

This chapter is the first of three that presents this study's findings. It traces the background history of Concert Properties, using interviews with people who were significant in its development. Next, the formation and development of Mortgage Fund One is described. This mortgage trust was designed to complement and support Concert Properties as an investment vehicle for pension funds. Both Concert Properties and Mortgage Fund One are examples of strategies for allocating the assets of pension funds. The success of these strategies is examined in this chapter.

It's Our Jobs; It's Our Money

In 1968, as the new president of the Telecommunications Workers Union (TWU), Bill Clark negotiated the right to bargain pensions, and then joint trusteeship of TWU's pension fund. Bruce Rollick, a young actuary working for union-employer pension funds at the time, was sent on the road. His job was to visit every union local to explain the importance of pensions, of collective control of this large pot of money, and of a collective agreement and a trust agreement to prevent abuse of these funds by the employer. Membership involvement was crucial to back up negotiations with the employer and support the union in its new role as trustee of the fund.

Bill Clark's starting point was the amount of investment money leaving British Columbia. His inspiration in gaining more control over pension fund investment came when reading Peter Drucker's book, entitled *The Unseen Revolution: How Pension Fund Socialism Came to America* (1976). When interviewed by a reporter from the *Vancouver Sun*, some years later, Bill Clark said: 'You can only drain a community so long and too late you realize it has a serious effect on employment and that has a serious effect on [payments into] pension funds' (Casselton, 1988, p. D.12).

Both Clark and Wayne Stone, then administrator of the Carpentry Workers' Pension Plan of B.C. (CWPP), attested to the continuing loss in British Columbia of unionized employment in the construction trades. The percentage of union work on construction sites had been decreasing for years, as developers used more and more non-union labour. In 1999, Clark estimated that the building trade unions were still only getting about 27 per cent of the commercial construction work in British Columbia, and even less of the residential construction. Construction workers, on average, are the lowest paid group of workers in the goods-producing industries, as reported by the government of British Columbia (2000), with gross weekly wages in 1998 of $723, or $20.67 per hour, based on a 35-hour work week. While the sector is predominantly non-union, there are both union and non-union wages represented. By comparison, an average Concert construction wage, based on Concert's on-site workforce, at unionized rates of pay, is $33 per hour. Both rates are gross, including benefits and vacation.

Getting control of pension funds, then, was a way for union members to fight union-busting in the construction trades in British Columbia, and create well-paid construction jobs.

Pooling Pension Funds and Company A

Clark's goal was to pull together a group of pension funds, and develop a new fund where 'nobody [had] to put in more than they're comfortable with, but you still end up with a huge pool of equity funds' (interview, April 1999). As he saw it, the pool of money would not be directly managed by the funds, but by experts hired by the funds, to invest according to the policies established by the trustees (ibid,).

First attempts at creating a model were too 'all-encompassing, too complex and scared people off' (ibid.). One model proposed was a trust company, funded by a multiplicity of pension funds with a board of directors to deal with real estate, mortgage funds, venture capital, and other financial services. Driven by a desire to own some of the B.C. corporations that were being bought up by foreign interests, this direction sought to use pension money to start buying up the B.C. corporate sector.

This model, called Company A, is shown in Figure 8.1. The model was developed by Bill Clark, Bruce Rollick, and others to provide economic development by investing pension funds British Columbia. As a result of resolutions pushing for pension funds to be used to rebuild the B.C. economy, and provide jobs for union members, the group was instrumental in getting a policy paper produced by the B.C. Federation of Labour, entitled 'A New Look at British Columbia's Economic Future.' Company A was to use union labour to make pension funds accessible as capital in the B.C. economy in a broad base of sectors. Pension funds would commit a certain percentage of their assets to the pooled fund.

The Company A model laid the groundwork for the pension fund investment vehicles that were to be created. It illustrated a basic shareholder structure for larger and smaller pension funds, reserving the directorships for the larger funds, who, by dollar amount (rather than percentage of assets) could invest more than the smaller funds. Company A was to be the management company of a number of specialized investment vehicles, designed to provide capital to different sectors of the economy.

At the time, Company A was considered ambitious, but it was approved by a number of unions. Ultimately, However, it failed to get the support of employer pension trustees (Baldwin et al., 1991). As Rollick later pointed out, this strategy did not fly with the employer trustees, because it often involved investing in competitors (Mortgage Fund One, interview, April 1999).

Finally, the new group settled on real estate 'because you can build it, you can see it and you can sell it' (Clark, interview April 1999). There was also a familiarity with real estate. Some of the building trade unions were already investing in construction, but were doing it individually. However, this project was to be different. The idea behind the earlier Company A proposal of pooling small amounts of money from a number of pension funds to spread the risk was retained from the original model, as was the concept of a management company and an investment vehicle. It was to be called Concert Properties.

One of Concert's earliest projects was 424 Drake Street on Pacific Point in Vancouver. This project was described as a 'precedent-setting first joint venture' in the *Vancouver Sun* (Casselton, 1988, p. D12) and financed by thirteen separate pension funds, with no more than 2 per cent of each fund's assets. It was a plan to construct residential housing in two phases, condominium and rental. The idea was that the sale of the condominiums would finance the rental accommodations.

For this plan, Bill Clark and others recruited the support of trustees of the pension funds. Some of the unions that committed funds were the

Figure 8.1   Company A: Proposed investment company of Federation of Labour.

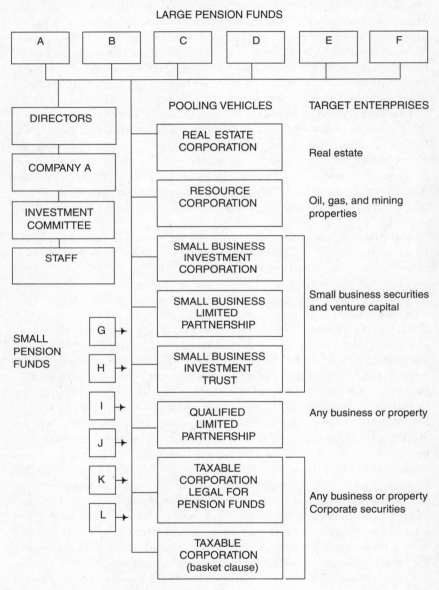

Source: Baldwin et al., 1991.

TWU, food and pulp unions, carpenters, floorlayers, shipbuilders, electrical workers, and piledrivers. In 1988, each phase was worth more than $14 million, with the long-term expectation of 14 to 15 per cent returns. First, the mortgage on the land would be paid off by rental returns. Once the mortgage was paid off, these payments would revert directly to the pension funds. In the meantime, returns would be approximately 9 per cent. At this point, there was no management company (Rollick, telephone interview, January 2000).

Pension Funds, Affordable Housing, and Rates of Return

While many pension funds were still moving their assets into the stock markets, Clark and Rollick were arguing that long-term investment of thirty or forty years in real estate was a perfect strategy for pension funds. They suggested a limit of 10 per cent of their assets to prevent overexposure. This investment strategy could be put to best use in the residential rental market, where long-term ownership over a long period could stabilize rents and provide a stock of affordable housing in the Vancouver region.

Developers were (and still are) reluctant to build rental accommodations. Building housing for sale provided immediate returns. Building rental accommodation is a longer term investment, with low returns in the short run unless the project is well capitalized. To avoid investment in longer term rental accommodations, developers have often sold rental buildings to get an immediate return. This has the consequence of increasing rents, since the new owner gears rents to the new purchase price. Pension funds could provide the guarantee of long-term investment, stabilized ownership, and affordable rents, if government had the land for development and the pension funds could gather enough capital to fund the project.

To this end, in 1988 under Bill Clark's leadership, five pension plans put together a real estate and property management company called Wescan, with employer and union representatives of jointly trusteed plans as shareholders. Wescan employed six experts in real estate development and property management. At the time, Clark said enthusiastically to the *Vancouver Sun*: 'If we're able to pull this together, we'd have available $300–400 million without anyone having to put up more than 10% of their assets. The potential is absolutely staggering' (Casselton, 1988, p. D12).

Clark pointed out that not long before this 'we had money and land, but nobody knew how to do anything' (David Podmore, interview, April 1999). The new management team, led by Jack Poole, now chairman of Concert Properties, was critical. A team of experts would put into action what the pension fund trustees had in mind.

Affordable housing was the leading criterion for development. The pension funds guaranteed that, in any given year, rents would not go up more than inflation plus 1 per cent. The City of Vancouver had unused land, and the partnership was ideal. Led by Mayor Gordon Campbell, city council was enthusiastic about this new cooperative venture (Casselton, 1988). The city was particularly interested in this partnership because Vancouver had been losing its stock of rental housing through demolition and conversion to condominiums. According to CMHC, the vacancy rate in west end Vancouver was under 1 per cent from April 1986 to October 1988 (David Podmore, interview, April 1999).

There was 'little prospect' of rental housing being built *without* the combination of capital from pension funds, land from the city, and the expertise of the management team assembled by the funds (Ibid.). The city agreed to be a financial partner and also agreed to the creation of a new entity. The city was to lease the land under long-term leases to the new company, and the new company would build and manage the rental housing.

In 1990, a new provincial government was elected, led by the New Democratic Party under Mike Harcourt. The Harcourt government was also an initial investor. The new company, popularly known as the Vancouver Land Corporation, was called VLC Properties. The province was prepared to contribute five-year mortgage subsidies under its rental supply program. Wescan was eclipsed by VLC.

Incorporated in May 1989, VLC Properties had a mandate to provide economically priced, multifamily rental and for-sale housing in British Columbia at a reasonable rate of return to shareholders. It was a remarkable collaboration of business, labour, and government. With an initial capitalization of $27.3 million, VLC had as shareholders the province, the City of Vancouver, pension funds, two banks, and private interests. Pension funds owned 75 per cent of VLC (see Table 8.1).

VLC's objectives were to provide quality, economically priced housing and job creation for skilled, unionized labour with reasonable rates of returns (Greystone Properties, n.d.). The city provided the land on long-term leases for which VLC would pay property taxes, and the pension funds were to put up the capital and expertise to build and manage guaranteed rental housing. Pension funds would get their returns through rental income (Podmore interview, April 1999).

Table 8.1   Initial VLC shareholders

Shareholders	Investment ($ thousands)	Ownership share (%)
16 pension plans	19,240	70.5
24 investors	3,560	13.0
2 banks	1,500	5.5
Province of British Columbia	1,000	3.7
City of Vancouver	2,000	7.3
Total 44 partners	27,300	100.0

Source: Personal communication from David Podmore, 14 October 2004.

Table 8.2 illustrates the housing projects built on city-owned land by VLC Properties from 1990 to 1992. Table 8.2 does not include later rental accommodation built by Concert Properties on city-owned land. At a cost of over $35.5 million, 460 rental units were built. Over this short period, almost 400,000 hours of on-site labour were put into the construction. Pension funds, most of them shareholders, gained over $1 million in additional contributions. From Table 8.1 it can be seen that:

1 Pension funds, for an original investment in VLC of $19.24 million, created in returns a total of $12.7 million in work, contributions to the health and welfare plans, and additional contributions to the pension funds themselves. (These returns are for the four projects which were to remain in VLC.)
2 Another way of expressing these gains is that for every dollar of investment sixty-six cents came back in returns in the form of work and contributions to health and welfare and pension funds.
3 On increased pension fund contributions alone, pension funds made returns of 5.6 per cent on their original investment.

This calculation does not include dividends returned to pension funds during these periods of construction. The calculation does assume that the work would not have otherwise been available to unionized construction workers. These points are discussed below. It is also important to note that the gains were made in unionized work for a broad group of construction unions, not all of whose pension funds have invested in Concert Properties.

The provision of rental housing capitalized by pension funds with

Table 8.2 Construction of rental housing projects by VLC Properties on land leased by the City of Vancouver, 1990–1992

Project	Rental units (n)	Construction date	Total project cost ($)	Construction hard costs[a] ($)	Total labour component[b] ($)	Hours of on-site labour[c]	Contributions to benefits plans[d]	Contributions to pension plans[e]
Parkside Village	52	Jan.–Aug. 1990	4,050,000	3,550,000	1,597,500	48,409	72,614	137,482
Fraser Pointe 1	177	Jun. 1990–Sept. 1991	13,850,000	10,600,000	4,770,000	144,545	216,818	410,509
Cassiar Court	48	Jan.–Sept. 1991	4350,000	3,250,000	1,462,500	44,318	66,477	125,864
Fraser Pointe 2	183	Apr. 1991–June 1992	13,200,000	10,750,000	4,837,500	146,591	219,886	416,318
Total	460		35,450,000	28,150,000	12,667,500	383,863	575,795	1,090,173

Source: Extracted from Summary of Company Activities, (Concert Properties, 1999).

[a] Construction hard costs represent labour costs as well as construction materials purchased for the construction project.
[b] The total labour component is the amount of hard costs spent on on-site labour (i.e., hard costs minus materials equals labour). This figure is the equivalent of gross pay, before deductions for taxes, vacation and benefits.
[c] Hours of on-site labour is calculated on an average rate of pay of $33 per hour.
[d] Contributions to benefit plans are calculated based on an average rate of $1.50 per hour deducted from pay for health and welfare.
[e] Pension fund contributions are calculated based on an average rate of $2.84 per hour deducted from pay.

land leased from the City of Vancouver has been extremely successful. In fact, David Podmore (interview, April 1999) has reported that 80 per cent of the rental housing built in Vancouver since 1989 was built by Concert Properties. Moreover, VLC met its target in not increasing rents beyond inflation plus 1 per cent. However, the actual rate of return resulting from these investments was reduced because the pension funds did not provide 100 per cent of the capital that was required to build the units. Therefore, VLC had to have mortgage debts on the properties, at the high borrowing rates that existed in the early 1990s.

While the decision to mortgage was vehemently opposed by Clark, shareholders at the time did not have the confidence to inject more pension fund capital into VLC Properties. One intimation is that employer trustees were not prepared to invest a higher level of capitalization. Podmore described the lack of capitalization as generated by 'a new initiative and a natural reluctance to go too far at the outset' (interview, 1–2 December 1999). Clark, however, has said that 'We don't like paying any profits to the bank. But that has always been the feeling in my union. That it's nuts to build a beautiful property and then borrow from the bank' (Podmore interview, April 1999). This experience, for Clark, formed the genesis of the concept of Mortgage Fund One, which will be described later in this chapter.

Structure of VLC Properties

When VLC Properties was originally structured, Podmore notes that twenty-nine pension plans were investors. There were also twenty-six private investors, including the City of Vancouver and the provincial government. Included in the private group were the Bank of Montreal, Toronto-Dominion Bank, several major property developers, and some business people in the community. Podmore described VLC as follows:

> We really set three goals for the company, and they were laid out in the offering. Obviously, the company was created with a social purpose, which was to address the housing needs at the time with the creation of rental housing. Secondly, [the company was] to generate a return on the invested pension capital *over a long term*. There was a deliberate emphasis to caution everyone that this was a very long-term investment, rather than an expectation of an immediate return. And the third objective was to create employment, union-only employment. We're a union builder, we build on an all-union basis. We've never conceived of this company as a buyer of real

estate product. This distinguishes us from Penreal, another pension fund investment group, where the main emphasis is on buying existing real estate. (Interview, April 1999)

In 1992, VLC Properties was restructured. There were a number of reasons for the restructuring. First, Podmore, Jack Poole (another founder), Clark, and Rollick reasoned that a real estate investment vehicle for pension funds should not be taxable, since pension fund investment itself is tax exempt. A partnership of pension funds and others as shareholders would be problematic in that it would provide a tax shelter for other investors simply because of their partnership with pension funds. This would not qualify for tax exemption under section 149 of the act.

During the 1970s, a number of Ontario pension funds had invested in real estate as active builders. Real estate development companies fought this competition by lobbying the federal government to change the Income Tax Act. They hoped to limit pension funds from becoming active builders. Section 149 of the act now exempts companies registered by pension funds before 11 November 1978. These 'grandfathered' companies have an intrinsic value as real estate companies and are permitted greater scope through having 'reasonable' freedom to be active builders. They also will likely receive the assurance in advance from Revenue Canada in the form of an opinion letter.

Tax exemption was not the only issue. To guarantee fiduciary responsibility, pension funds needed a shield from the liabilities of real estate development. While union trustees insisted that quality work was a natural outcome of union labour, civil suits were always a possibility. Given the proliferation of 'leaky condo' suits in British Columbia, they could not put members' pension benefits at risk. Pension funds setting up companies after 1978 had to make sure that their beneficiaries would be protected from liability suits by agreements with development companies which would essentially provide the shield from liability by being the active builders. This was not necessary for pre-1978 companies.

As part of the restructuring of VLC, a company that pre-dated 1978 was found and purchased from the Air Canada pension fund. The company, re-named Greystone, was registered as a pre-1978 company under section 149 (1) (o.2) of the Income Tax Act.

It was clear that more capital was needed for VLC and that the capital would come from pension funds rather than private investors. VLC Properties was to be restructured as a tax-exempt pre-1978 real estate development corporation, wholly owned by Canadian pension funds. This made it possible to raise capital from pension funds only. On restructuring, VLC went from $27.3 to about $80 million. One later additional offering took the company to $128 million.

At this point, in 1992, most of the land owned by the City of Vancouver had been developed. VLC Properties had completed four major buildings with the city on the land leased from it. To avoid tax penalties, these buildings (and their management) remained with VLC, which was re-named VLC Leaseholds; it retained the same ownership structure. Ownership shares were valued at $5.00, and shareholders were repaid $4.75 of their original share capital. They continued to hold shares valued at 25 cents, which, in 1999, were worth approximately $1.60. The long-term mortgages went with the new company. Returns, therefore, have been 'substantial' on the four buildings (Podmore interview, April 1999). Pension funds transferred the share capital returned to them into the new company at a dollar a share.

The new company, Greystone, had only pension funds as shareholders. The larger pension funds were represented on the board of directors, and the board also retained Ken Georgetti, the president of the B.C. Federation of Labour as a member. He retired from the board in July 2004. If VLC was a remarkable alliance of business, labour, and government, Greystone was an equally remarkable multisector collaboration across labour unions.

Concert Pension Fund Investment

The new company was to exist in the form of two companies, Greystone Real Estate Corporation and Greystone Properties. This enabled the pension funds, through the company, to both own and develop land. The name Greystone was challenged in 1995 by Greystone Capital Management, an investment management company based in Saskatchewan. To overcome this problem, a new name – Concert – was formally adopted in 1999.

The shareholders' major investment is in Concert Real Estate Corporation, effectively a holding company for equity and title of properties. Concert Properties Limited is a taxable corporation that exists to enable joint ventures with other groups besides the shareholder pension funds (David Podmore, personal communication, 14 January 2000).

Table 8.3 shows the present percentage shares held by shareholders in both Concert companies. Clark has maintained that for the model to

Table 8.3   Concert shareholders by sector (%)

	Concert Real Estate Corp.	Concert Properties Ltd.
Building trades		
Boilermakers' Pension Trust Fund	0.77	0.59
Bricklayers and Masons Pension Plan	0.30	0.23
Carpentry Workers' Pension Plan of B.C.	3.54	2.70
Ceramic Tile Workers Pension Plan	0.14	0.10
Floorlayers' Industry Pension Plan	0.27	0.21
GWIL Industries	0.08	0.06
Heat and Frost Local Union 118 Pension Plan	0.46	0.36
Labourers Pension Plan of B.C.	0.39	0.30
Local 213 Electrical Workers' Pension Plan	3.10	2.37
Marine and Shipbuilders' Local 506 Pension Plan	0.15	0.12
Operating Engineers Pension Plan	2.32	1.77
Piledrivers, Divers, Bridge, Dock and Wharf Builders	0.23	0.18
Sheet Metal Workers (Local 280) Pension Plan	1.23	0.94
Shopworkers Industrial Union Local 1928 Pension Plan	0.17	0.13
Teamsters Canadian Pension Plan	3.61	2.75
Teamsters (Local 213) Pension Plan	3.06	2.34
The Plumbers Union Local 170 Pension Plan	1.13	0.87
Subtotal	20.95	16.02
Food service		
Retail Wholesale Union Pension Plan and Trust Fund	2.73	2.09
United Food and Commercial Workers Union Pension Plan	11.25	8.59
Subtotal	13.98	10.68
Forestry		
Canadian Forest Products Ltd. Pension Master Trust Fund	4.89	3.74
Pulp and Paper Industry Pension Plan	11.06	8.45
The Trustees of the IWA Forest Industry Pension Plan	8.32	6.36
Subtotal	24.27	18.55
Telecommunications		
Telecommunications Workers Pension Plan	40.78	31.5
Subtotal	40.78	31.15
Other		
Concert Real Estate Corporation	0	23.62
	0	23.62
Total	100	100

Source: Concert (Dec. 1999).

work, there should be an anchor pension fund that is large and that can set the pattern for the other investor funds in terms of the proportion of funds it invests. In this case, his own fund, the Telecommunications Workers Pension Plan (TWPP), is clearly the anchor fund (Podmore, interview April 1999).

The shareholders in Concert are listed by sector in Table 8.3 The largest shareholder and anchor is the TWPP, with 40.78 per cent of Concert Real Estate and 31.15 per cent of Concert Properties shares. The second largest shareholder is the United Food and Commercial Workers Union Pension Plan, with 11.25 per cent of Concert Real Estate and 8.59 per cent of Concert Properties; its members do not derive on-site work from construction projects. The next three largest shareholders are pension plans with members in the forestry sector, which constitutes the largest sector after the anchor and also do not benefit from on-site work. The building trades pension plans constitute the largest number of investors, but none has investments exceeding 3.61 per cent of Concert.

Allocation of Concert Pension Fund Assets

Concert recommends that no more than 5 per cent of a pension plan's assets should be invested in its shares. Table 8.4 shows share ownership as a percentage of fund assets for selected owners of Concert Real Estate Corporation. Owners were selected based on the availability of data on their pension fund assets. The data were drawn from the *Canadian Pension Fund Investment Directory* (1999). The following points can be made:

1　None of the funds allocate a large percentage of their funds to Concert.
2　The TWPP remains the anchor fund, with the largest proportion of its assets in Concert at 2.3 per cent.
3　TWPP is closely followed by the Teamsters Local 213 Pension Plan which has 2.1 per cent of its assets in Concert.
4　Data are available for two of the three forestry funds, the Pulp and Paper Industry Pension Plan and the I.W.A. Forest Industry Pension Plan. Each has over $1 billion in assets, yet their asset allocations in Concert are 0.9 per cent and 0.5 per cent, respectively.

It is important to note that Table 8.3 does not show the total investments of each pension fund in the two Concert companies. Nor does it

Table 8.4   Estimates of selected ownership in Concert Real Estate Corporation as a percentage of fund assets

Pension fund	Fund assets[a] ($)	Ownership in Concert Real Estate Corp.[b] (%)	Outstanding share ownership in Concert[c] ($)	Ownership as % of fund assets
Building Trades Sector				
Heat and Frost Local Union 118 Pension Plan	51,500,000	0.46	475,000	0.9
Teamsters Local 213 Pension Plan	150,000,000	3.06	3,126,890	2.1
Carpentry Workers Pension Plan of B.C.	200,000,000	3.54	3,613,561	1.8
Operating Engineers Pension Plan	374,000,000	2.32	2,370,555	0.6
Food Service				
Retail Wholesale Union Pension Plan	209,000,000	2.73	2,791,666	1.3
Forestry				
Pulp and Paper Industry Pension Plan	1,250,000,000	11.06	11,301,599	0.9
I.W.A. Forest Industry Pension Plan	1,831,000,000	8.32	8,500,000	0.5
Anchor Pension Fund				
Telecommunication Workers Pension Plan	1,791,000,000	40.78	41,658,896	2.3

Source: Estimated from cited sources by author

[a] Drawn from the *Canadian Pension Fund Investment Directory* (1999).

[b] % ownership in Concert Real Estate Corporation taken from Table 8.2

[c] Letter from David Podmore, 14 January 2000.

show investments in VLC Properties. The percentage figure therefore does not reflect the full investment in Concert and its related companies. Nor does it reveal the total real estate asset class for the pension fund.

It can be concluded that the larger the pension fund, the larger the share of ownership in Concert. However, from the data available, the larger pension funds do not necessarily commit more capital in relation to their total assets. In fact, the converse may be true, that the smaller funds commit a larger proportion of their assets to Concert, compared with all sectors, with the exception of the anchor (Bruce Rollick, personal communication, 12 January 2000). Several reasons are cited for a lower commitment of pension funds to Concert. First, it has been suggested that there may be employer resistance to these investment strategies. Union trustees of pension funds that are trusteed by the union only (particularly in the building trades) have far greater freedom than union trustees of a jointly trusteed fund.

Second, some union trustees are reluctant to invest in Concert as their only real estate investment. Concert argues that pension funds should not invest more than 5 per cent of their assets in real estate, and a maximum of 5 per cent in mortgages (which count as fixed assets). Nevertheless, investing in one company, Concert maintains, is low risk because of its reliance on the rental residential market, the security provided by its assets, and its sound management. Even so, Concert did diversify by moving into housing sales (of condominium townhomes) in order to increase its short-term returns.

Third, as Clark had said earlier, a way to increase capitalization of Concert was to decrease borrowing from the banks and establish a financial institution owned by pension funds.

Mortgage Fund One

Concert has been, in some ways, too successful. While the attempt to build a real estate development company based entirely on equity did not worked since Concert was undercapitalized, the company, as Podmore has said, had a far greater capacity than it was delivering. Overall, the model worked. However, as Rollick said, if the company were to own everything it built, it would need much more funding. The idea was to manage both the equity and the debt. Thus, Mortgage Fund One (MFO) was created, and it could not have existed without Concert (MFO interview, April 1999).

Bill Clark called it a 'politically integrated company' (Podmore interview, April 1999) for the following reasons. First, MFO was conceived to decrease the influence of private lenders who may, in the long run, have interests antithetical to Concert. MFO would thus stabilize the long-term interests of Concert. MFO was set up in 1992 and essentially enabled the growth of Concert from $27.3 to approximately $130 million. Second, while MFO is independent of Concert, it exists to fund not less than 30 per cent and not more than 50 per cent of total loans to Concert projects. Concert, for its part, receives approximately 33 per cent of its financing from MFO and is working to increase borrowing to about 50 per cent of long-term requirements. In the long run, MFO should be about three times the size of Concert (MFO, interview, April 1999). However, this does not mean that there will be no borrowing from banks. Both Concert and MFO assert that lending to and borrowing from conventional lenders as well (without being dependent on the banks) provides an additional test to ensure non-preferential treatment. Third, the more Concert borrows, the more returns go back to MFO and thus to pension fund shareholders, who compensate for their lower short-term returns on Concert with their higher, short-term returns on the mortgage fund.

Its financial statements for 1998 describe MFO as an investment trust established under British Columbia law for the benefit of its unit holders by trust agreement originally dated by 30 September 1992 (Price, Waterhouse, Coopers, 1998, p. 1). MFO meets the conditions of a unit trust under the Income Tax Act, since all net income reverts to the unit holders; there is therefore no income tax paid (ibid., p. 3). There is one class of units and no limit on the number of units that can be issued. The work of the trust is managed by ACM Advisors Ltd., a company created for the purpose, which is paid fixed fees for portfolio management services (ibid.).

Pension funds investing in MFO achieve diversification in their fixed income portfolio by using the MFO investment as an alternative to bonds. ACM recommends that pension funds invest at least 5 per cent of their assets. The unit-holder or investor base is just slightly different from the Concert Properties shareholder group.

Union-Built Housing

The objective of Mortgage Fund One is to provide 'by way of investments in mortgages, interim and long-term financing to fund the development, re-development and construction of residential housing, office, retail,

Table 8.5   Capitalization and investment growth of Mortgage Fund One, 1992–1998

Investors	Capital invested ($ mil.)	Captial invested as a percent of MFO (%)	Investment growth ($ mil.)	Market value 31 Dec. 1998 ($ mil.)
Telecommunications Workers Pension Plan	45.0	57.4	18.8	63.8
United Food and Commercial Workers	6.0	7.7	1.0	7.0
Pulp and Paper Industry Pension Plan	3.0	3.8	1.8	4.8
Carpentry Workers Pension Plan of B.C.	7.6	9.7	1.8	9.4
Others	16.8	21.4	4.3	21.1
Totals	78.4	100	27.7	106.1

Source: derived from Mortgage Fund One (1999).

industrial and mixed-use buildings located in British Columbia, all of which will be constructed by contractors whose employees are represented by approved unions under a collective agreement' (MFO, 1999). MFO currently has fourteen investments, with an approximate value of $91 million in term and interim construction loans, all in British Columbia. MFO insists that any project funded, however partially, must be 100 per cent union-built. While all Concert projects are union-built, ACM staff report examples of projects of other developers that would not have been 100 per cent union-built and, therefore, would have paid lower non-union wages without MFO's involvement. 'Eight One Nine,' a high-rise condominium tower in Vancouver, and The Grande, another tower in North Vancouver, are two such examples. This condition is in the covenant the borrower has to sign. Building sites have also been inspected by MFO for potential violations of this condition of funding (MFO interview, April 1999).

Mortgage Fund One: Capitalization and Rates of Return

Table 8.5 illustrates a summary of MFO capitalization. MFO's other shareholders are:

- Local 213 Electrical Workers Pension Plan
- Teamsters Local 213 Pension Plan

Table 8.6   Rates of return, of Mortgage Fund One, 1993–1998 (%)

	1993	1994	1995	1996	1997	1998
Rate of return	8.26	8.11	8.22	10.02	7.69	8.40

Source: Mortgage Fund One (1999).

Table 8.7   Investment Comparison 1993–1998 (%)

	Mortgage Fund One	Wyatt Pooled Mortgage Funds	Scotia McLeod Mortgage Index
Cumulative yield	62.20	58.20	63.00
Annual yield	8.4	7.94	8.48
Management fee ratio	0.52	0.61	1.25
Net annual yield	7.88	7.33	7.23

Source: Mortgage Fund One (1999).

- Teamsters Canadian Pension Plan
- International Heat and Frost Union Local 118 Pension Plan
- Pile Drivers, Divers, Bridge, Dock, and Wharf Builders Pension Plan
- Ironworkers Local 97 Pension Plan
- Floorlayers Industry Pension Plan
- Marine and Shipbuilders Local 506 Pension Plan
- Sheet Metal Workers (Local 280) Pension Plan

Mortgage Fund One's shareholders, therefore, are very similar, but not identical to Concert. Again, the TWPP plays an anchor role with respect to the funding.

Since the average maturity of loans is approximately five years, Mortgage Fund One has already established its track record of returns. These are shown on Table 8.6.

Table 8.7 shows that MFO's management fees are less than two other Canadian mortgage benchmarks. In addition, MFO's net annual yield exceeds those other benchmarks and, therefore, provides a higher return to the pension plan investors (ibid.).

This chapter has described the history of Concert since its conception by a group of union leaders and their experts who advised them.

Through an innovative partnership of labour, business, and government, VLC Properties was formed to build and manage rental accommodations on land leased from the City of Vancouver, with 75 per cent of the funding provided by pension funds.

The original core of union pension activists reasoned that pension funds could provide the guarantee of long-term investment, stabilized ownership, and affordable rents, if government would lease land for development. Leased land was necessary to lower the need for capital. The pension funds guaranteed that rents would not increase by more than inflation plus 1 per cent. The City of Vancouver had unused land, and the partnership was ideal.

VLC, in a few short years, created 460 rental units with 400,000 hours of on-site labour at a cost of $35.5 million. Pension funds, most of them shareholders, gained over $1 million in additional contributions to their funds.

The next stage of development created Concert, a remarkable multi-sector alliance wholly funded and owned by pension funds. This form of organization protected the tax-exempt status of pension fund investment. Concert is, in fact, two companies – one to allow for land acquisition (which is tax exempt) and a second for real estate development (not tax exempt).

Concert, however, has not been able to provide total capitalization of rental housing projects and has mortgage debts on the VLC projects, reducing its short-term rate of return. Mortgage Fund One, a mortgage trust owned by pension funds, was developed primarily to provide debt financing to Concert. Financing union-built projects only, MFO yields a short-term rate of return to pension funds and, in effect, compensates for Concert's lower short-term rate of return. In the longer term, debts are repaid and rental income provides a reasonable rate of return to pension fund investors.

The next chapter examines models of social accounting at Concert and examples of shareholder gains from investment in Concert and Mortgage Fund One.

chapter 9

Carpenters and Concert: Social Accounting Models

This chapter describes the role of the Carpentry Workers' Pension Plan (CWPP) in Concert. It presents social accounting models for Concert using the variables of job creation, increased contributions to pension funds, and fiscal benefits to government and the broader community.

The Carpentry Workers' Pension Plan

The carpenters' union is the largest construction union in British Columbia, with over 9,000 members. Although its membership, and organizing policy, is not restricted to carpenters, that trade predominates. The Carpentry Workers' Pension Plan of B.C. (CWPP) has been in existence for over thirty years, and for much of that time Wayne Stone was its administrator. The CWPP is a special multi-employer plan under the Income Tax Act, and all contributions are technically classed as employer contributions. All seven trustees are from the union side. The plan has about 14,000 members.

The CWPP has been involved in real estate since the late 1970s. Its original involvement was buying land and building for cooperatives. Wayne Stone views this period as the only time when the CWPP was able to provide social housing, through government funding: 'With the wrap-up of social housing and the co-operative program, we started looking for other alternatives so that we could still provide good quality homes for people. We worked very closely with Bill Clark to set up VLC. That's been part of our history' (interview, 19 April 1999).

Wayne Stone and Bill Clark were the core union leaders working with Ken Georgetti, then at the B.C. Federation of Labour, first to set up Wescan and then VLC Properties. The three were the first union champions of pension fund investment. In 1988, in response to a question from a *Vancouver Sun* reporter (Casselton, 1988, p. D12) about a 'marriage of convenience' between labour and capital, Stone said: 'It's created some problems for us as individuals. We've overcome it from the point of view we've created employment and provided quality housing.' Stone goes on to say that if the WPP's money was with 'money managers whose main concern is best possible returns, ethical guidelines [will likely be] violated through investment in armaments and atomic power' (ibid.). Georgetti was more forthright at the time and is reported as saying: 'It's just the old tired attitude that if you believe in labour or social democracy, you have to be against capital and profits. We can use pension income to create jobs, union jobs, that pay a fair rate and get a fair return. We can make a profit ... but ... without exploiting people' (ibid.).

The CWPP continued its interest in real estate development by investing in Concert and, later, in Mortgage Fund One. However, it also set up a real estate development company of its own, Western Housing Development Corporation. Through this company, it undertook joint ventures with other development companies to build quality rental and affordable housing and purchase real estate. However, Revenue Canada determined that the company was not exempt under the Income Tax Act and assessed the CWPP $4.5 million in back taxes. This matter has been resolved out of court with no back taxes payable by the CWPP, but a guarantee that the company will be disbanded.

Stone concluded at the time that the only way pension funds could go into real estate development was through a model such as Concert (Wayne Stone, interview 30 November 1999). This sentiment flew in the face of overexposure of the pension fund to its real estate investments. The CWPP Annual Report of 1998 shows 8.76 per cent of the fund's assets invested in Western Housing Development Trust, 9.57 per cent in the Western Housing Development Corporation, 2.5 per cent in Concert, 4.81 per cent in 'projects,' and 22.04 per cent in unspecified mortgages and loans. This overexposure to real estate was based in an interest in investment related to job creation in the construction industry.

By 2000, it was clear that the pension fund had an unfunded liability. Real estate investments were no longer yielding good returns, and benefits – in particular a generous early retirement package designed to open up jobs for new apprentices – were too costly. Lower interest rates also reduced returns on investment. Contributions to the plan were also sinking because of a slump in the construction industry. The plan therefore had higher costs and lower returns than expected (CWPP, 2001).

An interim valuation of the plan in 1999 had also signalled trouble. With the early retirement of Wayne Stone, the board of trustees hired Jane Richey, an 'outside professional' as administrator. It became clear that the plan had not been managed well, and problems with assumptions, accounting, and valuation procedures emerged. Hiring a professional expert to manage the plan was critical to putting the plan on the road to recovery.

The previous administrators of the plan, Wayne Stone and Wayne Owen, were carpenters whose beliefs in worker control extended to administration of the pension plan. They therefore did not hire experts for the day-to-day administration of the fund or its investments. Owen had argued (Quarter, 1995) that the carpenters 'did not want to go to the bargaining table, negotiate an amount of money into the pension fund and turn it over to the the money managers and lose control of it. Right from day one, it was the carpenters' desire to maintain control of those funds within the Carpentry Workers' Pension Plan, and that's what we have done' (p. 178). In 2000, however, the board of trustees hired a team of professional advisors (including some with a previous association with the CWPP) to work with trustees and staff to undertake a complete audit and valuation of the plan's assets. A new governance structure was also initiated, marked by a greater collaboration between trustees, staff, consultants, and money managers and more complete communication with members. Trustees began to spend more time developing policy and procedures on investment. As Brent Rogers, the Central B.C. trustee from Dawson Creek, said: 'A system of checks and balances has been put in place ... The investment policy has to be reviewed at least annually ... probably bi-annually until we get everything cleaned up – and we must stick to it. We're builders, we'll get through it. If we run into a mistake in a structure, we rebuild it. If we see a problem, we fix it. Its not easy, some tough decisions had to be made' (CWPP, 2001, p. 11). Another trustee pointed out that the new approach to governance, with its system of checks and balances, no longer relied on the decision-making of one person. Trustees have been forced to learn more about investment management and take more responsibility for their decisions (CWPP, 2001).

A key to recovery was a new statement of investment policy. Investment in real estate was restricted to 8 per cent of assets, with 10 per cent as a maximum. Unsatisfactory real estate investments were to be liquidated, and minimum performance standards were delineated for future real estate holdings.

Table 9.1   Concert Properties, labour component by trade

Trade	%
Bricklayers	6
Carpenters	37
Cement masons / plasterers	3
Electrical workers	3
Elevator constructors	0.5
Ironworkers	4
Labourers	14
Operating engineers	2
Painters / drywall tapers / glaziers	10
Plumbers	9
Roofers and sheet metal workers	5
Teamsters	0.5
Tilesetters	3

Source: Concert Properties, 12 Nov. 1999.

Major cuts in benefits were delayed for three years in the hope that a new investment strategy combined with a change in the economy would drive up the value of CWPP's assets. But announced immediately were reductions in the early retirement provision, termination of active membership in the plan following a three-year break in service, reductions in contribution payouts, a revised schedule of personal top-up rates, and a disability pension only after ten years of pension credit (Ibid.).

In 2003, despite good performance in a poor economy, the plan's finances failed to improve, and across-the-board benefit reductions of 35 per cent were instituted, as well as a reduction in the early retirement subsidy, elimination of the 80 factor, and, finally, a reduction of up to 45 per cent in the pensions of recent retirees. These reductions were higher than anticipated and devastating to the membership of the CWPP.

The CWPP and Concert

Table 9.1 shows the estimated proportion of carpentry work Concert uses on its projects. At 37 per cent of the total labour component typical project, in a far more carpentry workers are needed than any workers in other trades. Nevertheless, as we have seen, job gains alone cannot be the driver of strategies for asset allocation. Table 9.2 shows the impact of nine years of Concert's construction activity on job creation and pen-

Table 9.2   Carpentry workers' construction activity in Concert, 1990–1999

	$	Hours
Project value (construction), completed by Feb. 2000	360,000,000	
Labour component ($360,000,000 × 45%)	162,000,000	
Hours of on-site labour created ($162,000,000 ÷ $33/h)		4,910,000
Hours of employment for carpenters (4,910,000 × 37%)		1,817,000
Contribution to carpenters' health and welfare plan (1,817,000 h @ $1.195/h)	2,171,000	
Contribution to carpenters' pension fund (1,817,000 hours @ $2.34/h)	4,252,000	
Total carpenters' benefit (wages, vacation, health and welfare, and pensions) [$21.62 × $1.12 + (1.195 + 2.34)] × 1,817,000 h	50,421,000	
Carpenters' pay net of contributions	43,998,000	
Estimated taxes paid by on-site labour of carpenters ($43,998,000 × 25%)	10,999,500	

Source: Concert Properties (12 Nov. 1999); Canada (1997).

sion fund contributions for the CWPP and on estimated tax revenues for the federal and provincial governments. Several points are to be made about the calculations in Tables 9.1 and 9.2 (some of these points are made more briefly in the notes to Table 8.1):

1 The construction value of a project represents its 'hard costs.' These costs are split almost equally between materials and labour. Labour costs are usually estimated by Concert at about 45 per cent of the construction value.
2 Concert calculates its average on-site labour costs at $33.00 per hour. This includes taxation, vacation, pension, and health and welfare payments. As has been noted, this should be compared with the average gross rate of pay for a construction worker in British Columbia of $20.67 per hour. A carpenter's gross union wage (including vacation, pension, and health and welfare) is $27.75 an hour.
3 A carpenter's contribution to the union's health and welfare plan is $1.195 per hour, as governed by the collective agreement.
4 Contributions to the pension fund are at the rate of $2.34 an hour, also governed by the collective agreement, they have remained unchanged for a number of years.

5 Tax revenues are estimated at 25 per cent of the carpenters' pay net of benefit contributions (which are tax exempt). This is an average tax rate also used by the Department of Finance.

Table 9.2 estimates that 4.9 million hours of work have been created by Concert projects, of which an estimated 1.8 million hours were for carpenters. The on-site work has an estimated value of $162 million, of which the total benefit to carpenters is estimated at $50.4 million. This does not include the 'soft' costs of professional or administrative services.

From all Concert's construction activity between 1990 and 1999, the CWPP is estimated to have received contributions of $4.25 million as a direct result of the work created by Concert. This increase in contributions flows directly from the insistence on union labour on construction sites, since the pension plan is a creation of the B.C. Carpenters Union. The pension plan would not have received this increase in contributions had it not been for Concert projects.

Table 9.2 also estimates that almost $11 million in tax revenues were collected from the employment of carpenters. This is an estimate of actual (rather than attributable) tax revenues. It recognizes that government is a stakeholder in pension fund investment, as has been discussed in previous chapters (particularly with reference to the value added statement examined in Chapter 6).

Politically Integrated Accounts

Savona is the name of a wood frame, four-storey building in west-side Vancouver. It has 103 residential apartments. It was designed for first-time homeowners and single people and sold by Concert. Table 9.3 illustrates a social accounting model for measuring pension fund investment in Savona. It was selected because it is also a project funded by Mortgage Fund One. It therefore illustrates how the two investments – Concert and Mortgage Fund One – complement one another in terms of their short-term rates of return.

The data are derived from a number of documents supplied by Concert and Mortgage Fund One. Some costs are actual rather than estimated. For example, project and labour costs and Concert equity data are actual figures supplied by Concert. Health and welfare and pension fund allocations are as outlined in collective agreements. Therefore, the formulas outlined in the previous table do not necessarily apply. There are several points of clarification:

Table 9.3 A social accounting statement of the Carpentry Workers Pension Pland of B.C. (CWPP) investment in Savona, a Concert project (construction period, 1998–1999)

	Concert	Carpenters
1 Concert's total project cost	$21,950,000	
2 Total equity required by Concert (20% of cost)	$4,390,000	
3 Carpenters' equity in Concert (@ 3.54%)		$155,400
4 Mortgage Fund One loan to Concert	$8,250,000	
5 Carpenters' equity in Mortgage Fund One (@ 9.7%)		$800,250
6 Total investment of carpenters		$955,650
7 Total value of on-site employment (169,224 h @ $33/h)	$5,584,392	
8 Carpenters' on-site employment (37% of 169,224 h)		(62,613)
9 Contributions to the CWPP of B.C. (@ $2.34/h)		$146,514
10 Contributions to the carpentry workers health and welfare plan (@ $1.195/h)		$74,823
11 Pay to carpenters, net of contributions		$1,515,663
12 Estimate of net on-site employment attributable to Concert		$572,712
13 Dividends paid by Concert to pension fund ($234,951 @ 3.54%)		$8,317
14 Return on investment to Mortgage Fund One (@ 8.4%)		$47,215
15 Total return to carpentry workers (add lines 9, 10, 11, 13, 14)		$1,792,532
16 Return to carpenters net of investments (subtract line 15 from line 6)		$836,882
17 Percentage gain to carpenters (line 16 ÷ line 6 × 100)		87.6
18 Net percentage gain to carpenters in work attributable to Concert as against investment [line 12 – (line 9 + line 10) as a percentage of line 6]		36.8
19 Total returns to CWPP (add lines 9, 13, 14)		$202,046
20 Percentage return to CWPP based on investment (line 19 ÷ line 6 × 100)		21.1

Sources: data derived from Concert Properties: Savona (12 Nov. 1999); letter from David Podmore 17 Jan. 2000; Mortgage Fund One (1999); Greystone Annual Report (1998); B.C.Stats: unemployment rates, labour average rates of pay.

1 Concert estimates that, as a rule of thumb, it provides 20 to 25 per cent equity in a project. Of the remaining financing, 66 per cent comes from the banks and 33 per cent from Mortgage Fund One (David Podmore, letter 14 January 2000).
2 The CWPP has a 3.54 per cent ownership in Concert (see Table 8.1) and a 9.7 per cent ownership in Mortgage Fund One (see Table 9.3). Therefore, their investments in Savona through Concert and MFO are prorated to reflect their ownership.
3 The data for actual hours of employment for Savona are supplied by Concert.

Hours of Work Attributable to Concert

An important question is how to account for hours of work created by Concert. It is always problematic to assert that this work would not have been created had it not been for Concert and that, therefore, all hours should be attributed to Concert. What is agreed by those interviewed at Concert, Mortgage Fund One, and some of the unions involved is that the *union* work would not have been created. For example, carpenters may have found work, but it would have been for lower wages on non-union construction sites. Concert, then, can at least be attributed with contributing to community wealth through providing higher (union) wage rates for its construction labour.

This point is conceded in row 12 of Table 9.3 of the accounting statement, where Concert is attributed with a net contribution of $572,712 in hours of work for carpenters. This is a conservatively low estimate. It assumes that, with a general (not industry) unemployment rate of 8.9 per cent in British Columbia in 1998, approximately 10 per cent of carpenters would have gone from unemployment to employment on a Concert construction site. In other words, their full hours of work can be attributed to Concert. The other 90 per cent, in the absence of Concert, would have been obliged to take non-union work, earning the average rate of construction pay for the province of $7.08 less per hour than the union (gross) rate. Even with this conservative estimate, the dollar value of job creation for carpenters that can be fairly attributed to Concert for its Savona project is $572,712. Furthermore, carpentry workers still make a gain on their pension fund's investment in the project of 36.8 per cent.

The social accounting statement represented in Table 9.3 sets off the total investments of the CWPP in a Concert project against its gains from the investment. It shows that, through work provided by Concert, members of the B.C. Carpenters Union make substantial gains of 87.6 per cent (set against their original investment in Concert and MFO). Table 9.3 further shows that the CWPP through its dual investments in Concert and MFO, makes a total rate of return of 21 per cent through increased pension fund contributions and returns on investment.

Table 9.4 has more similarity to a value added statement (vas). While it is not a balance sheet, it illustrates more clearly the investments and returns of several stakeholders in Concert – employees, shareholder pension funds, and government. Most of the calculations in Table 9.4 are drawn from Table 9.3 and therefore need no explanation. Foregone tax revenues on pension fund contributions and investment returns are estimated using the same method as the federal Department of Finance uses. A return on investment of 6.1 per cent is assumed, since it represents the 1998 rate of return on ten-year government bonds. (This rate of return is likely far in excess of that on Concert investments and slightly less than that of Mortgage Fund One.) An average tax rate of 25 per cent is also assumed.

Table 9.4 shows that government had a net loss of $2.1 million on the foregone revenue. However, there are a number of cautions about this result. First, the model only considers government as a stakeholder, without differentiation between different levels of government. Second, estimates of return relate only to income taxes for on-site employment. Information was not readily available for administrative staff of Concert and employees of all the professional services required in real estate development. Also, there are other taxes, primarily property taxes, which have not been taken into account. It can be assumed, therefore, that the estimate for tax revenue is extremely conservative. Third, this is only one project of several undertaken by Concert in 1998–9. Therefore, Table 9.4 does not present a complete picture of Concert's rates of return for that year.

Finally, in this case the limitations of the VAS model are apparent. It does not account for the impact beyond the walls of the project. Table 9.4 does not account for the indirect or induced effects of Concert's productivity, nor the jobs created by Concert, both of which have implications for tax revenues.

It is important to note that Savona housing construction was units for sale, rather than rental. As has been stated, 80 per cent of the rental accommodations in Vancouver built since 1989 are directly attributable to Concert. Given the vacancy rate in Vancouver at the 1980s, the reluc-

Table 9.4   A social accounting statement of stakeholder investment and returns in Savona, a Concert project (construction period 1998–1999)[a]

	$
Investments	
Total equity from Concert (20%)	4,390,000
Mortgage Fund One loan	8,250,000
Other loans	9,310,000
Total project	21,950,000
Estimated government foregone revenue on investment and returns:	
Concert	1,164,448
Mortgage Fund One	2,188,313
Total	3,352,761
Returns	
Employees	
Total value of on-site employment (169,224 h @ $33)	5,584,392
Benefits	
Health and welfare (@ $1.50/h)	253,836
Pension (@ $2.84/h)	480,596
Pay net of contributions	4,849,960
Total	5,584,392
Shareholders	
Estimated increased contributions to pension plans	395,984
Dividends from Concert[b]	234,951
Dividends from Mortgage Fund One[c]	693,000
Total	1,323,935
Rate of return	10.5%
Government	
Estimated tax revenues from on-site employment (25% of pay net of contributions):	1,212,490
Net loss	2,140,271

Source: Concert Projects (Dec. 1999; 12 Nov. 1999).
[a] All figures are estimates based on calculations used by Concert.
[b] This figure is extracted from the Annual Report, 1998.
[c] Mortgage Fund One reports annual rate of return is 8.4% (see Table 8.4).

tance of developers to build rental accommodations, and the history of the relationship between Concert and the City of Vancouver through VLC Properties, it seems reasonable to attribute the work created by construction projects of rental accommodations directly to Concert. The consequence of this will be seen in Table 9.5.

Table 9.5 A social accounting statement of the Carpentry Workers Pension Plan (CWPP) of B.C. investment in 600 Drake Street, a Concert project (construction period, 1992–1993)

	Concert	Carpenters
1 Concert's total project cost	$14,350,000	
2 Total equity required by Concert (25% of cost)	$3,587,500	
3 Carpenters' equity in Concert (@ 3.54%)		$126,998
4 Mortgage Fund One loan to Concert	$9,000,000	
5 Carpenters' equity in Mortgage Fund One (@ 9.7%)		$873,000
6 Total investment of carpenters		$999,998
7 Total value of on-site employment (129,545 h @ $33)	$4,275,000	
8 Carpenters on-site employment (37% of 129,545 h)		47,931 h
9 Contributions to the Carpentry Workers Pension Plan of B.C. (@ $2.34/h)		$112,159
10 Contributions to the carpenter workers health and welfare plan (@ $1.195 h)		$57,278
11 Pay to carpenters, net of contributions		$1,160,648
12 Estimate of on-site employment directly attributable to Concert		$1,151,751
13 Return on investment to Mortgage Fund One (@ 8.26%)		$72,110
14 Total return to carpentry workers (add lines 9, 10, 11, 13)		$1,402,195
15 Return to carpenters net of investments (subtract line 6 from line 14)		$402,197
16 Percentage gain to carpenters (line 15 ÷ line 6 × 100)		40.22
17 Net percentage gain to carpenters in work directly attributable to Concert as against investment [line 12 − (lines 9 + line 10) as a percentage of line 6]		98.2
18 Total returns to CWPP (add lines 9 and 13)		$184,269
19 Percentage return to CWPP based on investment (line 18 ÷ line 6 × 100)		18.4

Sources: data derived from Concert Properties (12 Nov. 1999); letter from David Podmore 17 Jan. 2000; Mortgage Fund One (1999); BCStats: unemployment rates, labour average rates of pay.

Union-Built Rental Accommodations

The building called 600 Drake Street was controversial when it was being built in 1992–3, because it aimed to provide housing for low-income people. Its design is contemporary, and it is a high-rise building of 192 small apartments, a mix of studio, junior one-bedroom, and one-bedroom apartments. Residents of 600 Drake Street could be on welfare or unemployment insurance. It is likely the closest a private developer has come to providing social housing in Vancouver.

Table 9.5 continues the social accounting model from the previous table. There is, however, one important difference. The project, 600 Drake Street, is a rental housing project. The following should also be noted: (1) This was one of the first Mortgage Fund One projects. MFO provided a twenty-year term mortgage for 63 per cent of the total cost of the project. In the absence of data, it is assumed that Concert financed 25 per cent of the total cost of the project, rather than all of the remaining 37 per cent. This is a conservative assumption since it lowers the individual union investment. (2) All figures relating to the B.C. Carpenters Union are based on the assumption of equal proportions of ownership in Concert and Mortgage Fund One; they are also based on the proportion of work on a construction site, as supplied by Concert.

The apartment building 600 Drake Street is a rental housing project built as a result of a unique arrangement between the City of Vancouver and Concert, as described earlier. As already stated, Concert has been credited with providing 80 per cent of rental housing built in Vancouver since 1989. It is, therefore, reasonable to assume that it is highly unlikely that this project or others would have been built without the intervention of Concert.

It is reasonable, based on the evidence, to assume that 80 per cent of the work would not have been created without Concert and, therefore, can be directly attributed to Concert. The formula used in Table 9.5 can be used for the remaining 20 per cent. It can be assumed that 10 per cent of the remaining hours of work would have been done by carpenters who otherwise would have been unemployed. In the absence of Concert, one can assume that 90 per cent of the remaining work would have been done by carpenters obliged to take non-union work, earning the average rate of construction pay for the province of $7.08 less per hour than the union (gross) rate. The calculations, then, would be as in Table 9.6.

Table 9.6 illustrates that just a 13 per cent deduction is actually made

Table 9.6   Calculation of hours of work and value of carpenters directly attributable to Concert from the 600 Drake Street (rental accommodation) construction project

Hours of work for carpenters (*n*)	47,931	
Value of carpenters' labour component		$1,330,085
80% of hours (*n*)	38,345	
Value of 80% hours of work @ $27.75		$1,064,068
Remaining hours of work (*n*)	9,586	
10% @ $27.75		$26,601
90% @ $7.08		$61,082
Total value of Carpenters' work directly attributable to Concert		$1,151,751

of the total labour component because 600 Drake Street is rental accommodation. Yet, the total labour component of Savona suffers a 67 per cent decrease. Both these social accounts show the difference between taking 100 per cent of the jobs created as a benefit for the carpentry workers' union and its pension fund, and a more accurate attribution of job creation.

The following chapters will discuss the fuller implications of these two models. However, it is important to note that investments by pension funds have financed both Concert and Mortgage Fund One. This can lead to substantial returns and help build up the pension funds through higher contribution levels; it can provide higher waged work for union members; and it can openly advocate a union presence in B.C. workplaces. Furthermore, pension fund investment can provide socially useful services to the community. Nevertheless, pension funds must take hold of overexposure to real estate in their investment portolios as well as the dangers of self-serving investments in job creation. The next chapter examines project in a working class neighbourhood in Vancouver – Collingwood – which is also a Concert project. It assesses the fiscal benefits provided by the Collingwood project and Concert to government and the broader community.

chapter 10

Collingwood and Concert: Union and Community

First, this chapter examines the Collingwood housing project and provides a short case study of the neighbourhood and a history of the development of housing projects within it from 1994 to 1999. It assesses the proportion of jobs created that are directly attributable to Collingwood and estimates the returns to stakeholders. Second, this chapter applies these same models to all Concert projects since its inception, providing an estimate of Concert's direct impact on the community, as well as its benefit to stakeholders. Finally, this chapter uses multipliers to estimate the impact of Concert on the economy of British Columbia.

Collingwood is a large ongoing project of urban redevelopment initiated by Concert Properties in 1993. Collingwood Village is a high-density residential community, that is still being redeveloped on 27.26 acres of industrial land. This land, assembled by Concert Properties, includes the remaining 2.276 acres of land owned by the City of Vancouver and leased to Concert and now completely developed. Potentially there could be up to 2,800 multifamily residential units, of which 15 per cent would be assured market rental units (the original pieces of land leased by the City of Vancouver). The rezoning of the land was completed in 1993.

According to the census data of 1991, the Renfrew-Collingwood community prior to redevelopment was a stable, family-oriented, and ethnically diverse community of lower income families. Eighty-eight per cent of the community lived in single-family homes, with an average household size of 3.2 persons. Forty-five per cent of women were in the workforce, with a high proportion of residents in low-paying work. Forty-eight per cent of families had incomes below the city average of $30,000. Eighty-five per cent of families had two parents living in the home. Nearly 60 per cent of families had English as a second language. Homes in the neighbourhood had the highest proportion of basement apartments in Vancouver. Renfrew-Collingwood was a safe, reliable community where a working-class family could own a home and raise a family (Paula Carr, Community Coordinator, Collingwood Neighbourhood House, interview, 8 November 1999).

In 1981, the government of British Columbia announced the selection of the Advanced Light Rapid Transit system, or the Sky Train, for Greater Vancouver. In a 1999 interview with the author, Chris Taulu, a long-time resident and community activist, describes her neighbourhood as having been a run-down east-side community before the Sky Train. It had, in fact, been left alone and starved of services for years. It was, she said, ready for redevelopment. The City of Vancouver initiated neighbourhood planning meetings, and the route and stations were built through neighbourhoods during the 1980s. The Joyce Street Station became the focus of redevelopment, as developers moved in to buy up land, and the city developed the Joyce Station Area Plan.

Fortunately, the city, working with community activists at the time, promptly rezoned land scheduled for redevelopment, effectively preventing land speculation. Developers sold the land to Concert for $65 million. The community, therefore, had one developer to deal with. This worked in the community's favour, according to city planners and community activists involved in the community negotiations (Chris Taulu, interview, 12 November 1999; Heike Roth, Economic Development Officer, City of Vancouver, interview, 13 November 1999).

Community Negotiations

Negotiations proceeded between the community, the city, and Concert on development of the new Collingwood community. Negotiations covered the planning, design, and construction of residential buildings, as well as the new site for the Collingwood Neighbourhood House. Prime concerns of the community were integration of the new and the older community residents, child care, and crime prevention. The Sky Train had created a 'crime corridor' across Vancouver, because it was a surface train system that was completely unstaffed. This quiet, forgotten east-side community had become vulnerable to substantially increased levels of crime.

A new 10,000-square-foot facility for the Collingwood Neighbourhood House (CNH), which had been in existence since 1985, became the focus of new services to the community. The new CNH contains offices and meeting rooms, an 8,000-square-foot daycare centre, and a gymnasium. As a result of negotiations with the community, the capital costs were paid by Concert and the City of Vancouver. Hard construction costs came to $5.4 million. The total cost of the building was $6.3 million, of which the city paid $3.6 million and concert paid $2.7 million.

Present operating funds for the neighbourhood house come from all levels of government, the United Way and other, smaller donors. It employs 120 people and more than 300 volunteers. Under a local hiring policy, the CNH recruits about 60 per cent of its staff from the local community. Although there have been union drives in the community services sector in British Columbia in the past few years, there is no doubt that the spotlight has been on the Collingwood Neighbourhood House – given the funding of the community by union pension funds (Carr, interview, 8 November 1999).

In addition, a new health care centre is being built by Concert and leased to the regional health board, and a new elementary school is being planned.

Crime Prevention

With the highest rate of crime in Vancouver, crime prevention remained the central issue for the community. In April 1994, a new community crime prevention office was opened with one staff person, Chris Taulu, and 120 volunteers. Within five months, Collingwood had dropped to third place among city areas for incidents of crime (Crime Prevention Office, 1994).

The crime prevention office works closely with community. It teaches prevention through the distribution of information leaflets, block watch programs, 'pooch patrols,' and bicycle programs. All training of volunteers is done by the Vancouver Police Department. However, Chris Taulu points out that the office is effective precisely because it is independent of the Police Department, unlike all other crime prevention offices in Vancouver.

Concert has provided office space free of charge, paid for its maintenance, and provided a $40,000 endowment over ten years, on the grounds that it, too, will benefit from strong crime prevention programs.

Collingwood, Pension Funds, and Job Creation

As of 1999, Collingwood Village was a project of seven years duration.

Table 10.1 shows projects totalling over $195 million, with labour costs for construction workers running at almost $57 million. Of this, almost $5 million had been contributed to pension funds.

It can be assumed that of this total cost, Concert invested 25 per cent in equity. Therefore, for an investment of $48,771,500, the pension funds gained a rate of return of 10 per cent in pension fund contributions.

Table 10.2 provides a social accounting of the amount of construction work that can be attributed to Concert in Collingwood. Because Collingwood is a community where both rental and market housing has been built, both models are used. The total number of hours of on-site work is divided into work on rental accommodations and work on housing units for sale. It is assumed that 80 per cent of construction work on rental accommodations would not have proceeded had it not been for Concert. Of the remaining hours, it is assumed that 10 per cent of the hours would have been taken by construction workers who would otherwise have been unemployed. The other 90 per cent would have been taken by construction workers at non-union rates of pay.

Therefore, work on housing sale projects is calculated by assuming that 10 per cent of construction workers would have been unemployed had it not been for the projects. These hours are calculated at full rate of the average wages paid by Concert. The other 90 per cent are calculated based on the difference between the full unionized average rate of pay and the average rate of pay for construction workers in British Columbia.

Table 10.2 shows that a total labour value of almost $38 million can be attributed to Concert from its on-site labour component of almost $57 million. This labour value is a direct effect attributable to Concert's economic activity in the Collingwood project since 1994. Its benefits flow to British Columbia.

Benefit to Stakeholders

It is also possible to calculate the direct benefit of the Collingwood project to various stakeholders. This is shown in Table 10.3, which estimates the benefits to employees, shareholders, and government of Concert's work in Collingwood for the construction period 1994 to 1999. It is based on information provided by Concert in Table 10.1 and calculations explained in Table 8.1.

The first group of stakeholders, that is, on-site employees, had 1,720,541 hours of work for a total benefit of $56.7 million, including

Table 10.1 Concert projects in Collingwood, 1994–1999

Project	Rental or sales	Construction date	Project cost ($)	Total cost of labour component ($)	Total on-site hours (n)	Contribution to pension funds ($)
Melbourne	R	1994–5	18,900,000	6,402,150	194,005	550,973
Wessex Gate / Earles Court	R	1994–5	23,850,000	8,278,200	250,855	712,427
Alexander Court	S	1994–5	6,102,000	1,530,450	46,377	131,711
MacGregor	S	1994–5	33,390,000	8,693,100	263,427	748,133
Collingwood Neighbourhood House		1994–5	6,300,000	2,430,000	73,636	209,127
Gaston Park		1994–5	1,210,000	456,750	13,841	39,308
Phase 1 Infrastructure			1,424,000	630,000	19,091	54,218
Emerald Park Place / Amberley	S	1997–8	36,227,000	9,617,400	291,436	827,679
Melbourne Park		1998	565,000	227,250	6,886	19,557
Remington	R	1998–2000	31,450,000	8,122,500	246,136	699,027
Bradford	S	1998–9	6,953,000	1,919,700	58,173	165,211
Phase 2 Infrastructure	R		1,613,000	558,900	16,936	48,099
Phase 3 Infrastructure			525,000	198,450	6,014	17,079
The Centro	S	1997–8	21,707,000	6,342,750	192,205	545,861
Joyce and Crowley	R	1998–9	4,870,000	1,370,250	41,523	117,925
Total			195,086,000	56,777,850	1,720,541	4,886,335

Source: Concert (Dec. 1999).

Table 10.2   A social account of on-site employment directly attributable to Concert on Collingwood projects (both rental and sales), 1994–1999

	$	hours (n)
Total hours of work		1,720,541
Total labour component (@ $33/h)		56,777,850
Value of work on rental accommodation projects to be attributed to Concert[a]		
Total hours of work		868,923
80% of hours		695,138
80% hours of work @ $33	22,939,554	
Remaining hours of work		173,785
10% @ $33		573,491
90% @ $12.33		1,928,492
(@ $33 – $20.67)[b]		
Total	25,441,537	
Value of work on housing sales projects to be attributed to Concert		
Total hours of work		851,618
10% of hours		85,162
10% hours of work @ $33	2,810,346	
90% of hours		766,456
90% of hours @ $12.33	9,450,402	
Total	12,260,748	
Total labour value to be attributed to Concert in Collingwood project:	37,702,285	

Sources: Concert (Dec. 1999); letter from David Podmore, 17 Jan. 2000.
[a] Included in this list of 'rental accommodation' are the Collingwood Neighbourhood House, several parks, a baseball diamond, and a Health Centre. All, with the exception of the Health Centre are on land owned by the city and leased to Concert. The Health Centre is on land owned by Concert and leased to the Vancouver / Richmond Regional Health Board.
[b] The average construction gross rate of pay for British Columbia is $20.67 (BCStats, 2000).

pension and health and welfare benefits. It should be noted that to denote that employees are an investment, this item could also have been included in the 'investment' category as a debit from project costs.

The second group of stakeholders, the shareholders, benefit from increased contributions to pension funds, as well as from dividends from their investment in both Concert and Mortgage Fund One. It is

Table 10.3 A social accounting summary of stakeholder investment and returns in Collingwood, a Concert project (construction period, 1994–1999)

	$
Investments	
Total equity from Concert (25%)[a]	48,771,500
Mortgage Fund One loans (34%)	49,746,930
Subtotal	98,518,430
Other loans (66% of remaining financing)	96,567,570
Total project	195,086,000
Estimated government foregone revenue on investment and returns	
Concert	12,936,640
Mortgage Fund One	13,195,374
Total	26,132,014
Returns	
Employees	
Est. hours	1,720,541
Est. pay net of contributions[b]	49,310,704
Est. benefits	
Health and welfare[b]	2,580,811
Pension[b]	4,886,335
Total	56,777,850
Shareholders	
Estimated increased contributions to pension plans	4,886,335
Dividends from Concert[c]	
Dividends from Mortgage Fund One, 1994–9[d]	3,518,766
Total	8,405,101
Rate of return	8.5%
Government	
Tax revenues from on-site employment	
(25% of pay net of contributions)	12,327,676
Property taxes	6,265,601
Net loss	7,538,737

Source: Concert (Dec. 1999; 13 Dec. 1999).
[a] This is Concert's estimate of their project financing in general (David Podmore, January 2000).
[b] see Table 7.1 notes.
[c] Information unavailable.
[d] See Table 8.4 An average of the rates of return (7.07%) was taken for the total investment.

noted that figures are not available for complete returns on investment in Concert. Nevertheless, shareholders still have averaged an 8.5 per cent return on their investment over these years of construction in Collingwood. Given that Collingwood has both rental and market accommodations, the rate of return will increase in the future, as outstanding loans other than those to Mortgage Fund One are paid off and rental income continues to be generated.

The third stakeholder is government. A simple calculation is made contrasting the estimated foregone revenue from pension contributions and the rate of return on investment with the taxes estimated to have been paid by on-site labour and in property taxes. The net loss to government is $7.5 million. The same cautions apply to Table 10.3 as applied to Table 9.4. The calculation is simplified because it does not account for other employment directly created by Concert; nor does it account for many other taxes paid such as corporate and sales taxes. Finally, the calculation does not take into account indirect and induced effects of Concert's productivity and job creation.

Concert and Community

The final question is the extent to which Concert's work has benefited the larger community. Table 10.4 provides another social accounting of Concert's work from 1989, since Concert's inception, to 1999. It summarizes the total number of hours of on-site employment and the value of that work that can be directly attributed to Concert. Table 10.4 measures the impact of Concert's work on the general community.

It is important to note that this is an account of on-site labour only. This work includes bricklaying, cement masonry, carpentry, electrical work, glazing, iron work, engineering, painting, plastering, plumbing, roofing, and carpentry. Table 10.4 is, therefore, a conservative account because there is also professional and administrative work to support the on-site labour. It is also important to note that this work was carried out on projects with a total cost of $498,585,000, or almost half a billion dollars.

Table 10.4 shows that of a total labour value (or component) of $129.4 million, only $79.2 million should be directly attributed to Concert. This is largely based on the proportion of hours spent on rental construction, as opposed to housing sales construction. This represents 2,400,752 hours of work, or 61 per cent of the actual labour component.

What impact does this work have on the community? The analysis and evaluation branch of the B.C. Ministry of Finance maintains an input-out-

Table 10.4   A social account of on-site employment directly attributable to Concert projects (both rental and sales), 1989–1999

	$	hours (n)
Total hours of work		3,922,527
Total labour component (@ $33/h)	129,443,400	
Value of work on rental accommodation projects to be attributed to Concert[a]		
Total hours of work		1,528,799
80% of hours		1,223,039.2
80% hours of work @ $33	40,360,293	
Remaining hours of work		
10% @ $33	1,009,007	
90% @ $12.33		
(@ $33 minus $20.67)[b]	3,393,017	
Total	44,762,316	
Value of work on housing sales projects to be attributed to Concert		
Total hours of work	2,393,728	
10% of hours	239,373	
10% hours of work @ $33	7,899,302	
90% of hours	2,154,355	
90% of hours @ $12.33	26,563,199	
Total	34,462,501	
Total labour value directly attributable to Concert	79,224,817	
Total hours to be directly attributed to Concert (@ $33/h)		2,400,752

[a] Included in this list of 'rental accommodation' are the Collingwood Neighbourhood House, several parks, a baseball diamond, and a Health Centre. All, with the exception of the Health Centre are on land owned by the city and leased to Concert. The Health Centre is on land owned by Concert and leased to the Vancouver / Richmond Regional Health Board.

[b] The average construction rate of pay for British Columbia is $20.67 per hour (B.C.Stats, 2000).

put model, with the assistance of Statistics Canada. This model has as its base year 1990. It has been used for many studies that assess economic impact, and it can be used to calculate approximately 13,000 different multipliers for the B.C. economy (B.C. Ministry of Finance, 1996).

Input-output models and their multipliers represent a simplified way of accounting for economic interdependence. In this case, they allow for an estimation of the indirect and induced effects of Concert's projects and the work it has created. They are somewhat crude and mechanistic. Therefore, for example, multipliers were not used to estimate the direct effect of Concert's production in creating jobs. Nevertheless, they are useful as estimates *in the absence of* information such as:

- The value added to capital by the Concert projects that have been built
- The impact of the value added on spending in British Columbia
- The impact on the suppliers of construction materials and services in the B.C. community in relation to their own economic growth and spending
- The number of jobs that have been created indirectly by suppliers or, more distantly, by commercial ventures benefiting from Concert projects
- The amount of spending, that has been created, or induced, by Concert, as a consequence of its production
- The amount of spending that has been lost to other provinces
- The amount paid in employment, property, and business taxes.

Table 10.5 uses multipliers against Concert's total project costs, for its ten years of existence, to attempt to provide estimates in response to these questions. Table 10.5 illustrates that, over the ten-year period, the indirect and induced effects alone of Concert outweigh the total project costs. Even though the multipliers chosen for employment effects are the more conservative, in that they take account of social safety nets in the absence of employment, indirect and induced employment increases the direct effect of Concert's estimated labour component by 71 per cent.

Using multipliers, the social accounting shows that Concert's impact on indirect and induced employment created 5,529,524 hours of work, more than doubling its direct, attributable on-site employment. This is in spite of the fact that the multipliers chosen for employment effects are the more conservative (as already stated). Furthermore, Concert's value added or contribution to productivity, in the community, through its indirect and induced effects is $508,556,700, which is just over its total project costs for the ten years.

Finally, the taxation revenues for all levels of government generated through Concert's productivity total $144,589,650, which amounts to 29 per cent of the total project costs. How does this compare with taxes foregone by government through tax exemption of pension contributions and returns on investment?

Table 10.5   Indirect and induced effects based on total project costs of Concert of $498,585,000, 1989–1999[a]

	Indirect	Induced	Total
Output	(.55) $274,221,750	(.15) $74,787,750	$349,009,500
GDP – Value Added	(.23) $114,674,550	(.09) $44,872,650	$159,547,200
Subtotal	$388,896,300	$119,660,400	$508,556,700
Employment			
(person years)	(4.4) 2191.2	(1.7) 847	3038.2
(person weeks)			157,986
(person hours)			5,529,524
Taxation[b]	Direct/Indirect	Induced	Total
Federal	(.14) $69,801,900	(.01) $4,985,850	$74,787,750
Provincial	(.11) $54,844,350	(.01) $4,985,850	$59,830,200
Municipal	(.02) $9,971,700	(.00)	$9,971,700
Total			$144,589,650

[a] Multipliers are shown in parentheses and are taken from the multiplier tables, item 154: Residential Construction (B.C. Ministry of Finance, 1996).
[b] Taxation collected on direct, indirect, and induced employment and businesses.

Table 10.6 shows estimates of taxes foregone by the federal government for both Concert and Mortgage Fund One. The calculations are based on methods used by the federal Department of Finance: the department calculates foregone revenue on pension fund asset returns by multiplying the total pension fund assets in Canada (as reported by Statistics Canada) by the reported interest rate on ten-year government bonds (6.1 per cent in 1997). This sum is multiplied by an 'average tax rate' (Ian Pomroy, Senior tax policy officer, interview 6 January 2000). If it is assumed that tax revenue is foregone by the federal government, this level of government more than recoups its investment through direct, indirect, and induced returns in the form of personal and business taxes. For all levels of government, it is clear that the work of Concert and Mortgage Fund One yields opportunities for tax revenue that far outweigh government subsidization. Clearly, the benefits of Concert extend beyond the interests of construction workers and their pension funds.

The Collingwood project is an example of urban renewal of a working-class community in the lower east side of Vancouver. Preliminary models have shown that the total project costs of five years of this develop-

Table 10.6   Foregone tax revenues for Concert and Mortgage Fund One – 1989–1999, on total project costs of $498, 585,000

Concert	
Equity (@ 25%)	$124,646,250
Foregone Taxes on[a]	
Investment	$31,161,563
Returns (@ 6.1%)[b]	$1,900,855
Total	$33,062,418
Mortgage Fund One	
Equity (33% of financing)	$123,399,788
Foregone taxes on	
Investment	$ 30,849,947
Returns (@ 7.07%)[c]	$2,181,091
Total	$33,031,038
Total Foregone taxes for Concert and Mortgage Fund One	$66,093,456

[a] As estimated by the Department of Finance.
[b] As estimated by the Department of Finance, in the absence of information on rates of return.
[c] Average rate of return, see Table 8.4.

ment are just over $195 million. This accounting itemizes the jobs created as well as monies flowing to union pension funds as a result of the development. The first social accounting model calculates the direct effects of this job creation on the broader community. It shows that a total labour value of almost $38 million can be attributed to Concert from its on-site labour component of almost $57 million.

A second social accounting model has estimated the returns from Collingwood to stakeholders – employees, shareholders, and government. Shareholders made an average rate of return of 8.5 per cent on their investment, with dividends from Concert unaccounted for. Governments made a net loss of $7.5 million, taking into account only revenues generated by on-site labour and property taxes, with indirect and induced effects unaccounted for.

The former model is then applied to all Concert projects since its inception, providing an estimate of Concert's direct impact on the community. Of a total labour value (or component) of $129.4 million, $79.2 million can be directly attributed to Concert, largely based on the proportion of hours spent on rental construction, as opposed to housing sales construction. This represents almost 2.5 million hours of work.

Finally, a multiplier model is used to estimate the impact of Concert on the broader community through its indirect and induced effects. It was found that the company doubled its direct, attributable hours of employment in the community. Furthermore, Concert's contribution to community productivity was more than double its total costs over a ten-year period. Finally, the tax revenues for all levels of government generated through Concert's productivity total $144.5 million, almost one-third of the total project costs. Foregone tax revenues on pension fund investment returns in Concert and Mortgage Fund One over ten years are estimated at $66 million. Therefore, the federal government had a net gain of $8.7 million on its investment. However, all levels of government benefited in the amount of $144.5 million.

The following chapter considers the implications of these findings for pension funds. It will propose and discuss a transferable model of social action that may guide pension trustees in setting up social, or economically targeted, investment.

Part 3

chapter 11

Accounting for Social Investment

One topic of this book has been an examination of the barriers confronted by union trustees in establishing meaningful, and implementable, social investment strategies. Part 3 offers an antidote, by proposing interpretations of the findings described in Part 2 and a way forward for union trustees to implement social investment strategies in managing their pension funds. This chapter is organized into two sections. First, definitions and standards for social investment are discussed. Integral to this discussion is consideration of the validity of using the term 'social investment' as a classification for ethical investment, shareholder activism, and asset targeting. Second, the measurability of social investment is discussed, and models of social accounting are considered, with particular attention to their transferability.

Definitions of Social Investment

This book examines three different vehicles for social investment: shareholder activism and corporate governance, ethical screens, and economically targeted investment (ETI). These three broad types are intended to provide a collateral, or social, benefit aside from the fiduciary responsibility to beneficiaries. All three satisfy the initially proposed definition of social investment (Chapter 5) as the 'inclusion of various social standards in investment decision-making to accompany financial standards.' Others (Bruyn, 1987; Lowry, 1991; Zadek et al. 1997) have suggested that the definition of social investment should include a challenge to conventional corporate behaviour, often because such a challenge arises in an arena of contested control.

If the challenge to corporate behaviour is included, this would effectively prevent the use of right-wing criteria, for example, anti-gay ones. Such criteria exist in the United States and could easily be taken up in Canada. The challenge to conventional corporate behaviour can be measured using accounting methods to assess the extent of social change. This process is called 'social accounting.'

One factor common to all forms of social investment is the need for collective action by unions and pension funds. Shareholder activism, corporate governance, and screens are more effective when more investors are working together in holding corporations accountable for their economic and social performance. As well, alternative investment strategies such as asset targeting can only work through the ongoing, long-term collective collaboration of unions and their pension funds.

The term 'social investment' appears to be valid for these apparently disparate ways of investment because of their social action component. To summarize, social investment, in relation to pension funds, can be defined as: collaborative action taken by unions and pension funds, leading to various types of collateral investment, which implicitly or explicitly challenge conventional corporate behaviour, and, through use of social accounting techniques, provide a verifiable contribution to the social and economic benefit of the community.

All forms of social investment are at but a beginning stage in Canada. The central area of research to date in the United States has been the impact of social investment on the rate of return. As I have already indicated, there is no body of evidence showing that any form of social investment inherently lowers returns. Types of social investment appear disparate and require different forms of organization, knowledge, and skills on the part of trustees, fund managers, and pension funds. This contributes to the practical difficulties in implementing social investment.

Shareholder activism assumes an involvement of investors' representatives in the daily life of the corporation. Pressuring for corporate accountability includes actions like meetings with corporate players, writing letters, and stacking annual meetings. These actions are directed at bringing about social change in the corporation's relationship with its shareholders, employees, or community, whether local or global. Pension fund involvement in shareholder activism is dependent on control over the proxy votes. When funds are pooled, they are often under the control of the financial industry.

As described in Chapter 3, in Canada it is extremely difficult for a pension fund to improve share value through either threatening to withdraw or, indeed, withdrawing its investment in a particular corporation. The cost of pulling out shares may diminish their value because of the lack of market liquidity and, therefore, call into question the fiduciary responsibility of trustees. There is evidence, however, that the use of corporate governance strategies by pension funds may be on the rise in Canada. Such strategies tend to revolve around issues of executive compensation, board structure, takeovers, and mergers, and they tend not to be considered social issues. Indeed, writing in the *Globe and Mail* in March 2000, Richard Blackwell (2000), reported a 'sea change' in corporate thinking on shareholder proposals. These proposals may influence corporate behaviour without reducing rates of return. However, while there is some disagreement over whether shareholder activism can actually increase rates of return, there is no evidence that it lowers rates of return.

An exciting shareholder proposal was submitted by Working Enterprises Limited. This is a company owned by seven unions in British Columbia, and it asked Placer Dome to provide shareholders with its risk management plans and liability insurance information. (This was described in more detail in Chapter 4.) The proposal requested a social accounting of the costs of risk management and liability insurance for all of Placer Dome's sites. Nevertheless, while addressing the social and economic behaviour of a corporation, this proposal is grounded in financial concerns. It illustrates how social accounting can be a tool to implement shareholder activism, even under the restrictive conditions imposed by legislation. It further shows how the impact of the behaviour of a corporation on its community can be shown by an internal accounting. For example, the social accounting requested by Working Enterprises Limited could be reflected in a value added statement (as described in Chapter 6).

Shareholder activism among pension funds in Canada is largely uncoordinated, although there have been attempts to provide a union focus through Working Enterprises, the B.C. Federation of Labour, and the Canadian Labour Congress under the leadership of Ken Georgetti, as well as the creation of SHARE, the Shareholder Association for Research and Education. However, pension funds tend not to coordinate efforts, and they are only just beginning to put organizational resources into their shareholder activities. More pension funds are now developing proxy voting guidelines. This lack of involvement in shareholder activism has been viewed as economically wasteful and possibly harmful to fiduciary responsibility through loss of shareholder value.

Ethical screens may be a valuable first step in exercising some control over investment. However, existing technical limitations inhibit their usefulness as measures of corporate social performance. For example, adding negative and positive factors together by definition means that the negatives are cancelled out by the positives. Thus, a company that has points against it for serious environmental violations can neutralize its score by, say, having women on its board of directors. Rigorous trade union or environmental values incorporated into an ethical screen may limit investment in the smaller Canadian market. Finally, screens cannot accommodate portfolio diversification.

Criticism of ethical screens is warranted because of the apparently low standards of social performance exacted by some of them. This can only be corrected through political pressure on corporations. Screens are not a substitute for other forms of activism exerted by pension funds, and they are a relatively weak tool with which to hold a company to account. In addition, there is no consensus on what the relationship between ethical standards and social and economic benefit should be. In the United States, for example, there are ethical screens to implement right-wing as well as left-wing value systems. Screens are a form of social investment to the extent that they lead to economic and social benefits. Accordingly, to be classified as a social investment, right-wing exclusionary values espoused by investment screens should be supported by an accounting of their social and economic benefit to the community.

There is no evidence that investments based on ethical screens lower the rate of return, even though they may not lead to better performance than unscreened investments. Most of the research on this issue has been undertaken in the United States, where there is a larger number of ethical funds. Also, the Domini Social Index (see KLD, 1998), which provides a benchmark for the performance of social investment portfolios, was developed there. In Canada, a similar index was recently developed by Michael Jantzi and Associates, based on the Domini index, and its availability will allow for more Canadian research on the performance of ethical funds.

Shareholder activism, corporate governance, and ethical screens are approaches to social investment, where the investor is attempting, if imperfectly, to hold corporations to account. However, this is difficult because pension funds are limited by law to investing no more than 10 per cent of their assets in any one corporation. Nevertheless, these are the only methods of social investment that can be applied by pension funds to stock market investment – when pension funds have control over their equity assets.

Stronger relationships with Working Enterprises, *Mining Watch Canada*, and others who are attempting to pursue strategies of shareholder activism would also be helpful in enabling trustees to hold funding staff and managers accountable for proxy voting of shares. Unions should have stronger relationships with organizations that are lobbying for change and developing strategies to pursue social investment goals. In this work, unions can provide much-needed support and resources to their pension trustees.

Economically targeted investment is the third form of social investment and the subject of the case study of Concert, which has been reported in this book. ETI involves using a portion of a fund's assets, often in conjunction with other investors, to create an investment vehicle that provides a reasonable rate of return and social or collateral benefits, as well. The pooled fund lowers the risk by spreading it among all the investors. This form of investment takes a very small proportion of assets – often (as the Concert study shows) between 1 and 2 per cent – and allocates it to affordable housing and other economic development projects.

In the United States, there is strong support for this form of social investment by pension funds, in the form of regulatory sanctions and federal investment guarantees to lower the risk. In Quebec, where a strong and unwavering commitment to economic development is linked to the nationalist aspirations of many institutions of the province, there is an even greater incidence of asset targeting. The pension activists in British Columbia who organized Concert and Mortgage Fund One have demonstrated a similar commitment to economic development.

Where there is an absence of strong regulatory or cultural support, economically targeted investment is dependent on leadership – from the union and the pension fund. For example, Concert was set up through the persistence of a small number of leaders in the trade union movement, with links to union pension funds and to experts in the real estate development industry. This is not to say that Concert is not replicable. However, we can see from the Concert example that (1) there is a strong need for training and education directed at union leadership, pension trustees, and the rank-and-file membership; (2) there should be improved communication between unions and their pension funds; (3) there should be increased collaboration between pension funds and between unions; regarding the investment of pension fund; and (4) union leaders need links to supportive experts in finance and real estate development. This particularly applies to the ability to pool funds, an issue that is dealt with more fully in Chapter 13.

Labour-sponsored investment funds are a strong Canadian example of social investment. These funds target sectors and regions of the economy in support innovative small- and medium-sized businesses. They invest in ethical funds and use shareholder activism techniques to encourage productive corporate behaviour. Some of them are union-based. They can all work with one another and learn from each other.

Models of Social Accounting

Social accounting methods should – and can – be used as tools to assess the collateral benefits of investment. Such accounting can provide evidence of productive or unproductive behaviour of corporations and of social benefits or social damage caused by corporations.

This study provides a first social accounting of an economically targeted investment by a pension fund in Canada, that of Concert. Through the use of social accounting, theory has been extended by providing measures of returns on pension fund investment that go beyond the narrow range of variables normally used in accounting. The social accounting methods used in this study can be put into two categories of benefits. In Category A are stakeholder benefits to (1) workers through job creation; (2) pension fund shareholders through increased contributions and dividends; and (3) government through increased employee taxes. In Category B, which describes the broader community impact, are the benefits of (1) job creation through construction of rental accommodations and market housing; (2) the indirect and induced effects of job creation; (3) the total costs of the project and (4) the indirect and induced effects on taxation of the project.

Category A models can be considered 'internal' in that such models only consider the benefit of the organization's investments to its various stakeholders, for example, workers, shareholders, and government. The value added statement is an appropriate model for illustrating stakeholder interest, although in reporting the Concert study the statements are not in the form of balance sheets because not enough information was available, (and, thus, it is unlike the model described in Chapter 6).

Category B models consider impacts on the broader community. First, in assessing the impact of Concert, an approach was developed to account for its direct impact on job creation through several projects. A net social gain was calculated, based on the differing social and economic contributions to the broader community of the construction of rental accommodations and market housing. Second, multipliers, from the B.C. input-output model, were used to estimate the indirect and induced effects of Concert's projects and the work they created. A further estimation was made of the impact on all levels of government of tax revenues from direct, indirect, and induced employment and Concert's productivity.

There are clear benefits to workers from investment of their pension funds. This is shown in Table 9.1 which, in employing the first category of models, shows that 4.9 million hours of work were created through Concert projects and that of these 1.8 million were for carpenters. Further tables corroborate this picture for on-site employment. However, it should be recognized that not all pension fund investors in Concert have their members represented in on-site employment. The Telecommunication Workers Union, which provides anchor funding to Concert through its jointly trusteed pension fund, is a case in point. Arguments for economically targeted investment based on direct job creation for members of the investee pension funds will have narrow appeal and miss the more important argument that such investment has a benefit and impact on a much broader community of interest. Such a limited strategy also runs the risk of overexposure and, ultimately, lower returns as we have seen in the case of the CWPP. It also calls into question the self-interest of union trustees.

Table 9.1 shows that the Carpentry Workers Pension Plan of British Columbia (CWPP) received additional contributions of $4.25 million because of employment on Concert projects. Again, although this is a significant gain for the pension fund, arguments for more productive pension fund investment that rely on increased pension contributions through job creation will have a narrow appeal (resting on self-interest) to those unions that can benefit from them directly. Furthermore, such investment may not meet the suggested definition of social investment because it offers no measurement of social and economic benefit to the broader community.

There is scant literature on pension fund investment. In the United States, the 'whole participant' approach has been proposed by Barber and Ghilarducci (1993) in recognition that pension funds benefit from higher levels of contributions when there is a strong economy that keeps fund members at work. Members, they argue, also benefit by working until they reach retirement age. This approach proposes that investment be measured according to its collateral benefits as well as its returns, as opposed to speculating for the best possible returns in a supposedly free market (Ghilarducci, 1994).

Quarter (1995, p. 213), in writing about Canada, has suggested that 'it is possible to have investment policies that take into account a broader range of criteria than the rate of return.' He notes that pension funds can be invested to provide additional contributions to the fund and jobs for members of the fund. He goes further, however, and suggests that funds can also be invested in social housing. However, this study has argued that the term 'collateral benefits' needs to be understood broadly enough to include the impact of a pension fund investment on the broader community. Social and economic indicators may reveal collateral benefits (or damage) to the community and, therefore, should be used as social accounting measures of investment return. Furthermore, job creation by its nature is not necessarily a social or economic benefit. This book has introduced the notion of net social gain from direct job creation (in Category B above) which is discussed in the second model below. Some housing work has more social value than other housing work because of the kind of housing created. This point could be extended to other industries besides residential construction, such as environmental technologies, health products, and mass transit.

Public policy should encourage a social return on investment that benefits contributors, beneficiaries, government, and the broader community. It is important to note that for Concert the anchor fund, the Telecommunications Workers Pension Plan (TWPP), was driven by a broader interest than simply creating jobs for its own members. TWPP's goal was to create economic growth in the province through pension fund investment from which everyone could benefit. Thus, the Telecommunications Workers Union was not self-serving in its use of pension funds. This position is supported by Deaton (1989), who argues that it is important to consider the broader impact of social investment strategies. Taxable benefits for those covered by pension plans already create an inequitable distribution of wealth. Therefore, further social investment policies that benefit members only increase these inequities.

The second model (see point 1 in Category B above, presented in Tables 9.2, 9.4, and 10.1) calculates the returns on investment for the carpentry workers' pension fund from investments in both Mortgage Fund One and Concert. This model introduces the idea of a net social gain from the direct creation of jobs. It assigns different values of job creation to two variables, (1) construction of rental accommodations and (2) construction of market housing, based on the differing social and economic value to the community of the two types of residential construction.

This accounting process is then applied to all of Concert's work from 1989 to 1999. The analysis shows that Concert can be directly attributed with $79,224,817 in labour value, or 2,400,752 hours of work, based on its mix of rental and affordable housing construction. This analysis relies on Robert Giloth (1997), who maintains that it is imprecise and unrealistic to assume that all jobs created in the course of a project would not have been created otherwise. However, Giloth submits, there are few rules governing the 'what if' of alternative job creation scenarios. The one offered in this book rests on the fact that rental housing was scarce in Vancouver because of the unwillingness of developers to invest the 'patient capital' needed for rental housing. The social accounting model ascribes a financial value to the social benefit provided by such investment.

The third model (see point 3 in Category A above) uses the value added framework to estimate the benefit to government of pension fund investment through job creation. It is introduced in Table 9.3. This is a fairly simplistic account of government revenue from a Concert project, since it only accounts for tax revenues from on-site job creation.

The final social accounting model (see points 2, 3, and 4 in Category B above) examines the impact of Concert's work on the broader community of British Columbia, using multipliers. The accounting shows that Concert's impact on indirect and induced employment created 5.5 million hours of work, which was more than double its directly, attributable on-site hours of employment. Furthermore, Concert's value added, that is, it contribution to productivity through its indirect and induced effects, at $508,556,700 is just over its total project costs for the ten years. Therefore, the value of Concert's benefit to the community is more than double its total costs.

Finally, the taxation revenues for all levels of government generated through Concert's productivity total $144.5 million, or almost one-third of Concert's total project costs. Foregone federal tax revenues on returns on pension fund investment in Concert and Mortgage Fund One over ten years are an estimated $66 million. Therefore, the federal government had a net gain of $8.7 million on its investment.

This case study of Concert has used well-established techniques such as profit and loss accounting and multiplier effects drawn from the fields of accounting and economics. Through a social accounting approach it has been possible to reveal some important components of the social value of pension fund investment. Social accounting models provide a practical method of measuring the value of the collateral benefits of pension fund investment. In so doing, they have redefined collateral benefits in terms of social and economic benefits. These accounting methods can theoretically be used in assessing all investments in all real estate development, and similar approaches could be developed to apply to all investment, generally. These accounting methods would then become an *evaluative* tool, measuring the extent to which an investment contributes to social and economic benefit.

Social accounting methods can also serve as ways of *reporting* on investment. The development of techniques such as the measures used in this book is conceptually possible for all investments, although unlikely in some political climates. However, it is always encouraging to remember that (as described in Chapter 6) a labour government in the United Kingdom introduced value added accounting statements as a reporting requirement for all corporations. This regulation was later rescinded by the Thatcher government which viewed labour costs as a liability that lowers profits. It is not inconceivable that collateral benefit statements could become a requirement of pension fund investment in general. This type of reporting would enhance the probability that investment of pension funds contributes to social and economic benefit. Needless to say, it would require a change in direction of government policy towards a regulatory support of productive investment.

In the current political climate, however, this kind of regulatory change may not be achievable. A more achievable scenario at the present time is that pension funds voluntarily provide more public (and membership) information on the social and economic benefits of their fund investments. This would be timely, given public (and membership) scrutiny of pension fund investment. Voluntary reporting may stimulate public debate about the value of investment, in general, and about the use of pension funds, more specifically.

The trade union movement has identified the need to develop standards for economically targeted investments that reflect principles of social democracy (OPSEU, 2004). The proliferation of public-private partnerships (P3s) in Canada using workers' pension funds, which promote collateral damage to workers and their communities, has created some urgency and renewed interest in social accounting.

This chapter has proposed a working definition for the social investment of pension funds. This definition calls for collaborative action by unions and pension funds to initiate various types of collateral investment, which may be demonstrated, using social accounting techniques, to provide social and economic benefit to the broader community. This is likely to provide an implicit or explicit challenge to conventional corporate behaviour.

All three types of social investment – shareholder action and corporate governance, ethical screens, and economically targeted investment – meet the conditions of the definition. None lower the rates of return. Shareholder activism can be improved through more collaboration between pensions funds and between unions and community organizations. Ethical screens can be strengthened through tests of economic and social benefit to the community. Where there is no regulatory or cultural encouragement, economically targeted investment has been shown to be dependent on union and pension fund leadership. This does not limit the transferability of Concert as a social investment model, but does call for intensive training and education targeted at union leadership and pension trustees.

This chapter has presented several models of social accounting that extend theory by providing measures of returns on pension fund investment that broaden the typical range of criteria. There are two broad categories, the first relating to stakeholder benefits and the second to broader community benefits. In the first, the stakeholders considered are workers, shareholders, and government. When pension funds consider only the first two, they leave out the broader policy implications of tax exemption and the ensuing argument that there should be benefit to the broader community. Such investment would also fail to meet the requirements of the definition proposed in this chapter.

In the second category of models of social accounting, the broader community impact of Concert, as an example, is considered in terms of job creation through construction of rental accommodations and market housing, of the indirect and induced effects of job creation, of the total project costs, and of the indirect and induced effects on taxation. A net social gain was realized based on the differing values, in terms of social and economic benefits, to the broader community of the construction of rental accommodations and market housing. Multipliers were used to estimate the productivity of Concert, the indirect and induced effects of on-site job creation, and the returns to all levels of government in increased tax revenues.

The use of social accounting techniques is essential in measuring the success of collateral investments and reporting results to members and the general public. The use of such techniques may encourage greater reporting on investment in general.

chapter 12

Two Models for Union Control of Pension Funds

Union control over investment of pension funds is a critical step, if unions are to participate in building more productive social investment strategies. First, this chapter will examine whether the Concert model is transferable. Second, as a guide for unions in pursuing union control and social investment strategies, two models are proposed that are transferable. The first model illustrates the levels of control necessary for unions to implement social investment strategies. The second is a social action model for union control over investment.

Concert as a Transferable Model

There is no easy formula for social investment that makes the Concert model directly transferable. First, it is not known whether a model of real estate investment similar or identical to Concert can be set up by other pension trustees. As was explained in Chapter 8, pension funds wanting to own and develop land can only do this with as much security through a pre-1978 company under Section 149(1) (o.2) of the Income Tax Act. It is unlikely that there are many pre-1978 companies available for purchase, and it is not known how many pension funds are registered to own and develop land. This section of the act needs to be changed. Unions and pension funds could enlist the assistance of labour-sponsored investment funds, experienced in federal government relations, to lobby the federal government for changes to the Income Tax Act to change this loophole.

Nevertheless, pension funds can invest in building real estate through agreements with development companies – the active builders. Pension funds can hire experts to protect the fund and its beneficiaries from liabilities.

Second, it might be argued that the need for specific types of leadership to build Concert effectively negates its ability to be a model for other trustees. On the contrary, both models proposed here illustrate how education of union leaders, training of trustees, and recruitment of expertise at various levels of control over investment enables pension funds to pursue social investment strategies.

What is remarkable about the genesis of Concert and Mortgage Fund One is: (1) the alliance of stakeholders from union, business, and government, and (2) the organizing ability of the union leaders to marshal the pooling of funds from their jointly trusteed pension funds. This could not have been done without fully informed union leaders who could network and learn from experts in investment and real estate and persuade employer trustees on their boards to agree to pool funds. One might argue that a limitation of sole trusteeships (common in the construction industry) is the lack of necessary rigour on boards composed solely of union trustees, where employer representatives do not also need to be persuaded of the wisdom of economic development strategies.

Pooling pension funds makes sense because it mitigates risk, shares experience and expertise, and provides more cross-accountability between partners. It also begins to make more productive use of the vast potential of pension funds. Real estate development is an important beginning in Canada. But there is an enormous need for capital for public sector infrastructure as well as private sector financing.

Unions can play a role in coordinating union trustees, providing them with the opportunities to network, developing resource lists of experts who are skilled in implementing social investment strategies, and providing the conferences where there can be genuine debate about the opportunities and strategies for progressive investment.

Levels of Control of Pension Funds

The experience of unions in British Columbia provides us with the elements of two models for union control of pension funds. The first model, shown in Figure 12.1, identifies the three levels of control that unions need to attain over their members' pension funds. These levels are developmental in that attaining the first level (negotiating pension plans) is needed before the second level (negotiating governance) can be achieved. Similarly, without joint trusteeship, it is unlikely that management of funds can occur.

The first level in gaining control of pension funds is gaining the right to negotiate pension plans, or exercising that right where it already exists.

Figure 12.1   Levels of control necessary for unions to exercise social investment strategies.

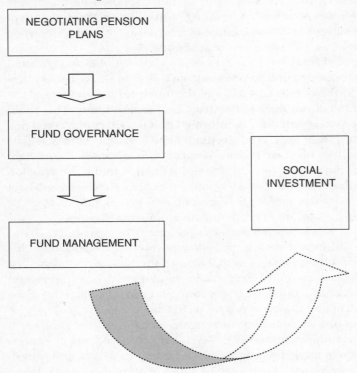

It is not uncommon for public sector unions, in particular, to have no statutory negotiability of their pension plans or funds. For example, the Ontario Municipal Employees Retirement System (OMERS) is not negotiable, even though there are some employee representatives (appointed by government) on its board of trustees. In the case of OMERS, changes in pension benefits or in the terms of the fund can be made unilaterally by the employer. In the case of Concert, Bill Clark was the principal initiator; he started his work as president of the B.C. Telecommunications Workers Union (TWU) with the goal of winning negotiability of his union's pension plan. Some unions, for example, the Canadian Auto Workers (CAW), have partial negotiability, that is, negotiability of the plan but not its management.

The second level is about governance. The Concert model presented here builds on the findings of a study identifying relatively little control by unions over pension funds in Canada, but identifying eight distinct models of control in the country's top twenty-three pension funds. These models range from little to full joint control over pension fund governance (see the Appendix). Among these top funds there is a distinct trend towards joint trusteeship among these top funds (Carmichael, 1998).

The TWU negotiated joint trusteeship in order to win meaningful control over investment of its pension fund: the third level. This was a strategy developed by Bill Clark and the union's actuary, Bruce Rollick. Clark knew the difference between real control and the appearance of control, and he had the power to achieve real control.

Unions in Quebec have a distinct advantage in having the legal right to an employee representative, as well as an alternate in training, on all pensions boards. The Quebec Federation of Labour has combined this right with a strong program of labour education on pensions from rank-and-file members to trustees to ensure that union trustees are fully informed and can make decisions in the interests of working people.

Often, joint trusteeship does not deliver an effective control over investment. For example, teachers' unions in Ontario have joint trusteeship through their federated union, the Ontario Teachers Federation. By law trustees must be 'financial experts,' so that relatively few teachers actually qualify as trustees. Furthermore, investment is handled by the vice-president of investment and fund staff. There are, therefore, many organizational barriers between a teachers' union and the investment process.

Within the third level – management of pension fund investment – there are different degrees of engagement ranging from access to information from investment staff or fund managers to the ability to hire fund managers, set their contracts, and fire them in the event they do not follow instructions.

Union control over investment of pension funds is a step towards a greater voice for unions in decisions about production (as discussed in detail in Chapter 5). Control over pension fund investment is a critical link between the trade union movement's goal of a decent living wage for everyone and any real transformation of the system. Moreover, pension funds are well placed to provide the capital needed to begin to build a more productive economy.

Figure 12.1 illustrates (by means of the arrow with shading) that unions may attain all three levels of control and not implement social investment

Figure 12.2 A social action model for union control of pension fund investment.

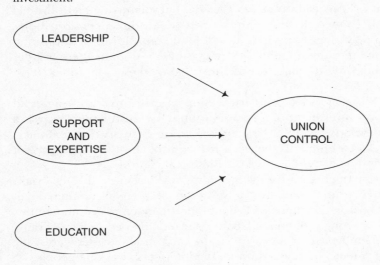

strategies. There are already union trustees with substantial control of fund management who have no record of implementing or even attempting to implement such strategies. Pension fund power, leadership, education, and specific types of support are all necessary elements to this end.

A Social Action Model for Union Control

The second model (Figure 12.2) is a social action model for union control of pension fund investment. It identifies three components necessary for effective action. These are: leadership, support and expertise, and education. In suggesting action strategies, each of these components interacts with each level of control. These components are based on an examination of Concert and Mortgage Fund One.

Leadership

Union leadership is essential in pursuing a strategy of pension fund control. In our case study, the key players remained consistent from the time when union investment strategies were first discussed with the B.C. Federation of Labour, even though the numbers in leadership grew.

All of the leaders were in positions of power. In spite of the lack of models to follow, and in face of a certain amount of scepticism, Bill Clark exerted an almost visionary leadership in his union. He was also president of his union, and union trustee of his members' pension plan. Thus, he was well-placed to execute his vision.

For many unions pensions may be an important item on the collective bargaining agenda. But involvement in pursuing the issue is not seen as a breeding ground for leaders or activists. Perhaps that is why the history of Concert is viewed by some as idiosyncratic and, therefore, not replicable. On the contrary, the activists – or champions – involved in Concert have uncovered a new arena for union activism. It is replicable through a change in union priorities and targeted leadership education.

Where union and pension fund leadership is separated, leadership from both the union and the pension fund is critical to the success of the investment strategy. In our case study, a good relationship and understanding of pension fund administration was shared by union and pension fund officials alike. Often, a union and its pension fund have leadership in common, through the president of the union, who also sits on the board of trustees. This was the case with the TWU. Where this was not the case, as in the CWPP, there were mechanisms for sharing information between the union and the pension fund, such as reports and resolutions at annual conventions, as well as fairly constant contact.

Where there is little or no relationship between trustees and their union, there can be problems, often because of a perceived threat to fiduciary responsibility and to the autonomous leadership of trustees. This is the case today with several unions and their pension funds across Canada (Carmichael, 1998).

Different types of leadership are necessary at different levels of control. For example, union leadership is critical in campaigns for negotiability of pension plans and joint trusteeship. However, union pension trustees become the new leaders of investment activism as governance of pension funds develops. This has clear implications for training programs on pension fund activism. There need to be clearly defined roles for both the union and the pension fund. Trustees have the legal obligation of fiduciary responsibility to make informed and independent decisions. The pension fund requires that its autonomy as a separate, bipartite organization be respected. However, the union has a clear role to play in research and education to train pension activists and trustees (see Figure 12.2).

A similar point was made in my study of the OPSEU Pension Trust, a jointly trusteed pension plan (Carmichael, 1996). Union and employer negotiators had to transform themselves into trustees, working in a 'different legal entity with very different responsibilities' (ibid., p. 53). Similar comments were made by Bill Clark and David Podmore, as they attributed much of the success of Concert to the ability of the main players to build a new organization without the politics and relationships of their respective unions and workplaces.

Unions are abandoning their responsibility when they leave their trustees to fend for themselves without any preparation and organizational policy direction on trusteeship and investment. In my 1998 survey (Carmichael, 1998), pension fund trustees complained about the lack of support and resources from their unions. When this occurs, the unfortunate outcome is the unavoidable reliance of trustees on fund managers, thereby perpetuating hegemonic approaches to investment. One factor contributing to counter-hegemonic work is the informed leadership of trade unions and pension funds working together. This is in spite of the fact, in the case of Concert, that the key players received no formal training from the union or the pension fund, but, as they said, they learned by doing.

Support of social investment strategies can be made more likely through union training that challenges the dominant thinking of the financial industry. This has implications for adult education strategies, which will be discussed later.

Formal leadership of the economically targeted investment was provided by the anchor pension fund, the Telecommunications Workers Pension Plan. As shown in Chapter 8, TWPP invested proportionately more in both Concert and Mortgage Fund One than other unions did. Having an anchor fund was necessary to provide stability to the pooled vehicles, although it is important to note that the TWPP still invested a very small proportion of its own assets. Therefore, had no risk of overexposure. This has implications for organizing strategies among pension funds. Pooling appears a natural move for smaller funds in order to spread the risk through asset targeting. However, smaller funds must ally themselves with at least one larger fund to provide the stable core. Larger funds, for their part must look to smaller funds to spread risk. Both large and small funds are required to exercise leadership in an economically targeted investment vehicle.

Similarly, collective action among large and small pension funds may be required by other forms of social investment. If either shareholder activism or ethical screens are to have an effect on holding a corporation accountable for its economic and social performance, it will be more effective if funds and unions act collaboratively.

Support and Expertise

Choosing allies, winning enduring support, and finding the right expertise were critical for Concert. Having negotiated joint trusteeship,
unions face steep learning curves in administering pension plan, as well
as pension fund investment. There fields of expertise are quite alien to
traditional trade union experience. It is unknown, for example, how
many fund managers there are with trade union experience or expertise
in social investment. Since the dominant view of the financial industry is
opposed to social investment, it has proven difficult for pension trustees
to find fund management support for alternative investment strategies.
This has been cited by the Canada Labour and Business Centre in its
survey of pension fund trustees (Falconer, 1998).

This inability to access knowledge about social investment strategies is
exacerbated by existing training for pension trustees, which is provided
primarily by the financial industry and by its representatives through the
Institute for Fiduciary Education, an American educational institution,
that has a corporate, unprogressive focus. Relying on this one institution reinforces hegemonic approaches to pension fund education and
training.

Nevertheless, unions can find the expertise necessary to pursue a
social investment agenda that enhances the viability of pension funds
and leads to economic and social benefits to the community. Bruce Rollick is an actuary, and David Podmore and Jack Poole are real estate
developers. All are experts identified by union leaders as union-sympathetic; all were instrumental in building Concert. As much as the union
and pension fund leaders, they are champions in the stories of Concert
and Mortgage Fund One. They do not make Concert a less replicable
model. On the contrary, they were sought out by leaders who wanted to
pursue social investment strategies but needed help in providing the
framework. Good referral networks among unions can put union leaders, pension trustees, and investment experts together.

In Canada, there is a growing cadre of expertise in labour-sponsored
investment funds. While regulatory frameworks are somewhat different,
investment strategies can be shared with pension trustees. In the United
States, the Heartland Project under the leadership of Leo Gerard, president of the United Steel Workers of America, involves a group of union
pension trustees, international researchers, and experts working on
innovative, 'high-road' investment strategies for pension funds. This
project may also provide a model for Canadian union trustees

The Center for Working Capital, an educational and research agency established by the American Federation of Labor and Congress of Industrial Organizations (AFL-CIO), is setting up an advisory committee of investment specialists who are willing to work with the trade union movement. It is hoped that this stable of experts will put flesh on the bones of a trade union pension fund investment agenda.

The trade union movement, itself, played a critical role in policy development and general support of Concert, providing legitimacy to the work of a relatively small group of trade unionists. Provincial federations of labour vary in their support of pension fund investment. In British Columbia, the Federation of Labour has shown positive, enduring, and informed support for Concert, to the extent that its (former) president, Ken Georgetti, has sat on the board of directors. Georgetti has now taken that informed support to the Canadian Labour Congress (CLC). This support has provided a link to other trade unions as potential shareholders and solidified the support needed to ensure the long-term viability of the investment vehicles. This formal support of the trade union movement through the CLC and the provincial labour federations is critical in pursuing a social investment strategy.

Labour federations do not always make the best use of their facilitative role. For example, the system of labour-sponsored investment funds in Ontario (or rent-a-union funds as they have been called) is an outcome of poorly managed conflict resolution by the Ontario Federation of Labour (OFL) between the Canadian Auto Workers Union (CAW), the Canadian Union of Public Employees (CUPE), and other unions. An old disagreement on policy direction resulted in laws that allowed for labour-sponsored investment funds run by unions in name only, and this brought discredit upon the trade union movement.

Federations of labour and the CLC are not the only unions in a coordinating role. The National Union of Public and General Employees (NUPGE) has recently started working with its component unions in organizing for joint trusteeship. The goal is to exchange experience and set standards for joint trusteeship. The NUPGE's components are unions of provincial employees with large, contributory pension plans. In the past, there has been little consultation or exchange of information on joint trusteeship, so it is no surprise that there are now eight models of control among the top twenty-three pension plans in Canada (shown in the Appendix).

Such coordination is effective in giving unionists a way to network and the opportunity to develop more supportive programming for pension activists. However, there is also a need for pension trustees themselves to set standards for joint trusteeship, fund management, social investment, and new methods of social accounting. This would be a project of union and employer pension trustees.

It is important to note that, for Concert to have succeeded, union trustees had to win the support of employer trustees sharing their pension boards. While the idea for Concert and Mortgage Fund One came from trade unionists, it was critical that they had the respect and support of their employer trustees.

Because of the nature of joint trusteeship, the relationship between employer and union trustees tends to be less combative than the adversarial process associated with collective bargaining in Canada. The following is a descriptions of more collaborative working relationships at the OPSEU Pension Trust: 'Because of the equal numbers of union and employer trustees, no decision can be made by one side or the other. There has to be some level of agreement between the trustees. Consensus has been established as the most comfortable form of decision-making; and there is an understanding that decisions need to be acceptable to most of them, even if it is not the personally preferred route' (Carmichael, 1996, p. 64). The process is not unlike other joint committee structures routinely negotiated in collective agreements. Informed union trustees reserve their distrust for financial managers who funnel institutional pension funds into the international capital markets.

Union control over investment of their pension funds is a critical step if unions are to participate in building more productive social investment strategies. There are distinct levels to union control requiring different types of leadership, support, and expertise. Winning negotiability and joint trusteeship of pension plans require focused union leadership to work with union membership. Pension trustees become the new leaders, once meaningful governance is achieved.

Leadership by union presidents, union trustees, and experts hired by unions tends to be visionary and well placed to pursue powerful strategies. This does not mean that Concert is not replicable. On the contrary, unions need to recognize that pension fund activism is a new arena for activism and leadership. The trade union movement, however, needs to continue to play a supportive role in coordinating unions in pooled investment strategies and facilitating relationships between unions. In Canada, labour-sponsored investment funds are centres of expertise that union leaders and pension trustees can learn from. In the United States, the Heartland Project and the Center for Working Capital are also good models for research and education.

In the next chapter, there is an extensive discussion of the implications for union education, based on the models of levels (Figure 12.1) and elements (Fig. 12.2) of union control. A strong role is proposed for trade unions in research and education in pension governance, investment issues, and social accounting. The limitations of this study are discussed and suggestions are put forward for future research.

chapter 13

Education and Research

This chapter provides an extensive discussion of the implications for education, based on the models provided in the previous chapter. While most of the discussion on education is devoted to the role of trade unions, joint trustee education is also proposed.

Education as Contested Terrain

Education is the third component of the social action model (see Fig. 12.2), but it is also a major issue in its own right and critical to an effective investment strategy. This book proposes a strong role for trade unions in research and education in pension governance, investment issues, and social accounting. Without a coordinated strategy within the trade union movement, it is unlikely that there will be more than isolated incidents of social investment of pension funds, except in Quebec where, as already noted, there is a more integrated tradition of union trustee education through the trade union movement.

The hegemonic control exerted by the financial industry over investment practice has been referred to in several chapters. Often this control is exercised in the absence of any alternative frameworks proposed by their unions. But coercion and undermining of 'lay' trustees by fund managers should also not be underestimated. As it becomes clear that more union members want joint trusteeship and some control over investment of their pension funds, opposition to union trustees mounts. Senator Kirby, as chairman of Canada's standing Senate Committee on Banking, Trade, and Commerce (1998) has called for 'the quality of direction and oversight needed in today's complex world' through 'highly knowledgeable people' to 'effectively monitor fund managers' (ibid., 1998, p. 6).

This can be achieved, it is often argued, through a model similar to the Ontario Teachers Pension Plan Board where, as a legislative requirement of the pension plan, 'union' trustees are selected from the financial industry. However, this would, in effect, cement control over workers' pension funds by the financial industry.

In an editorial in the *Financial Post*, Keith Ambachtsheer (2003, p. FP15), a leading pension industry consultant, described the pension crisis of low returns and 'ineffective' governance and management. Among several other best practice suggestions, Ambachtsheer recommends that company pension plans restructure their boards to be more representative of 'stakeholder interests.'

The Canadian Association of Pension Supervisory Authorities (CAPSA) has recommended to the federal government that pension laws be streamlined across provinces and, in particular, that pension boards have some employee or stakeholder representation. CAPSA has proposed regulatory principles for a model pension law (2004).

The trade union movement must follow the example of the Quebec Federation of Labour and begin to organize general membership as well as trustee education. The alternative will be more of the existing programming. As noted in the previous chapter, hegemonic approaches to pension fund education and training are exacerbated by existing training programs delivered primarily by the financial industry and by its representatives through the Institute for Fiduciary Education. This American educational institution has a corporate style and private sector approach to education and has weak links to the trade union movement, which it regards as a competitor. Nevertheless, its program is developmental and remains one of the few programs accessible to union trustees.

The results of a recent Canadian study (Carmichael et al., 2004) confirm anecdotal reports that opportunities for trustees are minimal and serve mainly to consolidate existing investment practices. Unions and trustees wishing to take a broader perspective towards investment are receiving little support from their pension funds. This is unfortunate because Canada needs new sources of capital to encourage emerging businesses and to rebuild crumbling infrastructure. Pension funds are ideal for this purpose because they can be invested in the long term. However, this will not happen unless there are radically different approaches towards investment of pension funds, a strategy that requires that the trade union movement develop a transformative educational agenda.

Undoubtedly, the argument will be made that existing training is 'neutral,' and that a training program supported by unions will be biased. There are several possible responses to such arguments. First, union trustees have complained that training received from the financial industry is delivered paternalistically and that, rather than providing critical decision points for investment, it tends to map out uncritically 'the way it is always done.' Furthermore, often it is the case that not enough information is supplied to allow trustees to pursue a critical learning path on their own (Carmichael and Quarter, 2003). Second, existing training offers few alternatives on different approaches to asset allocation, fails to discuss gaps in the market, and takes no account of policy discussions on economics or stock market behaviour. By providing insufficient information, trustees often come away from training programs feeling 'mystified.'

Union pension education, on the other hand, has traditionally been limited to enabling rank-and-file members to understand their rights to pension benefits when they retire. Freire (1973) refers to this type of training as involving a semitransitive consciousness, where the union might take credit for gaining benefits for its members, but there is little historical context for struggle and few connections are made between individual experience and social systems. In fact, some unionists remain unaware that their pensions constitute vast capital funds. It is clear that unions must develop their own body of knowledge on capital markets and their own strategies for investing their own pension funds; this will provide the impetus for a more collective discussion of investment in the interests of working people (Habermas, 1972; Comstock and Fox, 1993). At present, even where trade unions do have a role in investment, this role is not recognized. For example, an article on labour-sponsored investment in the Globe and Mail made no mention of union involvement (Won, 2000). Through education, this silence can be broken (Reinharz, 1992; hooks, 1988; Schrjivers, 1991).

Central to such an educational approach must be an 'unmasking' of the power dynamics of the capital markets, the self-interest of the financial industry, and the development of a union agenda based on the perspectives and interests of working people and their communities. This approach is particularly important since, in some cases, unionists – who have been trustees for many years – agree with the financial industry that they cannot 'wear a union hat' when making investment decisions for fear of being subjective. This belief has been bolstered by the *Cowan* v *Scargill* case (1984) in the British courts. This case has had a chilling effect on union involvement in investment decisions and union support and training of union trustees, in North America as well as in the United Kingdom (see Chapter 2). Such education needs to examine how participants are socially and historically located (Smith, 1987; Harding, 1992) as workers, trade unionists, community members, and future beneficiaries. Some union trustees are beginning to argue that fiscal prudence in the trusteeship of pension funds may be impossible in the absence of training that promotes critical reflection. Critical learning is needed to expose dominant thinking and show how alternative approaches may be initiated; and critical reflection is central to a transformative approach to adult learning (Mezirow, 1991). Transformative learning may be liberating at a personal level, or it may also be the outcome of education for radical social change through challenge to hegemonic ideology (Mojab and Gorman, 2002; Schugurensky, 2001). Critical reflection then becomes the process of revealing oppressive power dimensions in society (Brookfield, 2000).

Anecdotal evidence indicates that some employer trustees may also believe that responsible trusteeship requires more comprehensive training and that they would like to work with union trustees jointly on training issues. Obviously, both union and employer trustees need training that will enable them together to make prudent decisions based on a critical approach to their trustee work. Indeed, developing a prudent approach involves deciphering disparate interests in investment decisions.

This approach to transformative education is influenced by Paulo Freire's work on 'conscientization' (1970), as well as by the development of critical theory where critical reflection is a means of unmasking hegemonic ideology as a liberating step (Habermas, 1972). This direction is also supported by literature on socialist pedagogy (Youngman, 1986), popular education (Freire, 1970; Freire and Faundez, 1989), participatory research (Hall, 1993), social action (Newman, 1995), critical teaching (Shor, 1992), feminist theory (Smith, 1987; Harding, 1992), and labour education (Wertheimer, 1981; Martin, 1995; Taylor, 2001). This social activist approach has also been central to the practice of adult education by such educators Tomkins (1921), Coady (1939), and Freire (1970).

Strong arguments have been made for the trade union movement to expand its role in the economy through training pension trustees. Therefore, first initiatives in trustee training could attempt pilot programs that incorporate both union-only and joint union-employer training. Figure 13.1 illustrates some of the resources available for training in pension fund investment. All have been mentioned in previous chapters. There are academic institutions, a business and labour research centre, unions, economically targeted investment vehicles, venture capi-

Figure 13.1   Some educational resources for pension fund investment training.

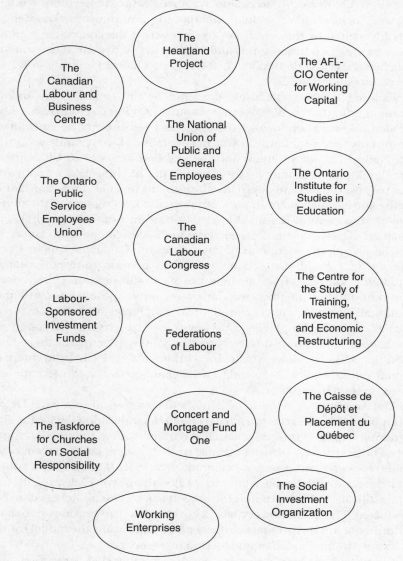

tal funds, a pension fund, a research project, and a social advocacy organization. All are readily accessible in Canada or in the northern United States. Such training should incorporate the informal knowledge already gained by the few union trustees across the country, as well as the expertise of pension funds undertaking innovative social investment (such as the Caisse de Dépôt et Placement du Québec) and labour-sponsored investment funds.

Training is more effectively delivered by the central trade union movement so that smaller unions without educational resources are not denied access. Traditionally, training has been internal to individual unions, as unions attempt to win negotiability. However, just recently, the National Union of Public and General Employees (NUPGE) started the development of training for a second tier of (future) pension trustees on governance and alternative investment practice, as a central initiative for its component unions. Support and involvement of the trade union movement at the third level – in fund investment (see previous chapter) – has been a positive element in the development of Concert.

The provincial federations of labour and the Canadian Labour Congress (CLC) could also become leaders in pension fund educational strategies. The CLC has now held two successful pension conferences for rank-and-file members of the trade union movement. Both the National Union of Public and General Employees and the Canadian Union of Public Employees have key roles to play with the congress, since both unions have a priority to seek joint trusteeship of their pension plans. Both unions are already working with the CLC and international union bodies to assemble a mechanism to track international pension fund investment.

The American Federation of Labor and Congress of Industrial Organizations (AFL-CIO) has provided a model by establishing the Center for Working Capital to provide research and training for union pension trustees. The goal of the centre is to enable trustees to both safeguard workers' deferred wages and promote economic prosperity. The AFL-CIO hopes that the centre will enable labour to speak with one voice, clearing the air of mystification that surrounds investment issues. This model needs to be evaluated. The CLC could establish a working group to provide up-to-date information on the progress of the centre and to assess the model for its relevance to the Canadian trade union movement.

Union trustees have called for pension training that is certified and reflects a strong depth of research. This is a new area of expertise which needs to be developed through reputable research. Training and education should be at all levels of the union membership – rank and file, second-tier leadership, and pension trustees. Rank-and-file members tend not to be trained unless there is a campaign for joint trusteeship. Otherwise, their education is restricted to information on benefits and other retirement issues.

Joint trusteeship is frequently described to rank-and-file members in terms of control over their future. However, there is no union education that makes this meaningful by connecting joint trusteeship to the economic agenda of social investment and economic development developed by the CLC; nor is there research or training on social accounting that could assess the success of social investment projects. There is no education or research to support the work that trade unionists have been doing and continue to do in British Columbia and Quebec and no encouragement for any such initiatives in other parts of Canada.

Informed debate at the rank-and-file level helps maintain joint trusteeship – and ultimately control over investment – through a succession of well-trained members who can aspire to becoming trustees. There is no planning in unions for leadership succession with regard to the responsibilities of pension fund trustees (Carmichael, 1998). Rank-and-file awareness and education is vital for continuity of the responsibilities of joint control.

Pension activists are the second tier of leadership. They will succeed trustees. They are, therefore, a critical link in the chain of trained unionists. The NUPGE is designing an education program for this group, using participatory learning techniques, and building on the research of this study. Unionists will learn how to identify structures for meaningful control of pension funds and get an introduction to social investment and some social accounting techniques. This program will be delivered for activists across the country.

As this study has shown, trustee education is critical. Union trustees need union space for training. Many have created their own space and survived. Those involved in Concert trained themselves. Some are accumulating a wealth of information on investment practice. For example, trustees are learning more about the respective advantages of some models of trusteeship, standards of accountability for fund managers, the intricacies of different techniques of investment, possible avenues for shareholder activism, and asset targeting. This information needs to be harnessed for educational and research purposes. However, many trade unionists have reported on the isolation from their unions, the steep learning curves to catch up with investment professionals, and the temptation to depend on funding managers for advice (Carmichael, 1998).

One tendency of both educational organizations and unions is a failure to share educational materials, course outlines, and curriculum. A successful trustee program in one union dies out through lack of resources, where another union could have picked up the work, updated the materials, and kept the program going in other forums. This is unfortunate. The trade union movement and its related organizations can make better collective use of resources.

Nevertheless, there are indications that active involvement of the trade union movement in initiatives that may be broadly called social investment are on the increase in Canada. The CLC has now held two conferences on pensions and it is extremely active in the international movement on corporate social responsibility. It has also endorsed the Shareholder Association for Research and Education (SHARE), a national organisation sponsored by the trade union movement to help pension funds 'build sound investment practices.'

SHARE is a non-profit agency established by Working Enterprises, a company which provides travel, insurance, and investment services to the trade union movement and is wholly owned by the B.C. Federation of Labour. SHARE works with pension trustees, plan administrators, and plan members to provide shareholder research, education, and policy. It is a relatively new initiative fully supported by the CLC that aims to work as part of the international movement to hold the corporate sector accountable through shareholder proposals. So far, SHARE has drafted and circulated proposals to be filed with the Hudson Bay Company and Sears concerning the use of sweatshop labour by suppliers. It has also developed critical research papers on fiduciary responsibility and investment policy.

The National Union of Public and General Employees has now instituted regular meetings of its union trustees and activists across Canada and recently held a first pilot educational meeting for trustees to establish a union agenda for investment strategies. The Canadian Union of Public Employees has held similar week-long workshops for trustees.

The CLC is also supporting a new trustee education initiative to provide training to union trustees. This is sponsored by Carleton University and the Ontario Institute for Studies in Education of the University of Toronto. It aims to design and deliver, through workshops and web-enabled methods, focused, practical training on fund investment for trustees with public-sector and private-sector pension funds across Canada. This group is supported by an advisory committee that includes representatives from the CLC, the NUPGE, CUPE, and other leading labour organizations.

Another new initiative, emerging from the Trustee Education Project is a three-year program funded by the Social Science and Humanities Research Council to develop a research/education program by and for union trustees. The CLC and every federation of labour in Canada has indicated an enthusiastic interest in playing a partnership role. This is a remarkable collaboration of the trade union movement and academic institutions, based at the Ontario Institute for Studies in Education of the University of Toronto. The trade union movement is clearly ready to work on pension fund investment issues and a comprehensive research/ education program reflecting a union perspective on investment. All research and education materials developed will be publicly accessible on its website, www.pensionsatwork.ca.

We are witnessing a change in organized labour's attitude to dealing with investment matters and a growing recognition that education – a transformative education – must play a central role in supporting trustees. While we know that training for trustees is dominated by the financial industry, there is a vacuum to be filled by unions and academic institutions that may stress a more transformative, holistic approach to pension fund investment, taking account of benefits to working people, their families, and communities.

There is an urgent need to train pension practitioners in Canada. The trade union movement is ideally placed to provide educational programs for rank-and-file members, second-tier activists, and union trustees. This education needs to take a critical approach to demystify the governance and investment of pension funds and allow pension trustees to make prudent decisions. In the interests of collaborative working relationships, there should be pilot projects for union and employer trustees since both suffer from a lack of training.

There are many resources in Canada and the northern United States for unions and pension funds to recruit educational and training help. However, there is no organization of education and research that provides effective support to pension practitioners. The CLC could appoint a working group to evaluate the progress of the AFL-CIO's Center for Working Capital and to determine its suitability as a model in Canada. Furthermore, this book can provide the basic research material for a handbook that will support the provision of educational training for all levels of pension practitioners.

chapter 14

Future Research

The limitations of this study and the implications for future research will now be considered. This study should be viewed as but a beginning of research on more productive ways to invest pension funds. Much more remains to be done.

Like all studies, this one have a number of limitations. It is unlikely that Concert itself can be replicated because of limitations imposed by the Income Tax Act. There are only so many pre-1978 real estate companies which can facilitate a role for pension funds as active builders. This is a somewhat startling discovery, particularly since much asset targeting in the United States is in real estate development. This section of the act was designed to protect developers from competition by pension funds. However, pension funds are not barred from working with development companies to invest in building real estate. Federal politics may now have shifted, though, with the federal government more interested in accessing the vast capital of pension funds for housing and infrastructure development.

Both Concert and Mortgage Fund One are in the real estate development market, an area of the market that possesses many unique features. The knowledge gained by Concert principals in real estate development in the Vancouver region and now Ontario is not readily transferable to other types of investment. So, for example, from this case study we cannot learn about investment in technology firms or the strategies around regional development or the rebuilding of manufacturing infrastructure. Nevertheless, we can learn something from the process that union trustees went through in the development of these two investment vehicles. We can also learn about the specialization necessary.

I have to ask though whether it is really necessary for pension funds to develop such a vast amount of specialized knowledge in all areas of economic development. Does this expose pension funds to unnecessary risk? Are there other ways in which pension funds can be accessed to contribute to housing and public infrastructure needs without such risk?

Further, does the present conventionally accepted asset mix of approximately 50 per cent equities not also expose pension funds to risk? I would argue that it is in the public interest to invest workers' pension funds productively, and that this could be achieved by investing pension funds wholly in government bonds, thereby guaranteeing an adequate return over the long term. What are the barriers to an investment practice that was routine in the 1960s?

This study used multipliers in the absence of specific information on the social and economic effects of Concert's productivity and the employment it created in British Columbia through residential construction. Admittedly, they are rather crude measures. However, the development of social indicators is a growing field of enquiry that in future should enable a more complete analysis of collateral benefit and damage. It is not assumed here that all productivity or job creation by their very nature are socially beneficial. Indeed, as discussed in Chapter 6, much social benefit remains unaccounted for, and as does much social damage (Mies, 1986; Waring, 1988).

Real estate development is an example of productive investment of pension funds. As one of its social accounting models, this study targets a working-class community in Vancouver. The model contrasts the differing social and economic value to the broader community resulting from the construction of rental accommodations and market housing. Conventional real estate developers are reluctant to build rental accommodations because of the poor short-term rate of return, unless they can immediately sell the development. The example of Concert illustrates a way of benefiting the broader community through stable rental accommodations built on leased land in partnership with the City of Vancouver. This is the first report of research examining the use of pension funds to increase affordable housing stock and rental accommodations. Because the focus is pension fund investment rather than housing, however, many questions about the provision of affordable housing are left unanswered. A more complete assessment is urgently needed since all urban centres in Canada are characterized by the same shortage of housing. Many more social indicators are being developed to assess the social and economic benefits of housing developments. For example, more attention is being paid now to the costs of urban sprawl versus the costs of affordable housing (the subject of future study). This topic is particularly important because there are increasing indications that pension funds will capitalize urban development in Ontario.

Questions about affordability of housing and its impact on homeless people are not addressed here. Because pension funds provide a potential source of capital for housing, research needs to be pursued on how these funds could provide a continuum of housing stock that would serve the whole community. This research would be particularly useful, since it would allow for more effective targeting of funds.

There is much to be done. This examination of Concert and Mortgage Fund One has presented the first opportunity for research into social investment by pension funds in Canada. The work should be continued and broadened so that we can have a greater understanding of economically targeted investment, shareholder activism, and ethical screens. In particular, a study is needed of the Caisse de Dépôt et Placement du Québec, where there is more variety of asset targeting, and thus more possibility of social investment models. Research could reveal important information about pension fund investment in regional development funds and in small- and medium-sized businesses in the communications, technology, biotechnology, health, and financial sectors. There are many examples of asset targeting in the United States that should be examined for their relevance to Canada; this in itself is a massive task.

Quebec offers important information about economic development. Legal frameworks, enabling regulations, and organizational processes need to be examined to assess what conditions allow asset targeting to flourish. It is interesting to note that Concert and Mortgage Fund One are also flourishing in Ontario.

Shareholder activism is a huge field. However, we need research into whether it adds value to a company. There is little to no research on how, for example, the California Public Employees' Retirement System (CalPERS) – a massive public pension fund – has set up standards of corporate accountability for sectors of the economy and to what extent the standards have been successful in changing corporate behaviour.

Much more needs to be done on social accounting. The models presented here are acknowledged to be narrow. The value added statement, in particular, promises to be fruitful. An implementation of the value added approach in a private or public sector setting would be extremely interesting, since this model has the advantage of that it can be scrutinized by professional accounting organizations using their professional standards.

Social accounting is a growing, international field of enquiry. An international organization that can assist Canadian unions in pursuing a better understanding of social accounting issues is the Institute of Social and Ethical Accountability (ISEA). Its function is to develop consensus on a set of standards that can establish 'a recognizable and accessible' level of quality in social accounting and auditing (Zadek et al., 1997, p. 57) and to legitimize the practice of social accounting so that it can be used more widely in the corporate sector. On the ISEA board are such organizations as the New Economics Foundation in the United Kingdom. Such informed liaisons are critical if the trade union movement is to move forward its own research in social investment. The controversy surrounding private-public partnerships (P3s) has added a new urgency to the need for standards for investment that add value to the community rather than profit to the providers of previously public services.

Compared with the United States, there is very little information on Canadian pension funds in general. For example, comparatively little is known about their respective investment practices and rates of return. In the absence of standards requiring greater levels of disclosure, it is optimistic to suggest that there should be more research. However, where a pension fund is willing, case studies could be undertaken. Far more information is needed about standards of care – the contracts governing fund managers – methods of reporting, and fee structures. All such information would be useful to a union agenda for exerting more control over fund managers.

Finally, consideration needs to be given as to how this research might be applied. The Canadian trade union movement must consider making a call for an organization devoted to research and education, strongly linked to the trade union movement, and with the ability to concentrate its work to develop an alternative, progressive agenda for the social control of capital.

All these areas of future research suggest that a working group should be formed on asset targeting in Canada. Although these are critical questions in real estate development, there are no doubt equally critical questions in each investment arena. A working group could focus on areas of research for social investment and social indicators to evaluate the progress of economically targeted investments.

We have examined here a case study of Concert, a real estate development company financed by union-trusteed pension funds. We have not, however, given close consideration to the many questions that remain on housing policy in Canada. The study developed social indicators to measure the fiscal impact of Concert's contribution to the broader community, but more reseach is needed on broadening the range of social indicators.

Many relevant research areas are in their infancy. Very little is known about the investment practices of occupational pension funds in Canada. There are few models of social investment of pension funds outside Quebec. Concert and Mortgage Fund One are two such examples.

Concert itself may not be directly replicable. Furthermore, the real estate development market tends to vary depending on the region and the type of development concerned. What is learned about Concert may not be directly transferable to other types of innovative investment in other sectors. Much more research is needed in asset targeting.

This study has provided some models of social accounting to measure the impact and benefit of investment on the broader community. In one, multipliers were used. However, more complete analysis is needed of the collateral benefits and damages caused by investments, in general, and pension fund investments in particular. This area of research is just beginning.

A centre for research and education should be established to begin to answer the many questions that this study raises about productive investment of pension funds. An assessment of the AFL-CIO's Center for Working Capital might lead to a model for such a centre in Canada.

Conclusion

Canadian pension fund assets are estimated to be at approximately $550 billion. In terms of financial assets, in Canada pension funds are second only to the combined assets of the country's major banks. Pension funds have become a critical source of capital for national and international markets. They are controlled by an intricate web of financial and legal standards such as fiduciary responsibility and yet, as deferred wages, they are largely beyond the control of workers or their unions.

Especially given their tax-exempt status, pension funds can provide the long-term capital needed to build a new economy based on real productivity. To test this assumption, a participatory research methodology was applied to Concert, a real estate development company in British Columbia. Concert is funded through the pooling of capital from twenty-six pension funds that have union trustees. The study focused on investments targeted to a working-class community in Vancouver. Models of social accounting, which broadened the criteria normally used in traditional accounting practice, were used to evaluate the investments.

Based on the results of the study, a new definition of 'social investment' is proposed. The definition contains the following elements: the collaborative action by unions and pension funds that leads to various types of collateral investments; such investments implicitly or explicitly challenge conventional corporate behaviour by contributing to the social and economic benefit of the broader community; and this benefit can be verified through the use of social accounting techniques.

A series of social accounting models was developed to assess the benefit of pension fund investment to workers through job creation, to pension fund shareholders through increased contributions and dividends, and to government through increased tax revenues. Another set of social accounting models uses multipliers to measure the impact of pension fund investment on workers, pension fund shareholders, and government.

The social accounting models applied to Concert's investments show that this real estate development company more than doubled its direct, attributable on-site employment for the broader community. Furthermore, from the time it was established, Concert's benefits have outweighed its total project costs. A net social gain of Concert's direct job creation was calculated based on the differing social and economic value to the broader community of construction of rental accommodations and market housing. Finally, it was shown that the federal government enjoyed a net gain of $8.7 million, notwithstanding its foregone revenues on pension contributions and return on investments.

It is unlikely that other pension funds can replicate Concert. Rather, it is recommended that both Concert and Mortgage Fund One be considered national investment vehicles for the provision of rental accommodation and affordable housing in Canada.

Two models are proposed for how to proceed. The first model identifies three levels of control: negotiability of pensions, trusteeship or governance, and the management of investments. All levels of control are essential for union trustees to implement strategies of social investment. The second model identifies three components necessary for effective action: leadership, support and expertise, and education. Taken together, these models recommend a strong role for research and education in the trade union movement. Without a coordinated strategy, it is unlikely that there will be more than isolated instances of social investment in Canada, outside Quebec.

There are signs that this strategy is under way, thereby signalling a move on the part of the trade union movement towards influencing how pension monies are invested. This was the intention of the original group of union activists who began Concert.

APPENDIX: CANADA'S TOP TWENTY-THREE PENSION FUNDS BASED ON ASSET SIZE

Funds with no union and no employee representation:

1 BCE Inc.
2 CN Rail
3 General Motors of Canada
4 Canadian Pacific
5 Air Canada

```
        ┌─────────────────┐
        │  Company Plan   │
        └─────────────────┘
           ▲ ▲   ▼ ▼
        ╭─────────────────╮
        │ Board of Directors/ │
        │     Trustees     │
        ╰─────────────────╯
```

Funds with little or no representation from the in-house union:

6 Ontario Hydro
7 Ontario Pension Board

```
        ┌─────────────────┐
        │      100%       │
        │    Employer     │
        │ representatives │
        └─────────────────┘
                │
                ▼
        ╭─────────────────╮
        │ Board of Trustees │
        ╰─────────────────╯
```

Funds with no joint trusteeship, but with 50% employee and retiree representation in selecting the government trustee:

8 Ontario Municipal Employees Retirement System (OMERS)
9 Alberta Local Authorities

```
        ╭─────────────────╮
        │  50% employees  │
        │  50% employers  │
        ╰─────────────────╯
                │
                ▼
        ┌─────────────────┐
        │   Government    │
        │    Ministry     │
        └─────────────────┘
                │
                ▼
        ┌─────────────────┐
        │  Legislated Plan │
        └─────────────────┘
                │
                ▼
        ╭─────────────────╮
        │ Board of Trustees │
        ╰─────────────────╯
           ▲
    Elected Chair
```

*This material is from Isla Carmichael (1998), *A Survey of Union Pension Trustees*.

Funds where unions are recognized, but only in an advisory capacity:

10 B.C. Municipal Employees*
11 B.C. Public Service Employees*
12 B.C. Teachers*
13 Nova Scotia Public Service Employees

Since 1998, B.C. pension plans have become jointly trusteed.

Jointly trusteed funds, where unions and the employer are equally represented, but the employer retains the chair:

14 Canadian Broadcasting Corporation (CBC)

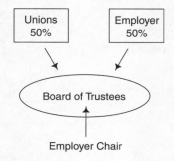

Jointly trusteed funds, where unions and employers are equally represented in selecting the government trustee, with a legislated chair:

15 Quebec Public Employees
16 Hydro Quebec
17 Quebec Teachers

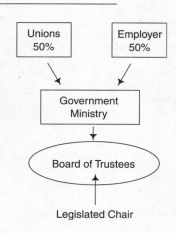

Jointly trusteed fund, where the affiliated union and the government are sponsors, with an independent chair:

18 Ontario Teachers Pension Plan

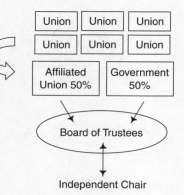

Jointly trusteed fund, where the union and the employer are equally represented, the government trustee is selected on union recommendation, and the trustees select the chair and vice-chair:

19 Alberta Public Service Pension Plan

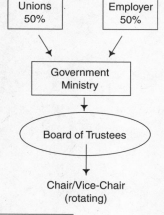

Jointly trusteed fund, where the union and the employer are equally represented as trustees, who select the chair and vice-chair (rotating):

21 Ontario Public Service Employees
    Union (OPSEU) Pension Trust
22 Hospitals of Ontario Pension Plan (HOOPP)
23 Community Colleges of Applied Arts and
    Technology (CAAT) Pension Plan

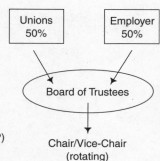

References

Adams, Roy. 1995. 'From Adversarialism to Social Partnership: Lessons from the Experience of Germany, Japan, Sweden and the United States.' In Roy Adams, Gordon Betcherman, and Beth Bilson, eds., *Good Jobs, Bad Jobs, No Jobs*, 19–61. Toronto: C.D. Howe Institute.

Aho, J.A. 1985. 'Rhetoric and the Invention of Double Entry Bookkeeping.' *Rhetorica* 3(1): 21–43.

Ambachtsheer, Keith. 2003. 'The Real Pension Crisis.' *Financial Post*, 16 July, FP15.

Ambachtsheer, Keith, and Don Ezra. 1998. *Pension Fund Excellence*. Toronto: Wiley.

American Federation of Labor and Congress of Industrial Organizations (AFL-CIO). 1998. *Economic Development: A Union Guide to the High Road*. Washington, DC: Human Resources Development Institute.

– 1993. *Pensions in Changing Capital Markets*. Washington, DC: author.

Amihud, Yakov, Bent Christensen, and Haim Mendelson. 1992. *Further Evidence on the Risk-Return Relationship*. Working Paper S-93-11. Salomon Brothers Center for the Study of Financial Institutions, Graduate School of Business Administration, New York University.

Ambrose, B. 1993. *Pension Fund Investment in Affordable Housing*. Background report for the secretary's conference on encouraging pension fund investment in affordable housing. Washington, DC: U.S. Department of Housing and Urban Development.

Andrews, Fred. 1999. 'Drucker Disdains Corporate Myopia.' *Globe and Mail* 18 Nov., B19.

Arnold, Patricia, and Theresa Hammond. 1994. 'The Role of Accounting in Ideological Conflict: Lessons from the South African Divestment Movement.' *Accounting, Organizations and Society* 19(2): 111–27.

Asmundson, P., and Foerster, S. 2001. 'Socially Responsible Investing: Better for Your Soul or Your Bottom Line?' *Canadian Investment Review* (Winter): 1–12.

Athanassakos, G. 1997. 'Firm Size Stock Return Seasonality and the Trading Patterns of Individual and Institutional Investors: The Canadian Experience.' *Journal of Investing* (Fall): 75–86.

Aupperle, K.E., A.B. Carrol, and J.D. Hatfield. 1985. 'An Empirical Examination of the Relationship between Corporate Social Responsibility and Profitability.' *Academy of Management Journal* 28(2): 446–63.

Baesel, J.B., and G.R. Stein. 1979. 'The Value of Information: Inferences from the Profitability of Insider Trading.' *Journal of Financial Quantitative Analysis* 14: 553.

Bak, Lori. 1998. 'The 1998 Top 100.' *Benefits Canada*, April, 28.

– 1997. 'The Top 40 Money Managers.' *Benefits Canada*, Nov. 36.

Bakan, Joel. 2004. *The Corporation*. Toronto: Viking.

Baker, Dean, and Archon Fung. 2000. 'Collateral Damage: Do Pension Fund Investments Hurt Workers?' In Fung, Hebb, and Rogers, *Working Capital: The Power of Labor's Pensions*, 13–43. Ithaca: Cornell University Press.

Baldwin, Bob, Ted Jackson, Michael Decter, and David Levi. 1991. *Investment Funds: Issues and Prospects*. Prepared for the Canadian Labour Congress (CLC).

Barber, Randy. 1997. 'Retirement, Pension and Capital Strategies: An Inventory of Major Issues Confronting Labor.' Washington, DC: Centre for Economic Organizing.

– 1982. 'Pension Funds in the United States: Issues of Investment and Control.' *Economic and Industrial Democracy* 3: 31–73.

Barber, Randy, and Teresa Ghilarducci. 1993. 'Pension Funds, Capital Markets, and the Economic Future.' In Gary Dymski, Gerald Epstein, and Robert Pollin, eds., *Transforming the U.S. Financial System*. 287–319. New York: M.E. Sharpe.

Bartik, Timothy J., and Richard D. Bingham, 1997. 'Can Economic Development Programs Be Evaluated?' In Bingham and Mier, *Dilemmas of Urban Economic Development*, 246–91.

Baucus, Melissa S. 1995. 'Halo-Adjusted Residuals – Prolonging the Life of a Terminally-Ill Measure of Corporate Social Performance.' *Business and Society* 34(2): 227–35.

Beebower, G., and G. Bergstrom. 1977. 'A Performance Analysis of Pension and Profit-Sharing Portfolios: 1966–1975.' *Financial Analysts Journal* 33: 31–42.

Beechy, T.H. 1990. *Canadian Advanced Financial Accounting*. 2nd ed. Toronto: Holt, Rinehart and Winston.

Benefits Canada. 1999. *Canadian Pension Fund Investment Directory*. Toronto: Maclean Hunter.

Benjamin, Dwayne, Morley Gunderson, and W. Craig Riddell. 1998. *Labour Market Economics*. Toronto: McGraw-Hill Ryerson.

Bertram, Robert. 1992. *Social Investment*. Toronto: Ontario Teachers Pension Plan Board.

'Beta Beaten.' 1992. *Economist*, 7 March, 87.

Bingham, Richard, and Robert Mier. eds. 1997 *Dilemmas of Urban Economic Development*. Beverly Hills: Sage.

– 1993. *Theories of Local Economic Development*. Beverly Hills: Sage.

Black, Bernard, S. 1992. 'Agents Watching Agents: The Promise of Institutional Investor Voice.' *UCLA Law Review* 39: 81.

Blackwell, Richard. 2000. 'Banks Give Shareholders a Voice.' *Globe and Mail*, 3 March, B10.

Blair, John, and Robert Premus. 1993. 'Location Theory.' In Bingham and Mier, eds., *Theories of Local Economic Development*.

Blair, Margaret. 1995. *Ownership and Control, Rethinking Corporate Governance for the Twenty-First Century*. Washington, DC: Brookings Institution.

Bodie, Zvi. 1976. 'Common Stocks as a Hedge against Inflation.' *Journal of Finance* 31: 459–70.

Bowen, Howard. 1953. *Social Responsibilities of the Businessman*. New York: Harper.

Bragdon, J.H., and J.T. Marlin. 1972. 'Is Pollution Profitable?' *Risk Management* 19(2): 9–18.

Breen, William J, and Robert A. Korajczyk. 1993. *On Selection Biases in Book-to-Market Based Tests of Asset Pricing Models*. Working Paper 167. Northwestern University, Evanston, Ill.

Brinson, G., L.R. Hood, and G. Beebower. 1986. 'Determinants of Portfolio Performance.' *Financial Analysts Journal* 43(39–44).

Brisbois, Cathy. 1997. 'Ranking Disclosure: Vancity Savings and Credit Union, Canada.' In Zadek, Pruzan, and Evans, eds., *Building Corporate Accountability*, 189–200.

British Columbia, Crime Prevention Office. 1994. *Evaluation Report*. Vancouver: author.

– Ministry of Finance and Corporate Relations, Analysis and Evaluation Branch. 1996. 'Provincial Economic Multipliers and How to Use Them: Draft.' Victoria, BC: author.

Bromiley, P., and Marcus A. 1989. 'The Deterrents to Dubious Corporate Behaviour: Profitability, Probability and Safety Recalls.' *Strategic Management Journal* 10: 233–50.

Brookfield, S. 2001. 'Unmasking Power: Foucault and Adult Learning.' *Canadian Journal of Adult Education* 15(1): 1–23.

Brown, B., and S. Perry. 1995. 'Focal Paper: Halo-Removed Residuals of Fortune's "Responsibility to the Community and the Environment" – a Decade of Data.' *Business and Society* 34(2): 119–214.

Brun, Leslie A. (n.d.) 'Economically Targeted Investing.' *Institute for Fiduciary Education Trustee Handbook*, 65–7. Toronto: IFE.

Bruyn, Severyn. 1987. *The Field of Social Investment.* Cambridge: Cambridge University Press.

Bryden, Kenneth. 1974. *Old Age Pensions and Policy-Making in Canada.* Montreal and London: McGill-Queen's University Press.

Caisse de Dépôt et Placement du Québec. 1998. *Annual Report.* Quebec: author.

CalPERS. 1995. 'Why Corporate Governance Today?' Sacramento: author.

Calvert, Geoffrey. 1977. *Pensions and Survival: The Coming Crisis of Money and Retirement.* Toronto: Maclean-Hunter.

Campbell, Beverley Ross, and William Josephson. 1983. 'Public Pension Trustees' Pursuit of Social Goals.' *Journal of Urban and Contemporary Law* 24(3): 43–120.

Campbell, John Y. 1987. 'Stock Returns and the Term Structure.' *Journal of Financial Economics* 18: 373–99.

Canada, Bureau of Statistics (1947). *Survey of industrial pension and welfare plans.* In pensions and welfare plans in Canadian Industry. Labour Gazette. Ottawa. Department of Labour, pp. 694–697.

Canada, Department of Labour. 1949. *Pension and Welfare Plans in Canadian Industry.* Ottawa: Labour Gazette.

Canada, Ministry of Finance. 1997. *Tax Expenditures.* Ottawa: author.

Canada, Pariliamentary Task Force on Pension. 1983. *Report of the Parliamentary Task Force on Pensions.* Ottawa: Queen's Printer.

Canada, Senate, Standing Committee on Banking, Trade, and Commerce. 1998. *The Governance Practices of Institutional Investors.* Ottawa: author.

Canada, Statistics Canada. 2004. Employer Pension Plans (Trusteed Pension Funds). Retrieved from: http://www.statcan.ca/Daily/English/040624/d040624d.htm

– 2001. *Quarterly Estimates of Trusteed Pension Funds. Fourth Quarter 2000.* Ottawa: Queen's Printer.

– 1997. *Pension Plans in Canada.* Ottawa: Queen's Printer.

– 1996a. *Trusteed Pension Plans: Financial Statistics 1994.* Ottawa: Queen's Printer.

– 1996b. *Canada's Retirement Income Programs.* Ottawa: Queen's Printer.

– 1980. *Pension Plans in Canada.* Ottawa: Queen's Printer.

Canadian Association of Pension Supervisory Authorities. 2004. *Regulatory Principles for a Model Pension Law.* Retrieved from http://www.capsa-acor.org

Canadian Institute for Chartered Accountants. 1999. *The CICA Handbook.* Toronto: author.

Canadian Labour and Business Centre (CLBC). 1993. 'Access to Capital Resources in Canada.' Ottawa: author (formerly the Canadian Labour Market and Productivity Centre).

Canadian Labour Congress (CLC). 1990. *A New Decade: Our Future.* Ottawa: author.

Canadian Pension Fund Investment Directory. 1999. Toronto: Maclean-Hunter Publishing.

Canadian Union of Public Employees (CUPE). 2003. 'Questions for Your Money Manager.' *Pension Talk* 1(4).

– 2002. *Pension Talk: Bringing Union Values to Pension Investing.* Ottawa: author.

– 1992. 'Pensions and Social Investment; Ethical Investment for the 1990s.' *CUPE Fact,* 29–32.

Carmichael, Isla. 2004. 'A New Role for Unions in the Economy.' In Anil Verma and Tom Kochan, eds., *Unions in the 21st Century: An International Perspective.* London: Palgrave McMillan.

– 1998. *A Survey of Union Pension Trustees.* A Joint Project of the Canadian Labour Market and Productivity Centre (CLMPC) and the Ontario Public Service Employees Union (OPSEU).

– 1996. 'The Development and Control of Occupational Pension Plans by Workers in Canada: The Ontario Public Service Employees Union Pension Trust, a Case Study.' Master's thesis, University of Toronto.

Carmichael, Isla, and Jack Quarter, eds. 2003. *Money on the Line.* Ottawa: Canadian Centre for Policy Alternatives (CCPA).

– 2003. 'Introduction.' In Carmichael and Quarter, *Money on the Line.*

Carmichael, Isla, Shirley Thompson, and Jack Quarter. 2004. 'Transformative Education for Pension Fund Trustees.' *Canadian Journal for Studies in Adult Education* 17(1).

Carpentry Workers Benefit Plan of B.C. and Carpentry Workers Pension Plan of B.C. 2001. *On the Level* 37, 1. Retrieved from http://www. carpentersunionbc. com/Level/PensionSpecialLevel2001.html

– 1998. *1998 Report.*

Carroll, Archie B. 1979. 'A Three-Dimensional Conceptual Model of Corporate Performance.' *Academy of Management Review* 4(4): 497–505.

Casselton, Valerie. 1988. 'The Hard-Hat Capitalists.' *Vancouver Sun,* 14 May, D10–D12.

CBC. 2002. *Venture.*

Clarkson, Max B.E. 1995. 'A Stakeholder Framework for Analysing and Evaluating Corporate Social Performance.' *Academy of Management Review* 20(1): 92–117.

Clement, Wallace. 1975. *The Canadian Corporate Elite.* Toronto: McClelland and Stewart.

Cleveland, Gordon, and Michael Krashinsky. 1998. 'The Benefits and Costs of Good Child Care.' Childcare Resource and Research Unit, University of Toronto.

Coady, M.M. 1939. *Masters of Their Own Destiny*. New York: Harper.

Coffee, John. 1991. 'Liquidity versus Control: The Institutional Investor as a Corporate Monitor.' *Columbia Law Review* 91(6): 1277.

Comstock, Donald E., and Russell Fox. 1993. 'Participatory Research as Critical Theory: The North Bonneville, USA, Experience.' In Park et al., *Voices of Change*, 103–25.

Concert Properties. 1999. 'Summary of Company Activities.' Document produced for internal use by Concert Properties. Vancouver: author.

Cooper, David J., and Michael J. Sherer. 1984. 'The Value of Corporate Accounting Reports: Arguments for a Political Economy of Accounting.' *Accounting, Organizations and Society* 9(3–4): 207–32.

Daly, Herman E. 1996. *Beyond Growth*. Boston: Beacon Press.

Daniels, Ronald J., and Jeffrey G. McIntosh. 1991. 'Towards a Distinctive Canadian Corporate Regime.' *Osgoode Hall Law Journal* 29(4): 863–933.

Daniels, Ronald J., and Edward J. Waitzer. 1994. 'Challenges to the Citadel: Recent Trends in Canadian Corporate Governance.' *Canadian Business Law Journal* 23(1–3): 23–44.

Davis, E. Philip. 1995. *Pension Funds: Retirement Income, Security and Capital Markets. An International Perspective*. London: Clarendon.

Deaton, Richard Lee. 1989. *The Political Economy of Pensions: Power, Politics and Social Change in Canada, Britain, and the United States*. Vancouver: University of British Columbia Press.

Diltz, J. David. 1995. 'The Private Cost of Socially Responsible Investing.' *Applied Financial Economics* 5(2): 69–78.

Drache, D., and H. Glasbeek. 1992. *The Changing Workplace*. Toronto: Lorimer.

Drucker, Peter. 1976. *The Unseen Revolution: How Pension Fund Socialism Came to America*. New York: Harper and Row, 1976.

Duttweiler, E. 1991. *Factbook, 1991*: New York: New York Stock Exchange.

Eisner, Elliot W. 1991. *The Enlightened Eye: Qualitative Inquiry and the Enhancement of Educational Practice*. New York: Macmillan.

Ellis, Patricia. 1990. 'Participatory Research Methodology and Process: Experience and Perspective of a Caribbean Researcher.' *Convergence* 23(4): 23–34.

Ellmen, E. 2000. 'Socially Conscious Investors Hobbled by Old Legislation.' *Globe and Mail*, 9 March, B15.

– 1997. *The 1997 Canadian Ethical Money Guide*. Toronto: Lorimer.

– 1996. 'Reforming Capitalism.' *Canadian Forum* (Jan.–Feb.): 9–14.

– 1990. 'Alternative Investing.' Proceedings of the Conference Strategies for

Responsible Share Ownership: Implications for Pension and Other Investment Funds. Sponsored by the Centre for Corporate Social Performance and
Ethics and the Task Force on the Church and Corporate Responsibility:
59–61.

Elton, Edwin. 1981. *Modern Portfolio Theory and Investment Analysis*, 2nd ed. New
York: Wiley.

Elton, E.J., M.J., Gruber, S., Das, and M. Hklarka. 1991. 'Efficiency with Costly
Information: A Reinterpretation of Evidence from Managed Portfolios.'
Manuscript, New York University.

Falconer, Kirk. 1999. *Prudence, Patience and Jobs: Pension Investment in a Changing
Economy.* Report prepared for the CLBC.

– 1998. 'Pension Barriers to Financing Small and Medium-Sized Business in Canada.' Notes for a Presentation to the Pension Investment Association of Canada.

Fama, Eugene. 1991. 'Efficient Capital Markets.' *Journal of Finance* 46(5).

– 1981. 'Stock Returns, Real Activity, Inflation and Money.' *American Economic
Review* 71: 545–65.

– 1970. 'Efficient Capital Markets: A Review of Theory and Empirical Work.'
Journal of Finance 25: 383–417.

Fama, Eugene, and Kenneth R. French. 1988. 'Permanent and Temporary Components of Stock Prices.' *Journal of Political Economy* 96(2): 246–73.

Fama, Eugene F., and A. Laffer. 1971. 'Information and Capital Markets.' *Journal
of Business* (July): 289–98.

Fama, Eugene F., and G. William Schwert. 1977. 'Asset Returns and Inflation.'
Journal of Financial Economics 5: 115–46.

Farrar, J.H., and J.K. Maxton. 1986. 'Social Investment and Pension Scheme
Trusts.' *Law Quarterly Review* 102(32).

Fazio, Hugom, and Manuel Riesco. 1997. 'The Chilean Pension Fund Association.' *New Left Review* 223 (May–June): 90–100.

Financial Post. 1997. 'Institutional Investors Should Have a Long-Term Perspective.' 1 July, 10.

Finlay, J. Richard. 1997. 'Governance Debate Just Beginning.' *Globe and Mail,*
28 March, B2.

Finlayson, Ann. 1988. *Whose Money Is It Anyway? The Showdown on Pensions.*
Markham: Penguin.

Fowler, D.J., and C.H. Rorke. 1988. 'Insider Trading Profits on the TSE.' *Canadian Journal of Administrative Science* 5(1): 13.

Freeman, R.E. 1984. *Strategic Management: A Stakeholder Approach.* Boston: Pitman
Ballinger.

Freire, Paulo. 1973. *Education for Critical Consciousness.* New York: Continuum.

– 1970. *The Pedagogy of the Oppressed.* New York: Seabury.

Freire, Paulo, and Antonio Faundez. 1989. *Learning to Question: A Pedagogy of Liberation.* New York: Continuum.

French, Kenneth, R., William Schwert G., and Robert F. Stambaugh. 1987. 'Expected Stock Returns and Volatility.' *Journal of Financial Economics* 19(Sept.): 3–30.

Friedman, M. 1970. 'The Social Responsibility of Business Is to Increase Its Profits.' *New York Times Magazine,* 13 Sept. 122–6.

Fryxell, G.E., and J. Wang. 1994. 'The Fortune Corporate "Reputation" Index: Reputation for What?' *Journal of Management* 20(1): 1–14.

Fung, Archon, Tessa Hebb, and Joel Rogers, eds. 2000. *Working Capital: The Power of Labor's Pensions.* Ithaca: Cornell University Press.

Ghilarducci, Teresa. 1994. ' U.S. Pension Investment Policy and Perfect Capital Market Theory.' *Challenge* (July–Aug.): 4–10.

Giloth, Robert. 1997. 'Commentary on "Can Economic Development Programs Be Evaluated?"' In Bingham and Mier, *Dilemmas of Urban Economic Development,* 278–84.

Gindin, Sam. 1997. 'Notes on Labor at the End of the Century.' *Monthly Review* 49(3): 140–58.

– 1992. 'Putting the Con Back in the Economy.' *This Magazine,* May.

Glaser, Barney G., and Anselm L. Straus. 1967. *The Discovery of Grounded Theory: Strategies for Qualitative Research.* New York: Aldine de Gruyter.

Glesne, Corine, and Alan Peshkin. 1992. *Becoming Qualitative Researchers.* New York: Longman.

Glickman, Murray. 1994. 'The Concept of Information, Intractable Uncertainty, and the Current State of the Efficient Markets Theory: A Post-Keynesian View.' *Journal of Post Keynsian Economics* 16(3): 325–49.

Gordon, Jeffrey, N. 1986. 'The Puzzling Survival of the Constrained Prudent Man Rule.' In Longstreth, ed., *Modern Investment Management and the Prudent Man Rule,* 195–231.

Goyder, G. 1961. *The Responsible Company.* Oxford: Blackwell.

Grant, J. 1976. *The Role of Private Pension Funds in the Financing of the Corporate Sector of the Canadian Economy.* Toronto: Wood Gundy.

Graves, Samuel B., and Sandra A. Waddock. 1994. 'Institutional Owners and Corporate Social Performance.' *Academy of Management Journal* 37(4): 1034–46.

Greenough, William Croan, and Francis P. King. 1976. *Pension Plans and Public Policy.* New York: Columbia University Press, 1976.

Greenwood, John. 1998. 'Index Funds in the Money.' *Financial Post,* 13 June, 1.

Gregg, Paul, Stephen Machin, and Alan Manning. 1994. 'High Pay, Low Pay and Labour Market Efficiency.' In Andrew Glyn and David Miliband, eds., *Paying for Inequality: The Economic Cost of Social Injustice*, 100–14. London: IPPR/Rivers Oram Press.

Greystone Properties n.d. 'A Developer with a Difference.' Vancouver: author.

Griffin, Jennifer J., and John F. Mahon. 1994. 'Corporate Social Performance and Corporate Financial Performance Debate.' *Business and Society* 36(1): 5–31.

Grossman, Blake R., and William F. Sharpe. 1986. 'Financial Implications of South Africa Divestment.' *Financial Analysts Journal* 42(4): 15–29.

Guerard, John B. Jr. 1997. 'Additional Evidence on the Cost of Being Socially Responsible in Investing.' *Journal of Investing* 6(4): 31–5.

Habermas, J. 1972. *Knowledge and Human Interests*. London: Heinemann.

Hall, Budd. 1993. 'Introduction.' In Park, et al., *Voices of Change*.

Hamilton, Sally, Hoje Jo, and Meir Statman. 1993. 'Doing Well while Doing Good? The Investment Performance of Socially Responsible Mutual Funds.' *Financial Analysts Journal* 49(6): 62–6.

Hanninen, Sakari. 1995 'Accountability Lost? An Environmental Struggle over the Economic Feasibility of Incineration.' *Accounting, Organizations and Society* 20(2–3): 175–92.

Harding, Sandra. 1992. 'Rethinking Standpoint Epistemology.' *Centennial Review* 36(3): 437–70.

Harrington, Diane. 1987. *Modern Portfolio Theory, the Capital Asset Pricing Model and Arbitrage Pricing Theory: A User's Guide*, 2nd ed. Englewood Cliffs, NJ: Prentice-Hall.

Harvey, David. 1985. *The Urbanization of Capital*. Baltimore: Johns Hopkins University Press.

Hayden, Anders. 1998. 'The Capitalist Crunch.' *This Magazine* (July–Aug.): 22–6.

Hebb, Tessa. 1998. 'Telling a New Economic Story.' *Making Waves* (Autumn): 42–4.

Helik, Jim. 1998. 'Simple Truths.' *Benefits Canada*, Oct., 15.

Henwood, Doug. 1997. *Wall Street*. New York: Verso.

Heron, Craig. 1996. *The Canadian Labour Movement: A Brief History*. Toronto: Lorimer.

Herremans, Irene M., Parporn Akathaporn, and Morris McInnes. 1993. 'An Investigation of Corporate Social Responsibility Reputation and Economic Performance.' *Accounting, Organizations and Society* 18(7–8): 587–604.

Hines, R. 1988. 'Financial Accounting: In Communicating Reality, We Construct Reality.' *Accounting, Organizations and Society* 13(3): 251–62.

Hodges, Charles, Walton Taylor, and James Yoder. 1997. 'Stocks, Bonds, the Sharpe Ratio, and the Investment Horizon.' *Financial Analysts Journal* 53(6): 74–80.

hooks, bell. 1988. *Talking Back: Thinking Feminist, Thinking Black.* Toronto: Between the Lines.

Hopper, Trevor, and Peter Armstrong. 1991. 'Cost Accounting, Controlling Labour and the Rise of Conglomerates.' *Accounting, Organizations and Society* 16(5–6): 405–39.

Hopwood, Anthony G. 1985. 'The Tale of a Committee that Never Reported: Disagreements on Intertwining Accounting with the Social.' *Accounting, Organizations and Society* 10(3): 361–77.

Hopwood, Anthony G., and Peter Miller, eds. 1994. *Accounting as Social and Institutional Practice.* Cambridge: Cambridge University Press.

Hopwood, Anthony G., Stuart Burchell, and Colin Clubb. 1994. 'Value-Added Accounting and National Economic Policy.' In Hopwood and Miller, *Accounting as Social and Institutional Practice.*

Hospitals of Ontario Pension Plan. 1994. 'Statement of Investment Policies and Goals.' Hospitals Of Ontario Pension Plan.

Hutchinson, James, and Charles G. Cole. 1980. 'Legal Standards Governing Investment of Pension Assets for Social and Political Goals.' *University of Pennsylvania Law Review* 128: 1340–88.

Hutchinson, Moira. 1996. 'The Promotion of Active Shareholdership for Corporate Social Responsibility in Canada.' Paper prepared for the Canadian Friends Service Committee, Toronto.

– 1990. 'Shareholder Action: Recent Canadian Experience.' Paper presented at the conference on Strategies for Responsible Share Ownership.

Iler, Brian. 1990. 'Shareholder Action: Recent Canadian Experience.' Paper presented at the conference on Strategies for Responsible Share Ownership.

Ilkiw, John H. 1997. *The Portable Pension Fiduciary.* Toronto: Maclean-Hunter.

Interfaith Center on Corporate Responsibility (ICCR). 1998. 'Inspired by Faith and Committed to Action: 1997–1998 Annual Report.' Washington, DC: author.

– 1995. 'Religious Groups Propose "Principles for Global Corporate Responsibility" – a New Business Philosophy for Responsible Corporate Action.' Washington DC: author.

International Labour Organization (ILO). 1998. *ILO Declaration on Fundamental Principles and Rights at Work.* Retrieved from http://www.ilo.org/dyn/declearis/DECLARATIONWEB.static_jump?var_language=EN&var_pagename=DECLARATIONTEXT

Ip, Greg. 1999. 'Maybe the New Economy Is Intangible.' *Globe and Mail,* 13 Sept. B2.

– 1996. 'Shareholders vs Job Holders.' *Globe and Mail,* 23 March, B3.

Jackson, Edward. 1997. 'ETIs: A Tool for Responsible Pension Fund Investment.' *Making Waves* 8(2): 2–3.

Jackson, Edward T., and Francois Lamontagne. 1995. *Adding Value: The Economic and Social Impacts of Labour-Sponsored Venture Capital Corporations and Their Investee Firms.* Prepared for the CLBC.

Jaffe, Jeffrey F., and Gershon Mandelker. 1976 'The "Fisher Effect" for Risky Assets: An Empirical Investigation.' *Journal of Finance* 31: 447–58.

Jagannathan, Ravi, and Ellen R. McGrathan. 1995. 'The CAPM Debate.' *Federal Reserve Bank of Minneapolis Quarterly Review* 19(4): 2–17.

Jagannathan, Ravi, and Zhenyu Wang. 1993. *The CAPM Is Alive and Well.* Research Staff Department Report 165. Minneapolis: Federal Reserve Bank of Minneapolis.

Jansson, Solveig. 1983. 'The Fine Art of Window Dressing.' *Institutional Investor* (Dec.): 247–50.

Johnson, Robert, and Gerald Jensen. 1998. 'Stocks, Bonds, Bills and Monetary Policy.' *Journal of Investing* 7(3): 30–6.

Kelsey, J. 1995. *Economic Fundamentalism.* London: Pluto.

Kinder, Peter D. 1993. 'Social Investing's Strength Lies in Readiness to Deal with World's Tough Questions.' *Pension World* 29(4): 10–12.

Kinder, Peter D., and Amy L. Domini. 1997. 'Social Screening: Paradigms Old and New.' *Journal of Investing* 6(4): 12–19.

Kinder Peter D., Steven D. Lydenberg, and Amy L. Domini. 1998. *The Domini Social Index.* KLD Research and Analytics, Inc. Retrieved from http://www.kld.com

Kothari, S.P., Jay Shanken, and Richard G. Sloan. 1995. 'Another Look at the Cross-Section of Expected Stock Returns.' *Journal of Finance* 50 (March): 185–224.

Kreiner, Sherman. 2003. 'The Role of Progressive Labour-Sponsored Funds as Tools for Advancing Economic and Social Goals: The Crocus Investment Fund Experience.' In Carmichael and Quarter, eds. *Money on the Line,* 219–36.

Kreps, T.J. 1936. *Business and Government under the National Recovery Administration.* American Council, Institute of Pacific Relations.

Kurtz, Lloyd, and Dan DiBartolomeo. 1996. 'Socially Screened Portfolios: An Attribution Analysis of Relative Performance.' *Journal of Investing* (Fall).

Lakonishok, J., Andrei Schleifer, Richard Thaler, and Robert Vishny. 1991. 'Window Dressing by Pension Fund Managers.' *American Economic Review.* Papers and Proceedings of the 103rd Annual Meeting of the American Economic Association 81(2): 227–31.

Lakonishok, J., Andrei Schleifer, and Robert Vishny. 1992. 'The Structure and Performance of the Money Management Industry.' *Brookings Papers: Microeconomics,* 339–91.

Lamontagne, François, and Edward T. Jackson 1995. *The Role and Performance of Labour-Sponsored Investment Funds in Canada.* Prepared for the CLBC.

Lane, Patricia. 1990. 'Obstacles to the Use of Union Pension Funds as Social Capital.' Paper presented at the conference on Strategies for Responsible Share Ownership.

Langbein, John H., and Richard A. Posner. 1980. 'Social Investing and the Law of Trusts.' *Michigan Law Review* 79: 72–112.

LeBaron, Dean. 1974. 'A Psychological Profile of the Portfolio Manager.' *Journal of Portfolio Management* (Fall): 13–16.

Lehman, C. 1992. *Accounting's Changing Role in Social Conflict.* New York and Princeton: Markus Wiener Publishing.

– and T. Tinker. 1987. 'The "Real" Cultural Significance of Accounts.' *Accounting, Organizations and Society* 12(5): 503–22.

Levine, Marc V. 1997. *The Feasibility of Economically Targeted Investment: A Wisconsin Case Study.* Brookfield, Wis.: International Foundation of Employee Benefit Plans.

Lincoln, Yvonna S., and Egon G. Guba. 1985. *Naturalistic Inquiry.* London: Sage.

Longstreth, Bevis, ed. 1986. *Modern Investment Management and the Prudent Man Rule.* New York: Oxford University Press.

Lorie, James H., Peter Dodd, and Mary Hamilton Kimpton. 1985. *The Stock Market: Theories and Evidence*, 2nd ed. Chicago: Dow Jones–Irwin.

Low, John. 1999. 'Valuing Intangibles: Results and Implications.' Paper presented at the the Second National Heartland Labor Capital Conference, Washington, DC, 29–30 April.

Lowry, R. 1991. *Good Money: A Guide to Profitable Social Investing in the 90s.* New York: W.W. Norton.

Luck, Christopher, and Nancy Pilotte. 1993. 'Domini Social Index Performance.' *Journal of Investing* (Fall).

Malkiel, B. 1995. 'Returns from Investing in Equity Mutual Funds 1971–1991. *Journal of Finance* 50(2): 549–72.

Manitoba Law Reform Commission. 1993. *Ethical Investment by Trustees.* Manitoba: Office of the Queen's Printer.

Manne, Henry. 1965. 'Mergers and the Market for Corporate Control.' *Journal of Political Economy* 73 (April): 110–20.

Markowitz, Harry. 1952. 'Portfolio Selection.' *Journal of Finance* 7 (March): 77–91.

Martin, D'Arcy. 1995. 'Street Smart: Learning in the Union Culture.' PhD diss., University of Toronto.

Maser, Karen. 1995. 'Who's Saving for Retirement?' *Perspectives on Labour and Income* (cat. 75-001E). Ottawa: Statistics Canada, 14–19.

McCritchie, James. 1996. *Ending the Wall Street Walk: Why Corporate Governance Now?* Retrieved from www.wp.com/CORPGOV/cgdiscussions.html

McDonald, John F. 1997. *Fundamentals of Urban Economics*. Englewood-Cliffs, NJ: Prentice-Hall.

Meek, Gary K., and Sidney J. Gray. 1988. 'The Value-Added Statement: An Innovation for U.S. Companies?' *Accounting Horizons* 2(2): 73–9.

Megarry, Robert. 1989. 'Investing Pension Funds: The Mineworkers' Case.' In T.G Youdan, ed., *Equity, Fiduciaries and Trusts*. Toronto: Carswell.

Meigs, W., R.F. Meigs, and Wai Lam. 1998. *Accounting: The Basis for Business Decisions*, 5th ed. Toronto: McGraw-Hill Ryerson.

Mercer, William Ltd. 1997. *The Mercer Pension Manual*. Toronto: Carswell.

Metro Credit Union. 1996. *Social Audit*. Toronto: author.

Mezirow, J. 1991. *Transformative Dimensions of Adult Learning*. San Francisco: Jossey-Bass.

Mier, Robert, and Joan Fitzgerald. 1991. 'Managing Economic Development.' *Economic Development Quarterly* 5: 268–79.

Mies, Maria. 1993. 'Towards a Methodology for Feminist Research.' In G. Bowles and Klein Duelli, eds., *Theories of Women's Studies*. London: Routlege and Kegan Paul.

– 1986. *Patriarchy and Accumulation on a World Scale*. London: Zed Books.

Miller, Peter. 1994. 'Accounting as Social and Institutional Practice: An Introduction.' In Hopwood and Miller, *Accounting as Social and Institutional Practice*, 1–39.

Mining Watch Canada. 2000. 'Shareholders Demand Placer Dome Disclose Environmental Risk.' 17 Feb.

Minns, Richard. 2003. 'Collateral Damage: The International Consequences of Pension Funds.' In Carmichael and Quarter, *Money on the Line*, 33–52.

– 1996. 'The Political Economy of Pensions.' *New Political Economy* 1(3): 375–91.

Minsky, Alan. 1988. 'Introduction to Trust Responsibility.' In *Canadian Employee Benefit Plans*, 81–90. Brookfield, Wis.: International Foundation of Employee Benefit Plans.

Moist, Paul. 2004. *P3s Rick the Public Rocket*. Retrieved from http://cupe.ca/www/33/ART404f7e991921e

Mojab, Shahrzad, and Rachel Gorman. 2003. 'Women and Consciousness in the Learning Organization: Emancipation or Exploitation?' *Adult Education Quarterly* 53(4): 228–41.

Montgomery, Kathryn. 1995–6. 'Market Shift – the Role of Institutional Investors in Corporate Governance.' *Canadian Business Law Journal* 26: 189–201.

Morley, Michael. 1979. 'The Value-Added Statement in Britain.' *Accounting Review* 54(3): 618–30.

Mortgage Fund One. 1999. 'Business Plan Summary 1999–2003: Investing in Today and Tomorrow.' Toronto: ACM Advisors Ltd.

Morton, Desmond, and Terry Copp. 1981. *Working People*. Ottawa: Deneau Publishers.

Mosher, A.B. 1952. 'Should Retirement at Age Sixty-Five Be Compulsory?' *Canadian Unionist*, 69, 77.

Moskowitz, Milton. 1972. 'Choosing Socially-Responsible Stocks.' *Business and Society Review* 1(1): 71–5.

Moye, M. 1997. 'A Review of Studies Assessing the Impact of Labour-Sponsored Investment Funds in Canada.' Paper.

Neimark, Marilyn, and Tony Tinker. 1986. 'The Social Construction of Management Control Systems.' *Accounting, Organizations and Society* 11(4–5): 369–95.

Nelson, Charles R. 1976. 'Inflation and Rates of Return on Common Stocks.' *Journal of Finance* 31: 471–83.

Newman, Michael. 1995. 'Adult Education and Social Action.' In Griff Foley, ed., *Understanding Adult Education and Training*, 246–60. St Leonards, Australia: Allen and Unwin.

Ogden, S.G. 1995. 'Transforming Frameworks of Accountability: The Case of Water Privatization.' *Accounting, Organizations and Society* 20(2–3): 193–218.

O'Grady, John. 1991. 'Whose Money Is It Anyway? The Next Stage in Pension Reform.' Presentation to the Canadian Bar Association. 20 June.

Ontario Arts Council. 1997. *Assessing the Local Economic Impact of the Arts: A Handbook*. Toronto: Informetrica.

Ontario Public Service Employee Union (OPSEU). 2004. 'Exposing the Truth: Building the Alternative. A Presentation on Public Private Partnerships in Ontario,' Toronto. Retrieved from http://www.opseu.org/convention/p32004.htm

– Pension Trust. 1997. *Annual Report*. Toronto: author.

Ontario, Royal Commission on the Status of Pensions in Ontario. 1982. *Report of the Royal Commission on the Status of Pension in Ontario*. Toronto: Government of Ontario.

Orren, K. 1974. *Corporate Power and Social Change: The Politics of the Life Insurance Industry*. Baltimore: Johns Hopkins University Press.

O'Sullivan, Mary. 1999. 'Shareholder Value, Financial Theory and Economic Performance.' Paper presented at the the Second National Heartland Labor Capital Conference, Washington, DC, 29–30 April.

Palameta, Boris. 2001. *Who Contributes to RRSPS? A Re-Examination. Perspectives on Labour and Income*. Ottawa: Statistics Canada.

Palmer, Bryan D. 1992. *Working Class Experience: Rethinking the History of Canadian Labour, 1800–1991*. Toronto: McClelland and Stewart.

Palmer, Geoffrey. 1986. *Trustee Investment: The Relative Merits of the Legal List and*

Prudent Man Approaches to Trustee. Wellington: New Zealand Joint Working Party.

Park, Peter, Mary Brydon-Miller, Budd Hall, and Ted Jackson, eds. 1993. *Voices of Change.* Toronto: OISE.

Parket, Robert I., and Henry Eilbirt. 1975. 'Social Responsibility – the Underlying Factors.' *Business Horizons* 18(4): 5–10.

Patry, Michel, and Michel Poitevin. 1995. 'Why Institutional Investors Are Not Better Shareholders.' In Ronald Daniels and Randall Morck, eds. *Corporate Decision-Making in Canada*, 341–78. Calgary: University of Calgary Press.

Pearce, P. and A. Samuels. 1985. 'Trustees and Beneficiaries and Investment Policies.' *Conveyancer and Property Lawyer.* Jan.–Feb.: 52–56.

Persky, Joseph, Daniel Felsenstein, and Wim Wiewel. 1997. 'How Do We Know That "But for the Incentives" the Development Would Not Have Occurred?' In Bingham and Mier, *Dilemmas of Urban Economic Development*, 28–45.

Press, Kevin. 2000. 'The Top Pension Funds of 2000.' April. Benefits Canada.

Press, Viva. 1997. 'Ethical Funds, Stocks Pay Off for Investors.' *Toronto Star*, 28 July, D4.

Preston, Lee E., and James E. Post. 1975. 'Private Management and Public Policy: The Principle of Public Responsibility.' Englewood Cliffs, NJ: Prentice-Hall.

Price, Waterhouse, Coopers. 1998. 'Mortgage Fund One. Financial Statements for the Year Ended December 31, 1998.'

Quarter, Jack. 1995. *Crossing the Line: Unionized Employee Ownership and Investment Funds.* Toronto: Lorimer.

Quarter, Jack, Isla Carmichael, Jorge Sousa, and Susan Elgie. 2001. 'Social Investment by Union-Based Pension Funds and Labour-Sponsored Investment Funds.' *Relations industrielles / Industrial Relations* 56(1): 92-114.

Quarter, Jack, Laurie Mook, and Betty Jane Richmond. 2003. *What Counts: Social Accounting for Nonprofits and Cooperatives.* Upper Saddle River, NJ: Prentice-Hall.

Ravikoff, Ronald B., and Myron P. Curzon. 1980. 'Social Responsibility in Investment Policy and the Prudent Man Rule.' *California Law Review* 68: 518–46.

Regional Data Corporation (RDC), and Perrin, Thorau, and Associates. 1998. *Analysis of Fiscal and Economic Benefits of the British Columbia Working Opportunity Fund.* Prepared for the Working Opportunity Fund.

Reinharz, S. 1992. *Feminist Methods in Social research.* Oxford: Oxford University Press.

Richmond, B.J. 1998. 'Counting on Each Other: A Social Audit Model to Assess the Impact of Nonprofits.' PhD. diss. University of Toronto.

Rifkin, Jeremy, and Randy Barber. 1980. *The North Will Rise Again.* Boston: Beacon Press.

Roe, Mark. 1991. 'A Political Theory of the Corporation.' *Columbia Law Review* 91: 10–67.

Romano, Robert. 1993. 'Public Pension Fund Activism in Corporate Governance Reconsidered.' *Columbia Law Review* 93: 795–853.

Rorke, C.H., and Al Ianet. 1976. 'The Random Walk Hypothesis in the Canadian Equity Market.' *Journal of Business Administration* 8(1): 23–8.

Rubenstein, Daniel. 1989. 'Black Oil, Red Ink.' *CA Magazine* (Nov.): 30–5.

Rudd, Elizabeth C., and Kirsten Snow Spalding. 1997. 'Economically Targeted Investment in the Policies and Practices of Taft-Hartley Pension Funds: Two Case Studies.' Paper presented at the conference on High Performance Pensions: Multi-Employer Plans and the Challenges of Falling Pension Coverage and Retirement Insecurity, Berkeley, California, 4–5 Sept.

Scane, Ralph E., QC. 1993. 'Occupational Pension Schemes: Is the Trust an Adequate Form of Provision?' In Donovan W.M. Waters, ed. *Equity, Fiduciaries and Trusts*, 359–82. Toronto: Carswell.

Schmitz, J.J. 1995. *The Performance and Consistency of Professional Portfolio Managers: A Review and Synthesis.* Mimeograph. Western Business School, University of Western Ontario.

Schrijvers, J. 1991. 'Dialectics of a Dialogical Ideal.' In L. Nencel and P. Pels, eds., *Constructing Knowledge: Authority and Critique in Social Science.* London: Sage.

Schugurensky, Daniel. 2001. 'Transformative Learning and Transformative Politics: The Pedagogical Dimension of Participatory Democracy.' In Edmund O'Sullivan, Mary Ann O'Connor and Amish Morrell, eds., *Transformative Learning Reader. Transformative Learning: Essays on Praxis*, 59–76. New York: Paragon.

Scott, A.W. 1987. *The Law on Trusts*, 4th ed. Boston and Toronto: Little, Brown.

Scott, Allan. 1980. *The Urban Land Nexus and the State.* London: Pion.

Sethi, S. Prakash. 1995. 'Introduction to AMR's Special Topic Forum on Shifting Paradigms: Societal Expectations and Corporate Performance.' *Academy of Management Review* 20(1): 18–21.

SHARE. 2004. *SHARE 2003 Key Proxy Vote Survey* SHARE. Retrieved from www.share.ca

Sharpe, William F. 1963. 'A Simplified Model for Portfolio Analysis.' *Management Science* 9(2): 277–93.

Shiller, Robert, J. 2000. *Irrational Exuberance.* Princeton: Princeton University Press.

Shor, Ira. 1992. *Empowering Education: Critical Teaching for Social Change.* Chicago: University of Chicago Press.

Smith, Dorothy. 1987. *The Everyday World as Problematic: A Feminist Sociology.* Toronto: University of Toronto Press.

Smith, M.P. 1996. 'Shareholder Activism by Institutional Investors: Evidence from CalPERS. *Journal of Finance* 51(1): 227–52.

Social Investment Organization (SIO). 2000. 'Canada Business Corporations Act Revisions. Submission to Industry Canada, February 14, 2000.' Toronto: author.

– 1996. *Best of the TSE 300: The First Annual List of the Top 50 Social and Environmental Performers.* Toronto: author.

Stack, Jack. 1992. *The Great Game of Business.* New York: Doubleday.

Stafford, James. 1987a. 'The Class Struggle and the Rise of Private Pensions 1900–1950.' *Labour / Le Travail* 20 (Fall): 147–71.

– 1987b.. 'The Rise of Pensions in Canada.' In *Working People and Hard Times,* 123–35. Toronto: Garamond.

Stanford, Jim. 1999a. 'Labour-Sponsored Funds: An Orwellian Charade.' *Canadian Dimension* (May–June): 41–5.

– 1999b. *Paper Boom.* Toronto: Lorimer and CCPA.

– 2001. *Quarterly Estimates of Trusteed Pension Funds. Fourth Quarter 2000.* Ottawa: Queen's Printer.

– 1997. *Pension Plans in Canada.* Ottawa: Queen's Printer.

– 1996a. *Trusteed Pension Plans: Financial Statistics 1994.* Ottawa: Queen's Printer.

– 1996b. *Canada's Retirement Income Programs.* Ottawa: Queen's Printer.

– 1980. *Pension Plans in Canada.* Ottawa: Queen's Printer.

Sullivan, L. 1999. *The Global Sullivan Principles.* Retrieved from http://www.chevron.com/newsvs/pressrel

Suret, J.M. 1993. *The Fonds De Solidarite Des Travailleurs du Québec: A Cost-Benefit Analysis.* Quebec: Université Laval.

Suret, J.M., and E. Cormier. 1990. 'Insiders and the Stock Market.' *Canadian Investment Review* 87(3): 2.

Taylor, Jeffery M. 2001. *Union Learning: Canadian Labour Education in the Twentieth Century.* Toronto: Thompson Educational.

Taylor, K. 1995. 'Return of the Index Fund.' *Benefits Canada,* 25–6 Feb.

Tesch, Renata. 1990. 'Qualitative Research: Analysis Types and Software Tools.' New York: Falmer Press.

'Tick Tock: Survey Fund Management.' 1997. *Economist,* 25 Oct., 10.

Tinker, Tony. 1985. *Paper Prophets: A Social Critique of Accounting.* New York: Praeger.

Tinker, Tony, and E.A. Lowe. 1984. 'One Dimensional Management Science: Towards a Technocratic Consciousness.' *Interfaces* (March–April): 7–14.

Tompkins, J.J. 1921. *Knowledge for the People: A Call to St Francis Xavier College.* Antigonish, N.S. (privately printed).

Toronto Stock Exchange, Committee on Corporate Governance in Canada.

1994. 'Where Were the Directors?' Guildelines for Improved Corporate Governance in Canada. Toronto: author.

Townson, Monica. 1997. *Protecting Public Pensions: Myths versus Reality*. Ottawa: CCPA.

Trades Union Congress (TUC). 1996. *Pension Fund Investment: A TUC Handbook*. London: author.

Ullmann, A. 1985. 'Data in Search of a Theory: A Critical Examination of the Relationship among Social Performance, Social Disclosure, and Economic Performance.' *Academy of Management Review* 10: 450–77.

U.S. Department of Labour. 1994a. *Bulletin* 94-1, 9 Feb. Reg. 32,606, 23 June.

– 1994b *Bulletin* 94-1, 59 Fed. Reg. 38,860, 29 July.

Urquhart, Ian. 1997. 'OFL's Wilson Bows Out with a Bang.' *Toronto Star*, A9.

Vance, S.C. 1975. 'Are Socially Respnsible Corporations Good Investment Risks?' *Academy of Management Review* (Aug.): 18–24.

Vancouver Stock Exchange (VSE). 1998. *Venture Capital: Risk and Reward*. Vancouver: author.

Vertin, James. 1974. 'The State of the Art in Our Profession.' *Journal of Portfolio Management* (Fall): 10–12.

Waddock, Sandra A., and Samuel B. Graves. 1996. *Finding the Link between Stakeholder Relations and Quality of Management*. Social Investment Forum, 1997 Moskowitz Prize Report. Retrieved from http://www.socialinvest.org

Wahal, Sunil. 1996. 'Pension Fund Activism and Firm Performance.' *Journal of Financial and Quantitative Analysis* 31: 1–23.

Waitzer, Edward. 1991. 'The Bishop of Oxford and Ethical Investment.' *Corporate Ethics Monitor* (Nov.–Dec.): 95–6.

– 1990. 'Legal Issues for Trustees and Managers.' Paper presented at the conference on Strategies for Responsible Share Ownership.

Waldie, Paul. 1998. 'OMERS Mulls Ranking Companies' Performance.' *Globe and Mail*, 19 March, B7.

Walker, Robert, and Tricia Hylton. 1998. 'Sri in Canada and the U.S.: I Can't See the Difference. Can You See the Difference?' *SIO Forum* (March–April): 2, 7.

Waring, Marilyn. 1988. *If Women Counted*. San Francisco: Harper and Row.

Warson, Albert. 2004. 'P3s Get Broader Role in Infrastructure.' *Globe and Mail*, 25 May, B18.

Wartick, Steven L., and Philip L. Cochrane. 1985. 'The Evolution of the Corporate Social Performance Model.' *Academy of Management Review* 10(4): 758–70.

Watson, Ronald D. 1995. 'The Controversy over Targeted Investing.' *Compensation and Benefits Management* (Winter): 1–9.

Wertheimer, Barbara Mayer. 1981. *Labor Education for Women Workers*. Philadelphia: Temple University Press.

Westell, Dan. 1997a. 'Ethics Audits on the Way.' *Financial Post*, 28 May, 6.
– 1997b. 'Proxy Votes Attract Significant Minority of Dissidents: Survey.' *Financial Post*, 25 Feb., 12.
Whittington, Les. 1998. 'Activist Claims Win at Royal Bank Meet.' *Toronto Star*, 6 March, D1–D2.
Won, Shirley. 2000. 'Labour Funds Rev Up.' *Globe and Mail*, 19 Feb., N1–N4.
– 1997. 'When Goodness Is Its Own Reward.' *Globe and Mail*, 11 Oct., B24.
Wood, Donna J. 1995. 'The Fortune Database as a Csp Measure. Research Forum Introduction.' *Business and Society* 34(2): 197–8.
– 1991. 'Corporate Social Performance Revisited.' *Academy of Management Review* 15(4): 691–714.
Woolverton, J.J. 1998. 'Investment Management throughout the Ages.' *Benefits Canada*, 14.
World Bank. 1994. *Averting the Old Age Crisis*. New York: Oxford University Press.
Yaron, G. 2002. 'Institutional Shareholder Activism in Canada.' *UBC Law Journal*. Retrieved from http://www.share.ca
– 2001. 'The Responsible Pension Trustee: Reinterpreting the Principles of Prudence and Loyalty in the Context of Socially Responsible Institutional Investing. *Estates, Trusts and Pensions Journal*, 20(4): 305.
– and Freya Kodar. 2003. 'How to Incorporate Active Trustee Practices into Pension Plan Investment Policies: A Resource Guide for Pension Plan Trustees and Other Fiduciaries.' In Carmichael and Quarter, *Money on the Line*, 71–138.
Yates, Charlotte. 1993. *From Plant to Politics: The Autoworkers' Union in Post-War Canada*. Philadelphia: Temple University Press.
Young, Margot. 1992. *Pensions and Social Investment: Ethical Investment for the 1990s*. Prepared for CUPE.
Youngman, Frank. 1986. *Adult Education and Socialist Pedagogy*. London: Croom Helm.
Zadek, Simon, Peter Pruzan, and Richard Evans, eds. 1997. *Building Corporate Accountability*. London: EarthScan.
Zanglein, J.E. 2000. Overcoming Institutional Barriers on the Economically Targeted Investment Superhighway. In Fung, Hebb, and Rogers, *Working capital: The Power of Labor's Pensions*, 181–202.
Zeikel, Arthur. 1974. 'The Random Walk and Murphy's Law.' *Journal of Portfolio Management* (Fall): 20–30.

Cases Cited

Blankenship v *Boyle*, 329 F. Supp. 1089 (1971).

Board of Trustees v *City of Baltimore*, 562 A.2d 720 (Md. 1989).

Cowan v *Scargill*, [1984] 2 All E.R. 750, [1985] 1 Ch. 270 (Ch.D.) [citing to Ch.].

Donovan v *Bierwirth*, 680 F.2d 263, 271 (2d. cir.) cert. denied 104 s. ct. 488 (1982).

Donovan v *Walton*, 609 F. Supp. 1221 (D.C. Fla. 1985), affirmed *Brock* v *Walton*, 794 F.2d 586 (11th Cir. 1986) at 586.

Guerin v *The Queen*, [1984] 2 S.C.R. 335.

Harvard College v *Amory*, 26 Mass. (9 Pick.) 446 (1830).

Martin v *City of Edinburg District Council*, (1998) S.L.T. 329 (Outer House).

Withers v *Teachers' Retirement System*, 447 F. Supp. 1248, 1254 (SDNY 1978) aff'd 595 F.2d 1210 (2d Cir. 1979).

Index